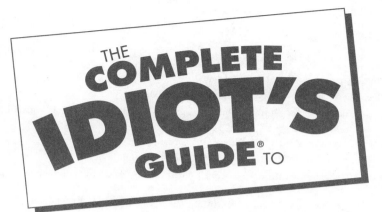

THE COMPLETE IDIOT'S GUIDE® TO

Feeding Your Baby & Toddler

by Elizabeth M. Ward, M.S., R.D.

ALPHA

A member of Penguin Group (USA) Inc.

To My Family

ALPHA BOOKS

Published by the Penguin Group

Penguin Group (USA) Inc., 375 Hudson Street, New York, New York 10014, U.S.A.

Penguin Group (Canada), 10 Alcorn Avenue, Toronto, Ontario, Canada M4V 3B2 (a division of Pearson Penguin Canada Inc.)

Penguin Books Ltd, 80 Strand, London WC2R 0RL, England

Penguin Ireland, 25 St Stephen's Green, Dublin 2, Ireland (a division of Penguin Books Ltd)

Penguin Group (Australia), 250 Camberwell Road, Camberwell, Victoria 3124, Australia (a division of Pearson Australia Group Pty Ltd)

Penguin Books India Pvt Ltd, 11 Community Centre, Panchsheel Park, New Delhi—10 017, India

Penguin Group (NZ), cnr Airborne and Rosedale Roads, Albany, Auckland 1310, New Zealand (a division of Pearson New Zealand Ltd)

Penguin Books (South Africa) (Pty) Ltd, 24 Sturdee Avenue, Rosebank, Johannesburg 2196, South Africa

Penguin Books Ltd, Registered Offices: 80 Strand, London WC2R 0RL, England

Copyright © 2005 by Elizabeth M. Ward, M.S., R.D.

International Standard Book Number: 1-59257-411-4
Library of Congress Catalog Card Number: 2005929446

07   06   05   8   7   6   5   4   3   2   1

Interpretation of the printing code: The rightmost number of the first series of numbers is the year of the book's printing; the rightmost number of the second series of numbers is the number of the book's printing. For example, a printing code of 05-1 shows that the first printing occurred in 2005.

Printed in the United States of America

Note: This publication contains the opinions and ideas of its author. It is intended to provide helpful and informative material on the subject matter covered. It is sold with the understanding that the author and publisher are not engaged in rendering professional services in the book. If the reader requires personal assistance or advice, a competent professional should be consulted.

The author and publisher specifically disclaim any responsibility for any liability, loss, or risk, personal or otherwise, which is incurred as a consequence, directly or indirectly, of the use and application of any of the contents of this book.

Most Alpha books are available at special quantity discounts for bulk purchases for sales promotions, premiums, fundraising, or educational use. Special books, or book excerpts, can also be created to fit specific needs.

For details, write: Special Markets, Alpha Books, 375 Hudson Street, New York, NY 10014

Publisher: *Marie Butler-Knight*
Editorial Director: *Mike Sanders*
Senior Managing Editor: *Jennifer Bowles*
Acquisitions Editor: *Tom Stevens*
Development Editor: *Nancy D. Lewis*
Production Editor: *Janette Lynn*

Copy Editor: *Tricia Liebig*
Cartoonist: *Chris Eliopoulos*
Book Designer: *Trina Wurst*
Cover Designer: *Bill Thomas*
Indexer: *Heather McNeill*
Layout: *Becky Harmon*
Proofreading: *John Etchison*

Contents at a Glance

Contents

Recipes for the Early Years

Foreword

Babies … those miraculous, mysterious creatures who come into our lives with some warning but no prior training or experience required. It seems they should arrive with some sort of owner's manual, but instead we receive much advice (some good, some not-so-good, and some conflicting) from mothers, mothers-in-law, friends, neighbors, doctors, and miscellaneous other well-meaning individuals. And what more important issue than nutrition to get some sound and solid input on? Especially when that seems to be one of only three basic functions of babies for the first several months of their existence: eating, sleeping, and elimination in one form or another. When it comes to the best food and methods of delivering it for babies and toddlers … controversies, strong opinions, and myths abound.

Scientists have made remarkable discoveries about the critical nature of good early nutrition. We have learned that diet in the first year of life can help determine whether children develop subsequent allergies and asthma, that breast milk provides protection from infections for the first several months of life when baby's immune system is immature, that inadequate iron intake in the first few years of life can lead to learning problems and later difficulties in school, and even that a particular fat present in human milk can influence our children's I.Q.!

We hear rules and proscriptions that may seem arbitrary: no solids before four months of age, no nuts or eggs in the first year, whole milk should be given between one and two years of age, but not thereafter. All of these facts and theories, and the knowledge of how important this issue really is, can make us feel overwhelmed and daunted. As parents, we would like to wade through everything we hear and read, and do right by our children.

The Complete Idiot's Guide to Feeding Your Baby and Toddler to the rescue! This guide provides practical, no-nonsense, guilt-free advice based on science and the real-life experience of a busy mother of three. It is easy to read, fun, and educational without causing "information overload."

The first several chapters walk us through feeding our baby and then toddler in a straightforward manner, giving us tips about behavior, development, and safety along the way. The next parts deal with specific nutrients, addressing common questions such as: Carbohydrates, good or bad? Is my child getting enough fiber? What about all these vitamins I see on sale? Then there comes an interesting assortment of useful topics like children as vegetarians, eating out with a toddler, and how to buy produce. But my favorite part of the book is the extensive collection of recipes. These give creative ways to present nutritious foods in appealing ways to suspicious toddlers. They are fast, easy, and will be useful well beyond the toddler years. Happy reading and feeding!

Alison M. Friedmann, M.D., M.Sc.
Pediatrician and mother of three

Introduction

It doesn't matter how smart you are, feeding a small child can really make you feel like a simpleton. When it comes to providing healthy meals and snacks for your little tyke, the adage that babies should come with instruction manuals rings true for you, and for the other caregivers who feed your child. Enter *The Complete Idiot's Guide to Feeding Your Baby and Toddler*, a comprehensive feeding manual to guide you from starting solids well into the toddler years. With this book in hand, you'll grow more confident in your feeding skills as you see your child develop and thrive during the coming years.

How to Use This Book

The Complete Idiot's Guide to Feeding Your Baby and Toddler is divided into five parts plus a recipe section, for easy use.

Part 1, "Starting Solids," supplies information about why, when, and how to begin feeding your baby solid foods. Each chapter tackles a different age group, discussing in detail the nutrition issues that apply to infants ages four to twelve months. This part supplies information about how your child's development affects your feeding choices. It also highlights fostering self-feeding skills, choking prevention, how much juice is okay for kids, organic baby food, and how to care for your child's teeth. And there are more than a dozen easy recipes for homemade food for you to try.

Part 2, "Feeding Your Toddler," delves into how the developmental changes that come after age one affects eating, with an emphasis on how a slower rate of growth influences food intake. This part serves up information on topics such as making the move to cow's milk and away from baby bottles; strategies for feeding erratic eaters; moving toward table foods; and snacking smarts. You also learn about the nutritional needs of toddlers beginning at twelve months and going well into two years.

Part 3, "Nutrition Basics," sets you straight on nutrition by providing clear, concise, and up-to-date nutritional information you can use to feed your child, and yourself. You learn about the role of carbohydrates, fat, and protein in a child's diet. This part also delves into critical vitamins and minerals your child needs to thrive, and explains the latest fluid requirements for kids.

Part 4, "Special Nutrition Concerns," covers three hot topics in childhood nutrition: overweight kids; food allergy and asthma; and vegetarianism. You learn how family lifestyle habits affect a child's body weight; how to foil food allergy and asthma with food; and whether vegetarianism is any good for children.

Part 5, "Let's Make a Meal!" is all about the savviest food choices in the supermarket, the kitchen, and restaurants. Don't have a clue about shopping for the healthiest kid-friendly ingredients? No worries. This part delves into smart supermarket choices. You might think you know about keeping foods safe, but even if you pick up one or two tips from the food safety chapter, you'll be doing your family a big favor. Lastly, what tired parent doesn't like to go out to eat? (No cleanup!) You learn all about the best way to dine out with a child in tow and how to make nutritious menu selections for your child in a variety of restaurants.

Recipes: You'll find more than 200 recipes for everything from avocadoes to zucchini, most of them in the recipe section. Don't worry: none of them use fancy or expensive ingredients, and many are ready in minutes.

Extras

Nutrition information can be daunting, especially when you're trying to figure out what to feed your little one. The following extras are designed to help demystify feeding advice as well as further explain some of the most important points of good nutrition for infants and toddlers.

Mother's Helper

These contain helpful hints from the author, a mother of three as well as a registered dietitian.

Nutrition Nugget

These provide news about the latest scientific studies that pertain to the topic at hand.

Safe at the Plate

These contain cautionary words to help keep your child as safe as possible.

Technically Speaking

These explain definitions of terms used in the text that are also found in the glossary.

Details, Please

These are full of more information on interesting topics that pertain to your child's health, often including recent scientific studies.

Acknowledgments

They say write what you know. With three children and a career as a registered dietitian, this book was right up my alley. Thank you to Marilyn Allen, my literary agent, who started the ball rolling and brought me together with Tom Stevens, one of the many editors who made this book better.

Special thanks also go out to my favorite chef, Laura Lewis, for contributing several recipes and holding my hand through the recipe development process, and to Sheah Rarback, M.S., R.D., and Alison Friedmann, M.D., M.Sc., for taking time from their busy schedules to offer their technical expertise.

Most of all, I thank my family. Hayley, Hannah, and Emma have unwittingly schooled me in the realities and joys of feeding young children. As always, I am most grateful to my husband Tom for his patience and support, no matter what the project.

Special Thanks to the Technical Reviewer

The Complete Idiot's Guide to Feeding Your Baby and Toddler was reviewed by an expert who double-checked the accuracy of what you learn here, to help ensure that this book gives you everything you need to know about feeding your children in the first couple years. Special thanks are extended to Sheah Rarback, M.S., R.D.

Sheah Rarback, M.S., R.D., is on the faculty of the Department of Pediatrics, University of Miami School of Medicine, and is director of nutrition at the Mailman Center for Child Development. In this position she is responsible for counseling children and adults on nutrition, teaching medical and nutrition graduate students, and participating in clinical research. Her areas of expertise are pediatric nutrition, pediatric obesity, food allergies, inborn errors of metabolism, and pediatric gastrointestinal disorders.

Trademarks

All terms mentioned in this book that are known to be or are suspected of being trademarks or service marks have been appropriately capitalized. Alpha Books and Penguin Group (USA) Inc. cannot attest to the accuracy of this information. Use of a term in this book should not be regarded as affecting the validity of any trademark or service mark.

Part 1 Starting Solids

Starting solids is a new and strange experience for babies and their parents. A baby must adjust to the foreign concept of spoon-feeding while his parents discover a child's food preferences and feeding quirks. Whether you know a thing or two about infants or you're completely clueless, you're in the right place. This part takes you step-by-step through the first year of feeding stages. You might feel like an idiot now, but by the time you're done scouring this part of the book for strategies and techniques, you'll be an old hand at feeding your baby.

Feeding Your Baby: From 4 to 6 Months

In This Chapter

- Determining when your child's ready for solid foods
- Feeding equipment every family needs
- Detailing the first meal
- Developing the brain and eyesight through nutrition

Baby, it's time to eat! By any measure, adding solid foods is an exciting nutritional and developmental milestone—for babies, their parents, and other caregivers, including sitters and relatives.

Ironically, although junior's initial spoonful of food is a major event worthy of recording, his first few weeks of solids are more about becoming accustomed to spoon-feeding than they are about good nutrition. Even so, there are guidelines for what to feed when the time is right.

Why You Must Wait to Serve Solid Foods

Four months is the earliest age for safely starting solid foods in most children, according to The American Academy of Pediatrics. Yet, you've probably heard of others who didn't wait that long. Perhaps your neighbor fed her daughter infant cereal at two months without any obvious repercussions. Or maybe your mother has hinted over and over that she "fed you kids at three months and you all turned out fine."

Based on these and other testimonials, you might be tempted to try solids before your child is developmentally ready. Resist that urge. Until at least four months, your child's digestive tract is unable to break down and absorb foods more complex than breast milk or infant formula. Feeding solids too early sets the stage for allergic reactions and other feeding problems.

> **Safe at the Plate**
>
> Unless directed to by your pediatrician, reserve baby bottles for infant formula or breast milk. There's no validity to the claim that adding cereal to a baby's bottle promotes sleeping through the night. In fact, the practice can lead to choking and overfeeding, and undermines the development of eating skills.

do not add cereal

Ready to Eat, Baby?

Age is only one of the criteria for judging your child's readiness for solids. There are several other signs to look for, including the following:

- She holds her head up. Your child should be able to hold her head up with good control for short periods of time. The ability to voluntarily move her head allows a baby to lean toward food and away when she's not interested, helping you to avoid overfeeding her. Developed head and neck muscles also prevent choking.

- She accepts food. The first few times your baby encounters a spoonful of food, she'll probably spit it right back at you. That reaction is normal, but it shouldn't last if she's really ready to eat. Baby's urge to eject an object from her mouth is called the *extrusion reflex*. If she continues to reject the spoon and its contents for a few meals running, hold off for a few days and then try again.

> **Technically Speaking**
>
> The **extrusion reflex** is a baby's instinctive way of rejecting something that could choke her. It's an automatic response in younger infants to anything other than liquid in their mouth.

- She's eyeballing your meal. Your baby might lean toward your food and try to grab it. She may even open her mouth when food passes in front of her or is close to her.

- She seems hungrier. Crying between feedings that had been holding her could mean she needs more food. If she's drinking upward of 35 ounces a day of infant formula and wants more or is nursing 8 to 10 times daily, she's probably ready for solids.

Nursing and bottle feeding are relatively straightforward feeding techniques that involve very little equipment; once baby is ready for solid foods, you'll need to make some additions.

Get the Gear: Must-Have Feeding Equipment

Starting solids requires an investment in certain low-tech gear. Here's what you need when your baby is ready to move on to more than fluids: highchair, bowls, spoons, towels, and bibs.

You can certainly start off feeding your child solid foods while he's sitting on your lap, but you might not want to make a habit of it. Why? He may balk when you decide it's time for him to eat in the highchair. To get baby interested in the highchair, let him sit in it for a few minutes at a time before his first meal is served there.

Highchairs can be hard to figure out. You, and anyone else who feeds your baby, should feel comfortable using the highchair. It pays to know how to secure your child in the highchair, and how to get him out quickly, if need be. The safest highchairs have a waist strap and a strap that runs between the legs. Whenever your child is in the highchair, use both straps to keep him secure and to prevent him from standing. Prevent slipping by padding the highchair with a towel or small blanket. Don't stray too far from the highchair; crafty older babies and toddlers may learn how to unfasten safety straps. The majority of highchair injuries occur when adults don't use the restraining straps and when children are not closely supervised.

Several small, sturdy plastic bowls are convenient for mixing and serving infant foods. And have a few spoons on hand that are specially designed for baby feeding. Small, shallow spoons with no hard edges work well; spoons coated with plastic are more comfortable for teething babies when they bite down to soothe their irritated gums. Spoons with long handles may be more comfortable for you to use because you don't have to lean in so far over the highchair tray to get the food to baby's mouth. Spoons with shorter, curved handles are ideal for baby to hold because they are difficult to poke themselves in the eye with. Curved handles are even handier later on when your child takes over the job of feeding himself because they are easy for little mitts to hold.

Small towels (face-cloth size) or paper towels work well for cleanup. Wipe the cleanest thing first—usually baby's face and hands—then clean the highchair and other surfaces covered with food.

Bibs with Velcro or snaps are easier to put on a squirming infant. Some babies are not messy eaters, so you may not need bibs. Other babies might need a bib, but are so distracted by it during the meal that it's just easier to go without. In the warm weather, you can feed a topless baby—it makes for a much easier cleanup!

Details, Please

A safe and sturdy highchair can take you from his first bite all the way through the toddler years. When purchasing a new highchair, choose one with a wide base for stability. Be sure that the waist belt has a buckle that cannot be fastened unless the crotch strap is also used, and look for easy-to-use straps. What about hand-me-down highchairs? They should be clean and sturdy. Be sure the straps are in good condition, are securely attached, and work properly.

The First Meal

Today's the day. You've assembled the necessary feeding gear and the video camera is charged. You've even invited the grandparents to view your child's foray into solid foods. What should you serve, and how should you go about it? Read on.

Timing Is Everything

Plan on introducing your child to solids when he's well rested and not overly hungry—this will make it easier for him to accept this new experience. A couple of hours after his first bottle and before his first nap of the day may be the ideal time for the first bite. Avoid introducing a ravenous child to spoon-feeding. You'll frustrate yourself and confuse him, because he's accustomed to eating from a bottle or the breast.

On the Menu

Today's special is: soupy iron-fortified rice cereal! For first-time eaters, this is the perfect choice for tickling their taste buds. It might not be your idea of a delectable meal, but rice cereal is the best food for babies just starting out. Why? Because it is free of

gluten, a component of grains that can be aller-
genic, and it is fortified with iron. (Read more
about the importance of iron in Chapter 11.)

No culinary talent is required to execute the
recipe for the first of baby's many meals. In a
very small bowl, combine the following:

> 1 teaspoon iron-fortified infant rice cereal
>
> 4 to 5 teaspoons expressed breast milk or
> infant formula

> **Technically Speaking**
>
> **Gluten** is the protein por-
> tion of some grains, including
> wheat, barley, oats, and rye,
> that can sometimes trigger an
> allergic reaction in susceptible
> babies. Gluten intolerance can
> show up at any age, but may
> first appear during infancy.

Mixture will be soupy. As for the temperature of baby's food, keep it cool to lukewarm. Your child's mouth is far more delicate than yours, and much more sensitive to
burns.

You've probably noticed by now that baby's food is not actually solid. Semi-solid or
semi-liquid more aptly conveys the best texture for a four- to six-month-old, or any
beginning eater. That's because runny cereal resembles breast milk and infant formula
so it's more likely baby will readily accept it. It also reduces choking risk. Around six
or seven months, when children typically become more experienced eaters, they can
make the transition to a thicker cereal/fluid mixture. Premature babies might take
longer to tolerate thicker cereal.

Most likely, your child will tolerate rice cereal without a problem. After a week or
so, feel free, but not obligated, to move on to other single-grain fortified infant cereals, including oatmeal. Children of parents who have allergies should hold off on
gluten-containing grains, however. See Chapter 14 for more on food allergies.

Bon Appétit, Baby!

The moment has arrived. She's in her highchair, with bib securely fastened. You've mixed
the infant cereal according to instructions and
you're prepared with the proper infant feeding
spoon. What now?

Face your baby and talk to her. Wait for her
to look at you, but avoid putting on a show to
get her attention (the start of a hard habit to
break). After she's ready, place the spoon on her
lips and try to gently slip it into her mouth.
Because the cereal mixture will be runny, she

> **Safe at the Plate**
>
> Always pitch infant cereal
> and the contents of baby bottles
> (breast milk and formula) that your
> baby does not finish. Bacteria
> from baby's mouth makes its way
> into the food where it multiplies,
> even when refrigerated. Refeeding
> contaminated foods can give
> baby an upset tummy. Serve
> smaller portions if you're con-
> cerned about wasting food.

may suck it right off the spoon. Or, she might spit it out—a natural reaction to a strange sensation. Try again, but only if she seems interested.

She'll probably take a few teaspoons of food at her first meal, or less. If she's more interested in touching her food than eating, don't worry. Touching is part of how babies experience the world. Repeat the process tomorrow at about the same time, feeding your baby in the same area of the house. Babies are creatures of habit, and they take comfort in ritual and routine.

Sorry, I'm Just Not into Solids

Maybe baby's first bites weren't the memorable moments you expected. In fact, it was a total washout. You tried to feed her a few teaspoons of cereal for what seemed like an eternity, but she wanted nothing to do with the highchair, the spoon, or the food on it.

Not to worry. Starting solids is unfamiliar territory for infants. So is understanding that she should keep food in her mouth, work it toward the back of her throat, and then swallow it. Look at it this way: first meals whet a baby's appetite for bigger meals later on.

It never pays to force the issue with an unwilling baby; it makes her tense and more likely to refuse food the next time around. You might win the battle (manage to stuff a few teaspoons full of food into his mouth), but you won't win the war (establishing healthy eating habits).

Try feeding your reluctant eater again in a few days. Some children just need lots of time to develop eating patterns that feel familiar and comforting to them. It could take weeks of gentle prodding before eating solids becomes second nature for your child. As long as your baby is consuming solids by six months, there's really no reason for concern.

Mother's Helper

Your child may not be interested in solids at four months, but it pays to keep trying every few days or so for health reasons. A recent *Journal of the American Medical Association* study suggests children who start on infant cereal between four and six months run a lower risk of developing type 1 diabetes later on. Although no one knows for sure what causes it, the study results reinforce the notion of introducing solid foods between four and six months.

How Much Formula or Breast Milk Your Baby Needs Now

Your child may start solid foods at four, five, or six months old. No matter when he begins, breast milk and infant formula will continue to provide the bulk of his nutritional needs for months to come.

For a while, solid food is just a supplement to baby's liquid nutrition. The likes of infant cereal and other grain products, fruits, vegetables, and meats slowly take over for breast milk and infant formula. By about a year, solids should dominate your child's diet (consult their pediatrician if fluids dominate your child's diet). Don't worry that your child isn't eating heaps of solid foods yet. Use the time to expose him to an array of cereals, meats, fruits, and vegetables.

There is no reason to alter how you prepare infant formula because you have added solid foods to your child's diet. Always adhere to the directions for formula use given on the product's label, unless your doctor tells you otherwise. Changing the concentration of infant formula can overwork a child's kidneys or it could mean he fails to get the nutrients he needs to grow properly.

If you're still nursing after solid foods are introduced, be sure to eat right. Nursing moms need extra calories found in highly nutritious foods; adequate rest; and enough fluids to produce the most nourishing breast milk.

Breastfeeding women aren't the only ones who should pay attention to good nutrition. All women in their childbearing years who are capable of becoming pregnant should pop a daily multivitamin containing 100 percent of the Daily Value (DV) for folic acid to help prevent birth defects should a pregnancy occur. A daily multivitamin is a good idea for filling other nutrient gaps, including iron.

Nutrition Nugget

If you've headed back to work, or just need a break from nursing, you probably bank breast milk for baby for when you're not around. Recent research suggests that the longer you freeze or refrigerate breast milk, the lower the levels of antioxidants drop (components that ward off cell damage). Don't fret, however, even stored expressed breast milk beats out several infant formulas for antioxidant content in the study. Bottom line: you can store breast milk for up to two days in the refrigerator and upward of six months in the rear of a freezer, but the fresher the beast milk, the better for baby.

Breastfed Babies Need Extra Vitamin D

A shortfall of vitamin D in infants sets them up for rickets, a bone-softening disease. Babies drinking enough infant formula will likely get the vitamin D they need, but breastfed children may come up short.

Ask your pediatrician about over-the-counter vitamin D supplements. If you're nursing exclusively, your doctor will probably agree with The American Academy of Pediatrics' recommendation that nursing babies consume 200 International Units of supplemental vitamin D every day beginning within the first two months of life. Babies fed a mixture of breast milk and infant formula may not need supplemental vitamin D, so explain in detail to your doctor what your child is drinking.

Handling the Voices of Experience

When you were pregnant, friends, strangers, and relatives came out of the woodwork to provide commentary about pregnancy, delivery, life after baby, and a host of other topics related to parenthood. It probably won't stop there. People will have plenty to say about feeding your infant, especially if your tactics are not commonplace, such as breastfeeding past one year or making your own baby food.

Here's how to avoid letting well-meaning people get the best of you:

- Don't second-guess solid advice from experts. As long as you abide by current feeding guidelines recommended by health experts, there's no need to think you're in the wrong.

- Don't talk too much. Discussing every little detail with anyone who will listen leaves you wide open to criticism.

- Be gentle but firm. Let them know that your methods are working well for your child.

- Let them talk, and smile politely. Don't let what they say get under your skin. Most people love the sound of their own voice.

If others cause you to doubt yourself, call your pediatrician with any questions.

Nurturing Your Baby's Brain Development and Eyesight

Your infant's brain is developing at lightning speed. During the first two years of life, neurons (the nerve cells in the brain) responsible for communicating feelings; storing and retrieving memories; and processing information from the outside world, reach out to each other to form a sprawling communications network. At the same time, your infant's body is also busy securing speedy communication by laying down *myelin* around nerve cells.

> **Technically Speaking**
>
> **Myelin** is the sheath surrounding nerve cells that serves to protect them while preventing "short circuits" in communication.

Children require a balanced diet for peak brain function and vision. Although no single nutrient trumps another in importance, docosahexaenoic acid (DHA) is a type of fat that's particularly vital to proper development and function of the brain, nervous system, and vision. Nursing moms provide their babies with preformed DHA (the kind best used by the body) through breast milk; DHA-rich foods, including tuna, salmon, trout, sardines, and halibut, boost milk DHA levels. Pregnant and nursing women who avoid fish can get DHA in a supplement called Expecta LIPIL.

Bottle-fed babies reap the benefits of DHA from infant formula, also a good choice for breastfed babies making the switch to formula. Studies show formulas with DHA help maintain DHA levels in baby's body after weaning from the breast. Call infant formula makers to find out how much DHA is in their formula. Read more about DHA and brain development in Chapter 9.

The Least You Need to Know

- You must wait until at least four months to begin solid foods, but should start baby on solids by six months of age.

- At this stage, infant formula and breast milk supply the lion's share of baby's nutrient needs.

- It takes time for children and their parents to adjust to spoon-feeding. When a child doesn't seem ready, wait a few days and try again. Persistence pays off.

- Age is just one way to judge a child's readiness for solid foods; being capable of holding up her head is another. If your child shows an interest in food and is willing to open her mouth when you feed her, and if she seems hungrier, she's probably ready for more than fluids.

- During pregnancy, lactation, and the first two years of life, your baby's brain development and vision depend on a healthy diet. Docosahexaenoic acid is a fat that promotes peak brain development and eyesight.

Baby Food Basics

In This Chapter

- Knowing the pros and cons of prepared and homemade baby foods
- Learning about organic baby food
- Making your child's food at home
- Having recipes for baby's first foods

After your child is ready for more than infant cereal, you might be wondering whether to purchase prepared baby foods or make them yourself. Perhaps you'd like to know if organic foods really are better for your child. Of course, there are advantages and disadvantages to each type of baby food. But the truth is you don't have to choose one or the other. This chapter is devoted to helping you figure out a feeding style that best suits you and your baby.

Prepared Baby Foods

Store-bought baby food might cost a bit more, but it is not without its benefits. Parents appreciate prepared baby foods for myriad reasons, including the following.

Nutrition

Don't let the word "processed" put you off. Manufacturers maintain high quality standards for the ingredients that go into baby foods. For example, fruits and vegetables are often processed immediately after being picked to preserve quality and nutrition. Many first foods for babies supply added vitamin C, which is beneficial because vitamin C promotes the body's absorption of iron. That's important because young infants may not get vitamin C from natural sources yet, such as orange juice, because they are too acidic. Other products contain added docosahexaenoic acid, a type of fat important to baby's brain development and vision. And with the exception of the dessert category, processed infant foods are generally free of added salt, sugar, and starchy fillers.

Safe at the Plate

Fruit is plenty sweet for children on its own, and does not require added sugar or other sweeteners, especially honey. Children under the age of one must avoid honey, even when it's been cooked as part of a recipe. Honey may harbor a bacterium that causes infant botulism, which can be fatal. After his first birthday, your baby's digestive tract is mature enough to thwart the potential threat from honey. Until then, it's just not worth it.

Safety

Despite the specter of mass production, prepared baby foods may be safer than some of their homemade counterparts. Why's this? Manufacturers take many safety precautions; testing for nitrates is among them. Nitrates, chemicals that are part of natural and synthetic fertilizers used to grow fruits and vegetables, can penetrate plants. (Nitrates may also be found in water.) Excessive nitrate intake can cause *methemoglobinemia*, a dangerous form of anemia, in infants. According to the American Academy of Pediatrics, processed infant foods are not associated with methemoglobinemia.

Keep the following in mind to help keep your baby safe:

Technically Speaking

Methemoglobinemia causes a defect in the iron attached to hemoglobin, the part of the red blood cell that carries oxygen to cells. Symptoms include lack of energy, shortness of breath, and bluish tinge to skin, and are considered a medical emergency.

- Avoid purchasing (or using) jarred baby food when the vacuum seal button on the lid has popped up. A popped top signifies the food is unsafe to eat.

- Use baby food by the "use by" date on the container.
- Immediately refrigerate unused baby food. It's okay to reseal the jar and leave it in the refrigerator for one to two days, as long as you haven't fed your baby directly from the jar. You can feed directly from the jar when you plan on using all the food, however.
- Store dry baby cereals and unopened jars of baby food in a cool dry place.
- Follow manufacturer's directions for heating baby foods. Check the label.

Convenience and Portability

Stocking up on small jars of puréed vegetables, fruits, and meats, as well as boxes of infant cereal, can save time for parents with hectic schedules. And it's so simple to open the jar, box, or container of prepared baby food, take what you need, and refrigerate the rest if necessary.

You can tote small jars of baby food with you to daycare, restaurants, and on vacation without worrying about refrigeration (unless opened). Some brands of infant cereal even come in single-serve packets, great for on-the-go families who don't want to lug a cereal box with them.

Variety

Prepared baby foods offer an array of flavors, flavor combinations, and textures ranging from puréed for young infants to chunkier selections designed for older babies and young toddlers. Organic baby food is readily available and typically located alongside conventional baby foods on supermarket shelves, too. (See the next section for more on organic food.)

Organic Food for Thought

Organic food is a feeding option that's growing in popularity with parents. Should you fork over the extra dough for puréed fruits, vegetables, and meats with organic ingredients for homemade baby food?

Don't do it for the sake of nutrition. Although organic foods may contain more nutrients than their conventionally grown counterparts, the differences are so slight that they don't matter in the long run.

Parents interested in cutting the risk of chemical exposure in their children are best served by organic foods. A recent study by researchers at the University of Washington found children ages two to five who ate mostly pesticide-free foods had blood levels of organophosphates six times lower than kids who consumed mostly conventionally produced foods. Organophosphates are a category of pesticides linked to nervous system damage, leukemia, and other cancers. As a group, they constitute about half of all pesticides used in the United States, according to the Centers for Disease Control and Prevention.

The Meaning of Organic

Designating a food as "organic" signifies that the food meets standards set by the United States Department of Agriculture (USDA), including the following:

1. Ingredients are grown without using synthetic fertilizers and pesticides or sewage sludge as fertilizer (yes, you read right!).
2. The land used for organic food production has been free of synthetic pesticides for at least three years.

3. Animal products, such as meat, poultry, and milk, are derived from livestock that is fed only organic grain and never given antibiotics or growth hormones.
4. Foods are not genetically engineered nor do they contain genetically engineered ingredients and have not been subjected to *irradiation*, a way of making foods safer.

It's easy enough to determine whether meat, poultry, produce, and milk are organic because they contain a single ingredient. Processed foods are another story because the USDA allows the word "organic" on food labels even when the product is less than entirely organic.

Organic Labeling Simplified (Sort Of)

The Term	Means
100 percent organic	The food must contain 100 percent certified organic ingredients.
Organic	The food must contain at least 95 percent certified organic ingredients.
Made with organic ingredients	The food must contain at least 70 percent organic ingredients.

Homing In on Homemade Baby Foods

Sure, it takes time and energy, but that doesn't prevent parents from preparing their own baby foods. Gourmet cooks and avowed kitchen klutzes alike often try their hand at kiddie cuisine. The following are among the perceived benefits:

- Provides a sense of satisfaction.
- It may be healthier.
- Better variety.
- He or she is having what you're having.

When you cook for your baby, you run the show. The home cook gets to decide on the ingredients, organic or not; the flavor combinations; and the seasonings that go into baby foods (save herbs and spices for later in the first year, however). Making baby food also creates memories and it's a lot of fun.

Homemade baby food is perceived as better for you, and it may be—as long as you use the freshest fruits and vegetables as soon as they are picked—which is what baby food companies tend to do. Out-of-season fresh fruits and vegetables may pack less nutrition than you think because they are typically transported hundreds or thousands of miles from the field to the supermarket, losing nutrients along the way.

The many different flavor combinations home cooks are able to concoct help broaden their child's palate early on. Early acceptance of a

Safe at the Plate

Stick with iron-fortified infant cereals. There's no suitable homemade or store-bought substitute, especially in the early stages of feeding your child solid foods. Nursing babies, in particular, run the risk of coming up short of iron when they cut back on breastfeeding and don't consume enough iron from fortified cereals and puréed meats.

wide range of tastes could make him more accepting of novel foods later. Avoid giving young infants homemade beets, spinach, celery, and lettuce, however. They may contain dangerous levels of nitrates.

Depending on what you're serving, your child can dine on adult cuisine in a child-friendly form (as long as it's not a burger and fries or other fatty, low-nutrient fare). A meal of roasted chicken, mashed potatoes, and steamed broccoli can become baby food in no time. Simply remove the bones and skin from chicken and add it to a food processor or blender along with potatoes, broccoli, and breast milk or infant formula. Prepare a thinner mixture for younger infants and a thicker version for older babies who can handle it.

Let's Get Cooking, Baby!

You're sold on making your own baby food and you're eager to begin. Great! There's just one thing to consider first: food safety. Please read Chapter 18 before you begin your foray into homemade baby food making, or cooking anything, for that matter.

After you've completed the required reading, it's time to take stock of your kitchen. In addition to the usual appliances, including a refrigerator, oven, microwave, freezer, knives, spoons, potholders, and other basics, you'll also need the following tools for at-home baby food production.

- Stainless steel saucepan with steamer basket insert. Having two sets speeds baby food production, especially if you're cooking for older twins or triplets. Avoid copper cookware because it robs foods of their vitamin C. Collapsible steamers work well, too. Plus, they fit into different size saucepans.

- Shallow glass bowls and microwave-safe covers for microwave cooking. (See Chapter 18 for more on safely cooking in microwave ovens.)

- Food processor or blender. Larger food processors work wonders for preparing batches of baby food. Mini food processors and handheld blenders are better for mixing up smaller amounts of food, such as single meals.

- Two cutting boards: one for raw animal products and one for fruits, vegetables, and grains. Having two cuts down on time spent washing between uses when you're cutting meat on one board and fruits and vegetables on the other. Plastic and wood are equally safe, although you might prefer plastic because you can put it in the dishwasher. Replace heavily nicked or cracked cutting boards.

- A paring knife. Especially helpful for produce.

- Vegetable and fruit peeler. For, well, peeling.
- A colander. For rinsing and draining.
- Fine-mesh strainer. To separate solids, such as seeds, pulp, and chunks, from liquids.
- Kitchen shears. To trim fat from poultry; open meat packages; chop herbs; and open bags of frozen fruits and vegetables.
- Ice cube trays, baking sheets, or muffin tins. For freezing infant-size portions.
- Plastic wrap and small plastic freezer storage bags. For storing frozen baby foods.
- Markers or pens, and masking tape or labels. For identifying frozen baby food and the date it was prepared.
- Instant-read meat thermometer. To be sure you cook meat and poultry to temperatures that cut down on the risk of food-borne illnesses.

Now that you have what you need for the kitchen, you're ready to start learning how to cook for your baby.

How to Cook Your Child's Fruits and Vegetables

With the exception of bananas and avocadoes, always cook a beginning eater's fruits and vegetables. (Older babies can have soft mashed or diced fruits and vegetables.) Cooking tenderizes produce and it kills germs that may be present. Water leaches nutrients from fruits and vegetables during cooking, so boiling is out. Of course, overcooking food using any method destroys nutrients to some degree.

Steaming fruits and vegetables maintains nutritional integrity, but use as little water as possible to get the job done, and don't let it touch the food. The heat generated by steam saps some of the food's nutritional value.

Roasting and baking vegetables, including apples, winter squash, broccoli, cauliflower, and sweet potatoes, are also suitable cooking methods for making baby's food. Dry heat preserves nutrition and brings out the natural flavors in produce.

Microwave ovens are perceived as a boon for preparing fruits and vegetables because they cook food faster with less water and no pots and pans. However, there is some concern that cooking fresh produce in a microwave might not retain as many nutrients as steaming or roasting. Nutrient loss may be due to using excessive water when cooking produce, so use as little as possible.

How to Cook Your Child's Meat and Poultry

Roasting or baking chicken, turkey, beef, and pork is the best for baby as long as the finished product is tender, making it easier to chew and digest. Fried meats, such as chicken cutlets, are typically too fatty. Broiling and grilling meat and poultry can cause the formation of carcinogens, or cancer-starters, that have no place in a baby's diet or in yours.

Never eyeball meat or poultry for doneness. Always use a reliable meat thermometer. There's no need to add salt to baby's meat, or any other food he eats. Avoid seasonings such as ground black pepper and garlic until your child is closer to his first birthday. Heavy seasonings may be too harsh for his taste buds and hard on his delicate digestive system.

Your Frozen Assets

There's nothing like knowing you've got a meal that's ready in minutes when your infant is clamoring for food. Here's how to get baby's food into the deep freeze.

Assemble ice cube trays, baking sheets, or muffin tins. Ice cube trays, which hold about two tablespoons of food, are more practical for beginning eaters than muffin tins, which supply more food that could go to waste. Reserve muffin tins for babies with bigger appetites. Baking sheets lined with plastic wrap are trickier to use because they must stay level in the freezer while the food sets, but they allow you to personalize portion sizes as you plop food down to freeze.

Safe at the Plate

You might be hooked on making your own baby food, and start thinking: why not make homemade infant formula? Not a good idea. You can't possibly duplicate, or improve upon, store-bought infant formula. Here's why. Homemade formulas based on cow's milk, goat's milk, or soy beverages don't meet all of an infant's nutritional needs, particularly for iron. Goat's milk is low in vitamin D and it is also low in vitamin B12, folate, and iron, which can lead to anemia in infants. In addition, cow's milk protein that has not been cooked or processed is difficult for an infant to digest. The high protein and electrolyte (salt) content of cow's milk can strain an infant's kidneys, which are still maturing. Substituting evaporated milk doesn't make formula any more nutritious and still may stress the kidneys.

Whatever you use, be sure it's clean. Spoon cooked and cooled baby food into the container of your choice, leaving a bit of space for liquid to expand in ice cube trays or muffin tins. Cover food tightly with plastic wrap and place in freezer.

When the food freezes, transfer it to small, sturdy freezer bags or durable plastic containers with snug lids. Label containers with the name of the food and the date prepared. Frozen food that's stored in durable containers is good for one to two months.

Thawing Homemade Baby Food

Why warm baby's food? Because lukewarm food is more flavorful and appealing to a child than cold food. And very cold foods can damage mouth tissue as badly as hot foods can, so slightly warm is a happy medium.

There are several ways to defrost baby food, not all of them safe. Thawing baby food (or any other food, for that matter) on the counter is a huge mistake. Why? No matter how many precautions you take, food is never completely devoid of germs. When you leave food out to warm to room temperature, any bacteria present in the food can multiply and cause trouble for baby. Pick one of these methods instead:

- Take out a day's worth of food from the freezer the night before and leave it, covered, to defrost in the refrigerator.

- If your baby gets hungry before the estimated mealtime and you have no thawed food on hand, or when baby wants more food at a meal than you planned for, you can defrost his food in the microwave. Allow about 30 seconds for each frozen cube to thaw. *Always* test the temperature of baby's food before you feed it to him, and make sure you stir thoroughly to avoid hot pockets of air.

- Use a double boiler, which is a two-part pot in which one pan sits inside the other, and the lower pan holds water that you boil to generate heat. Place frozen food portions in the top portion of the double boiler to gently melt food.

Make sure you throw away any baby food that's been left out of the refrigerator or freezer for more than two hours (at 70°F) or for one hour in warmer weather. No matter what method you choose, never refreeze the unused portion of defrosted baby food.

After you're sure your baby can tolerate certain foods, it's okay to combine them. You can use homemade or prepared baby foods to come up with any number of meal combinations and consistencies. The table that follows lists a few of the many ways to mix infant foods.

Mix It Up

Combine	With
Tofu	Acorn or butternut squash; avocado; fruit
Chicken or turkey	Rice cereal and pears; sweet potato; apples; potato; green beans; carrots
Beef	Broccoli; carrots
Bananas	Berries or applesauce; infant oatmeal cereal
Pears	Acorn or butternut squash

Timesaving Tips for Making Baby Food

Making baby food is a worthy investment of your time. You're busy, so you won't want to waste precious hours in the store or at the stove. Here's how to have time to spare without cutting corners.

- Shop regularly. Keep a running list of what you need and take it with you.
- Organize your kitchen cabinets, refrigerator, pantry, and freezer to prevent time-sapping rummaging for ingredients.
- Keep baby food–making equipment in a central location in the kitchen.
- Save a trip to the store by stocking up on canned fruit in its own juices; frozen fruit and vegetables as a backup for fresh; canned legumes; and frozen meat and poultry.
- Prepare several foods simultaneously. For example, steam green beans, bake sweet potatoes, and roast a small turkey at the same time.
- Make a double batch using the recipes that follow.

The Least You Need to Know

- There are myriad feeding choices for parents and their children. You can combine prepared and homemade infant foods in any way that works for you.
- Even if you're not much of a cook, making your own baby food can be a satisfying experience.
- Making your own baby food can be more efficient and relaxing if you organize your cooking gear and ingredients.

- Organic baby foods contain ingredients grown using fewer chemicals.
- Whether you're using store-bought or homemade baby foods, baby's safety is paramount. Always abide by manufacturers' instructions and basic food safety principles.

Recipes

Making extra means you'll always have meals and snacks on hand for your child, and you won't have to cook for her every day. Read "Your Frozen Assets," earlier in this chapter, for more about how to store baby food for months. The following recipes provide at least two cooking methods and all end in how to fix the food for baby's consumption.

Avocado

1 ripe avocado   **Infant formula or breast milk**

1. Slice and pit a ripe avocado, and scoop out the insides.
2. Place avocado in a food processor or blender and purée, adding infant formula or breast milk if you need to thin mixture.
3. Serve mashed avocado to older babies. Mashed avocado is also useful for thickening baby's food.

> Fat fosters growth in infants. Avocadoes are rich in monounsaturated fat, one of the healthiest fats around.

Banana

1 ripe banana   **Infant formula or breast milk**

1. Peel banana and break into four pieces.
2. Place banana in a food processor or blender and purée until smooth, adding infant formula or breast milk if you need to thin mixture.
3. Serve mashed banana to older babies. Mashed banana is also useful for thickening baby's food.

> Bananas pack potassium and B vitamins to help keep cells in top form.

Acorn/Butternut Squash

Dark orange vegetables, including winter squash, supply vitamin A and fiber.

1 medium acorn or butternut squash or 1 (10-oz.) bag of fresh chopped squash   **Infant formula or breast milk**

1. Prepare using the following methods:

   To roast (whole squash): Heat oven to 400°F. Cut squash in half lengthwise. Scoop out seeds. Brush cut sides with one teaspoon canola oil and place on baking sheet cut-side down. Place baking sheet in preheated oven and roast squash until easily pierced with fork and tender, about 30–40 minutes. Remove from oven and turn right-side up to cool. Let stand for about 15 minutes. Scoop out soft inside of squash and reserve. Discard skins.

   To microwave: Empty contents of squash package into a shallow, microwave-safe dish with 2–3 tablespoons of water. Cover with a microwave-safe cover or with plastic wrap, but do not let the wrap touch the food. Cook on high for 8–10 minutes, stopping once to determine doneness. The squash is ready when easily pierced with a fork.

   To steam: Empty package of squash into the top of a saucepan with steamer basket insert. Steam over high heat for 5–10 minutes, stopping once to determine doneness. The squash is ready when easily pierced with a fork.

2. Place cooked squash in a food processor or blender and blend with infant formula or breast milk until you achieve a smooth, uniform consistency.

3. Strain if necessary before serving.

Broccoli/Cauliflower

Broccoli and cauliflower have phytonutrients, beneficial plant compounds that boost your child's immune system and ward off cell damage.

1 head broccoli or cauliflower or 1 (10-oz.) package of frozen chopped broccoli or cauliflower   **Infant formula or breast milk**

1. If using fresh broccoli or cauliflower, cut off stalks and chop top portion into one-inch florets. Wash thoroughly and drain.

2. Prepare using the following methods:

   To microwave: Place fresh or frozen chopped broccoli or cauliflower in a large, shallow microwave-safe dish in one-half inch water. Cover with a microwave-safe cover or with plastic wrap; but do not let the wrap touch the food. Cook on high for 3–5 minutes. The vegetables are done when easily pierced with a fork. Cook for 1–2 minutes more if not tender enough. Remove from microwave and immediately drain water from the dish. Let stand for 5–10 minutes to cool.

   To steam: Empty frozen broccoli or cauliflower into top of a saucepan with steamer basket insert. Steam over high heat until tender, about 7–10 minutes. When tender, remove from heat. Let stand for 5–10 minutes.

3. Place cooked vegetables in a food processor or blender and blend with infant formula or breast milk until you achieve a smooth, uniform consistency.

4. Strain if necessary before serving.

Carrots

½ lb. fresh carrots or 1 (10-oz.) pkg. frozen carrots, thawed   **Infant formula or breast milk**

> Carrots contain carotenoids, a raw material for vitamin A production in your baby's body and a pigment that contributes to carrots' brilliant color.

1. Cut off both ends of fresh carrots. Wash and peel.

2. Prepare using the following methods:

   To microwave: Place carrots in a large, shallow microwave-safe dish in one-half inch water. Cover with a microwave-safe cover or with plastic wrap; do not let the wrap touch the food. Cook on high for 8–10 minutes. The carrots are done when easily pierced with a fork. Remove from microwave and immediately drain water from the dish. Let stand for 5–10 minutes to cool.

   To steam: Place carrots in the top of a saucepan with steamer basket insert. Steam over high heat until tender, about 10 minutes. The carrots are done when easily pierced with a fork. Let stand for 5–10 minutes to cool.

3. Place cooked carrots in a food processor or blender and blend with infant formula or breast milk until you achieve a smooth, uniform consistency.

4. Strain if necessary before serving.

Green Beans

<table>
<tr><td>½ lb. fresh green beans</td><td>Infant formula or breast milk</td></tr>
</table>

Sometimes foods are note-worthy for what they do not contain. Fresh green beans qualify as a healthy baby food because they are nearly sodium-free.

1. Wash and remove both ends of green beans.
2. Prepare using the following methods:

   To microwave: Place green beans in a shallow microwave-safe dish in one-half inch of water. Cover dish with a microwave-safe cover or with plastic wrap; do not let wrap touch food. Cook on high for 7–10 minutes, checking once for doneness. When done, remove dish from microwave and drain water. Let stand for 5–10 minutes.

   To steam: Place green beans in the top of a saucepan with steamer basket insert. Steam over high heat until tender, about 7–10 minutes. Beans are done when easily pierced with a fork. Remove from heat. Let stand for 5–10 minutes.

3. Place cooked green beans in a food processor or blender and blend with infant formula or breast milk until you achieve a smooth, uniform consistency.
4. Strain if necessary before serving.

Peas

<table>
<tr><td>1 (10-oz.) pkg. frozen peas or
½ lb. fresh-shelled peas</td><td>Infant formula or breast milk</td></tr>
</table>

Peas, actually from the legume family, are filled with folate, a B vitamin your child needs to prevent a type of anemia.

1. Prepare using the following methods:

   To microwave: Place peas in a shallow microwave-safe dish in one-half inch of water. Cover dish with a microwave-safe cover or with plastic wrap; do not let wrap touch food. Cook according to package directions. When done, remove dish from microwave and drain water. Let stand for about 5 minutes.

   To steam: Place peas in the top of a saucepan with steamer basket insert. Steam over high heat until tender, about 5 minutes. Remove from heat. Let stand for about 5 minutes.

2. Place cooked peas in a food processor or blender and blend with infant formula or breast milk until you achieve a smooth, uniform consistency.
3. Strain if necessary before serving.

Potatoes/Sweet Potatoes

1 medium white or sweet   **Infant formula or breast milk**
potato

> Color counts. White potatoes are a healthy choice for baby, but deeply colored sweet potatoes offer more nutrients overall.

1. Prepare using the following methods:

   To bake: Heat oven to 400°F. Scrub the outside of white or sweet potato. Prick the potato with a fork in several places. Place directly on oven rack. Bake until tender, about 45 minutes to an hour for white potatoes; 35–40 minutes for sweet potatoes. Remove and let cool until easy to handle. Slice lengthwise and remove inside of potato. Reserve. Discard skins.

   To steam: Peel one medium white or sweet potato. Chop into one-inch cubes. Place in top portion of double boiler. Steam until tender, about 15–20 minutes. Remove pan from heat and cool for 10 minutes.

2. Place cooked potato in a food processor or blender and blend with infant formula or breast milk until you achieve a smooth, uniform consistency.

3. If you're cooking for an older infant, mash potato before serving.

Apples

3 Golden Delicious apples   **Infant formula or breast milk**

> Babies love the mild and sweet taste of apples. That's a good thing, because they offer water, fiber, and vitamin C. Golden Delicious apples tend to be sweeter, but you can use whatever apples you have on hand.

1. Prepare using the following methods:

   To bake: Heat oven to 350°F. Wash apples and core. Peel a strip from the top of each apple. Place apples in a one-quart casserole dish. Add two tablespoons water. Bake 40–45 minutes or until tender. When done, remove from oven and let stand for 10 minutes to cool. Scoop out insides and discard skins.

   To microwave: Peel apples. Cut in half and remove core and seeds. Chop into one-inch pieces. Place apples in shallow microwave-safe dish with two tablespoons water. Cover dish with microwave-safe cover or with plastic wrap; do not let wrap touch food. Cook on high 5 minutes or until tender. Remove from microwave and drain water. Let stand for 5 minutes.

To steam: Peel apples. Cut in half and remove core and seeds. Chop into one-inch pieces. Place apples in top portion of double boiler. Steam until tender, about 5 minutes. Remove pan from heat and cool for 5 minutes.

2. Place cooked apples in a food processor or blender and blend with infant formula or breast milk until you achieve a smooth, uniform consistency.

Apricots/Plums

Apricots and plums are brimming with the potassium and fiber your tyke needs.

4 to 5 apricots or plums   **Infant formula or breast milk**

1. Peel fruit, cut in half and remove pits, and dice into one-inch chunks.

2. Prepare using the following methods:

   To microwave: Place fruit in a shallow microwave-safe dish in one-half inch of water. Cover dish with a microwave-safe cover or with plastic wrap; do not let wrap touch food. Cook on high 3–5 minutes or until tender. Remove from microwave and drain water. Let stand for 5 minutes.

   To steam: Place fruit in top portion of double boiler. Steam until tender, about 3–5 minutes. Remove pan from heat and cool for 5 minutes.

3. Place fruit in a food processor or blender and blend with infant formula or breast milk until you achieve a smooth, uniform consistency.

4. Strain if necessary before serving.

Nectarines/Peaches

Peaches and nectarines are one and the same; only the fuzz differentiates them. Both provide carbohydrates and vitamin C, among other nutrients.

3 to 4 medium peaches or nectarines   **Infant formula or breast milk**

1. Peel fruit, cut in half and remove pits, and dice into one-inch chunks.

2. Prepare using the following methods:

   To microwave: Place peaches or nectarines in a shallow microwave-safe dish in one-half inch water. Cover dish with a microwave-safe cover or with plastic wrap, but don't let wrap touch food. Cook on high for 3–5 minutes or until tender. Remove dish from oven and drain water. Let stand for 5 minutes.

To steam: Place chopped fruit in top portion of double boiler. Steam until tender, about 5 minutes. Remove pan from heat and cool for 5 minutes.

3. Place cooked fruit in a food processor or blender and blend with infant formula or breast milk until you achieve a smooth, uniform consistency.

4. Strain if necessary before serving.

Pears

3 or 4 Bartlett or Anjou pears   **Infant formula or breast milk**

1. Peel pears, cut in half and remove core and seeds, and dice into one-inch pieces.

2. Prepare using the following methods:

   To microwave: Place pears in a shallow microwave-safe dish in one-half inch of water. Cover dish with a microwave-safe cover or with plastic wrap; don't let wrap touch food. Cook on high for 5 minutes or until tender. Remove dish from microwave and drain water. Let stand for 5 minutes.

   To steam: Place pears in top portion of double boiler. Steam until tender, about 5 minutes. Remove pears from heat and cool for 5 minutes.

3. Place pears in a food processor or blender and blend with infant formula or breast milk until you achieve a smooth, uniform consistency.

4. Strain if necessary before serving.

> Pears are among the top fiber sources. They also pack carbohydrates to energize your little one.

Meat and Poultry

Two ounces of cooked chicken, turkey, pork, or beef   **Infant formula or breast milk**

1. Chop meat or poultry into very small pieces.

2. Place meat in a mini food processor or blender and purée with infant formula or breast milk until meat mixture is uniform and smooth.

3. Remove any chunks before serving.

> Meat and poultry pack protein, B vitamins, zinc, and iron—nutrients that promote growth and good health.

Tofu

1 pkg. silken or firm tofu

Tofu is a good source of vegetable protein and healthy fats.

1. Remove a piece of tofu from the container and pat dry with a paper towel.
2. Mash tofu with a fork until smooth or put into a food processor to purée. Cube firm tofu into small cubes for older babies.

Safe at the Plate

Serve tofu to baby only if you're sure he's not allergic to soy.

Legumes

Legumes are loaded with carbohydrates to fuel your child's cells. They provide fiber and protein.

**1 14- to 16-oz. can legumes or   Infant formula or breast milk
1 cup dried legumes, cooked**

1. Prepare using the following methods:

    If using canned legumes, drain and rinse to remove any excess sodium.

    If using dried legumes, pick through beans, discarding any debris. Rinse well. Soak overnight in about three times their volume of water. Drain and rinse. Place soaked beans in a saucepan and cover generously with water. Simmer over medium-low heat until beans are tender. Simmering times vary with type of bean. Or, put beans in saucepan, adding cold water to cover generously. Over medium-high heat, bring beans to a simmer and cook for 2 minutes. Remove from the heat and let stand, covered, for 1 hour. One cup dried beans makes about 2 cups cooked, the amount found in a typical can.

2. Place legumes in a food processor or blender, and purée with breast milk or infant formula for beginning eaters. Mash for more accomplished eaters.

Safe at the Plate

If you're using garbanzo beans, remove skins before blending or mashing.

Feeding Your Baby: From 6 to 8 Months

In This Chapter

- Learning what foods to serve and why
- Knowing if your child is eating enough
- Explaining pediatric growth charts
- Serving juice to your child
- Taking care of your infant's teeth and gums

Chances are your baby has adjusted to eating infant cereal and he's become comfortable with the feeding routine. He's ready to add puréed fruits, vegetables, and meats, if he hasn't already. (If your baby is just starting solids, refer to Chapter 1 for advice.)

Although age guidelines are important to consider when introducing solids, you should also account for developmental readiness. By six months, many children are becoming adept at moving thicker foods to the back of their mouth and swallowing. In fact, at this point, slightly lumpier meals benefit baby's oral (mouth) skills and build muscle tone, affecting the way she eats, speaks, and makes facial expressions.

This is also the time when parents begin establishing eating patterns that take hold in their tykes. No guilt trip intended, but you should know that the feeding habits you encourage from now on could affect your child's food choices for years to come.

May I Introduce: When to Serve Baby What

After cereal is old hat, parents often ponder which food to next offer their child. The advice they get from friends, family members, and health professionals usually says serving puréed vegetables to baby first is the best move. The rationale goes something like this: Infants prefer sweetness and if you introduce fruit first, it will be harder for your child to accept stronger-tasting vegetables and meat.

However, the idea of serving vegetables before fruit and meat is more anecdotal than scientific. Recent research published in the *Journal of the American Dietetic Association* suggests it's okay to serve your baby fruit, vegetables, or puréed meats as first foods and in any order.

Meat? Yes, you read right. The Centers for Disease Control and Prevention actually recommends serving plain puréed meats beginning at six months to reduce the risk of iron deficiency. According to the American Dietetic Association research, parents tend to hold off on serving meat until at least nine months.

Of course, the order of introduction beyond infant cereals depends on your child's food allergy risk. See Chapter 14 for more on food allergies.

Mother's Helper

What's the 411 on so-called follow-up formulas? These commercial infant formulas are designed for infants as young as six months. Some are even touted as useful for up to 24 months. Follow-up formulas generally contain more calcium, iron, protein, and calories than infant formulas. Does your child need a follow-up formula? Not necessarily, but it won't hurt. Babies with food allergies, those who are very sensitive to different foods, and those with a history of poor growth may benefit from follow-up formula.

The Terms of Texture

Your baby is ready for more than puréed foods, but not yet developed enough to handle diced fruits, vegetables, and meats. The following foods can be used to thicken puréed foods from a jar or baby foods prepared from the recipes in Chapter 2: mashed banana, mashed avocado, mashed tofu, infant cereal, and cooked pastina (tiny pasta).

Making Time for Meals

He's not exactly a chow hound yet, but your baby is probably eating more than he did a couple of months ago. As he moves through the six- to eight-month stage, chances are he'll eat solid foods at least twice daily, maybe more. Plan on devoting some extra time to each meal, including cleanup.

What about sticking to a schedule? It helps to have set times for breakfast, lunch, and dinner, but don't expect baby to always eat on cue. Flexibility is a big plus with babies, especially when it comes to food. Your infant may eat according to an inner clock that mystifies you, but satisfies him. And sometimes children don't feel well or are too tuckered out to eat.

Is Your Child Eating Enough? Too Much?

What's the right amount of food for a six-, seven-, or eight-month-old? That depends. Some children might be consuming breast milk or infant formula only at the six-month mark (although will hopefully soon start on solids to maximize nutrition and development). Some eight-month-olds are enjoying three meals a day of infant cereal and puréed fruits, vegetables, and meats.

Your baby may eat half as much as your friend's, despite the fact that you offer him just as much food. Is something wrong with your child? Probably not. Calorie needs vary among infants. Healthy children typically eat according to the energy they require. Most pediatricians will tell you that as long as you offer your son or daughter enough age-appropriate foods, they will get what they need to grow.

These guidelines are suggested targets for an infant six to eight months old. However, don't be concerned if your child doesn't eat everything on the list every day, especially if he is thriving.

> **Mother's Helper**
>
> Crying doesn't always signal hunger. Crying is a baby's way of communicating with you. Sometimes they are tired, uncomfortable, or sick, or just need comforting. If you do offer the breast or bottle every time he whimpers, he might become accustomed to taking food even though he needs something else.

Food	Amount (in a Day)
Infant formula	20–32 ounces in 3–4 feedings
Breastfeeding	4–5 feedings daily or on demand
Dry-fortified infant cereal	8–10 teaspoons (mix with breast milk or infant formula)
Fruits and vegetables	1–2 jars or 1 cup puréed and strained or mashed, cooked fruits and vegetables (total)
Meat	½ to 1 jar or a few ounces puréed

Mom, Dad, I'm Full!

Were you a member of the Clean Plate Club as a kid? You know, that group of children required to devour every last bit of food on their plates before leaving the table? Well, it's time to renounce your membership.

Your parents' motivation for not wasting food was worthy. Unfortunately, it was misguided. Encouraging a child to finish his food when he's not hungry helps set the stage for overeating later in life. Learning to trust a child's instinct to eat when he's hungry and stop when he's satisfied is the greatest gift a parent can give their child, especially when the parent must work hard to overcome his or her own eating issues.

You might pride yourself on being able to sneak in some spoonfuls when your child is distracted, but resist the urge. Starting at six months, and even before, children are capable of showing their interest in eating. Use this time to make eating as pleasurable as possible for your baby. Smile and offer praise and encouragement for his eating efforts.

Learning to take no for an answer will help you avoid feeding frustration. Don't take her food refusal personally. And avoid reading into her facial expressions. When you give her the first spoonful of a new food, she may screw up her mug and spit the food back out at you. Keep in mind she could be reacting to the novelty of it, not to the eating.

Of course, there is a chance that a child's poor appetite is related to an underlying medical condition. Speak to your pediatrician if her lack of appetite persists.

Chances are your child has had enough food when she does one or more of the following:

- Swats the spoon
- Turns away

- Purses her lips tight when she sees the spoon coming
- Plays with the food, but doesn't put any in her mouth
- Spits out every spoonful of food you give her
- Becomes cranky or cries

Details, Please

A study in the *Journal of the American Dietetic Association* shows that when mom snubs certain foods, particularly vegetables, it's highly unlikely she'll offer those foods to her child to try. That's unfortunate, because the study also found food preferences are shaped as early as two years of age. Introducing your child to an array of flavors early on helps broaden her food choices down the road and may help her to choose a more varied diet. That means serving foods that may not be appealing to you, but that your baby might like.

The Juicy Details About Juice

Juice is perceived as a good-for-you beverage, head and shoulders above soda and other sugary soft drinks. And it is. Beverages containing 100 percent fruit juice supply calories, vitamins, minerals, and phytonutrients. Phytonutrients are disease-fighting plant substances that soda and other beverages lack. Juices for infants and toddlers often contain added nutrients, including vitamin C; and yogurt and juice blends work in several nutrients, including vitamins and the mineral calcium. Although juice is a nutritious beverage that can be used in place of fruit, it does not offer the fiber found in whole fruits.

How Much Juice for Your Child?

There is such a thing as too much juice, according to the American Academy of Pediatrics (AAP). The AAP suggests waiting until at least six months to introduce juice to infants. Furthermore, they suggest limiting a child's juice intake to just six ounces (three-quarters cup) a day until he's six years old. The high natural sugar content of juice can cause diarrhea in otherwise healthy children.

Never fill a baby's bottle with juice. That's the beginning of an unhealthy habit that can be very difficult to break. Children may come to prefer a juice-filled baby bottle to one that contains much-needed infant formula or breast milk. Your child might be less likely to give up a juice bottle, which could result in nutrient deficiencies, cavities, and excess calories. Because there is no real need for juice, you can wait until your baby has begun using a sippy cup around eight months or so. Dilute juice by half to cut the amount of sugar.

Choosing the Best Juice for Your Child

Only beverages that contain 100 percent juice are worthy of your baby. Look at the top of the Nutrition Facts Panel for the percentage of juice in a beverage. You'll find that juice concoctions with the terms cocktail, drink, beverage, and any word ending in -ade (such as lemonade) on the front of the label contain less than 100 percent juice. These beverages, although fortified with nutrients such as calcium and vitamin C, contain lots of added sweeteners that kids don't need. Children (and adults) should always consume juice that's undergone *pasteurization* to reduce the chance of illness from germs. Check the label.

> **Technically Speaking**
>
> **Pasteurization** is the process of heating juice and other liquids, including milk, to a high heat to kill bacteria that can make you sick.

Does Size Matter?

Let's face it. We live in a society obsessed with size. Chances are you've been quizzed about your baby's birth weight by friends, family, and complete strangers. Maybe your baby weighed much less or much more than others you know of and you felt odd about it. Forget about it. Sometimes it's difficult to feel good about your child's size, but it's important to consider that healthy kids come in all shapes and sizes.

Pediatric Growth Charts

At every pediatrician's visit, the doctor or nurse weighs your child and measures his length and the circumference (distance around) of his head, then plops him on a chart called the Centers for Disease Control (CDC) Growth Chart. What's that all about?

The CDC Growth Charts assist doctors, dietitians, and nurses in determining whether children are growing within the norm for their age. Growth chart assessments are used as part of the child's overall examination and determination of health. After two, your child's *Body Mass Index (BMI)* will be added to the growth chart equation. Use the CDC Pediatric Growth Charts available for downloading at www.cdc.gov/growthcharts to track your child's growth. There is also a website run by the Neonatal Research Network, which does research for the National Institute of Child Health and Human Development. Parents can go to this website and track the growth of their low-birth-weight baby: neonatal.rti.org/birth_curves/dsp_BirthCurves.cfm.

As your child gets older, you might be inclined to discuss where his height, weight, and head circumference fall on the growth charts. You may feel badly when your child doesn't weigh as much as others, or is not as tall, or just the opposite. Avoid comparing children, because their rate of growth can differ. For example, exclusively breast-fed babies tend to gain weight more rapidly during their first two to three months, but weigh less than formula-fed infants from six to twelve months. As long as your child is a healthy weight and is growing at the right rate, then there's little to worry about. Here are some red flags when it comes to weight:

- Your infant has gained no weight for two to three months.

- Your child's weight and height are both below the fifth percentile.

- Your child has suddenly lost weight, which could signal a developmental or feeding problem or illness.

Technically Speaking

Body Mass Index (BMI) assesses a person's weight as it relates to his height to determine body fat. The growth charts used after age two include a BMI component to help determine if a child has too much body fat.

Your Child's Adult Size: Nature or Nurture?

When you're wondering about your infant's full-grown self, remember this: The weight of a healthy full-term baby has no bearing on his full-grown size. Genetics plays a role in the size of your child, although environment (sedentary lifestyle and too many calories) can overcome a propensity for thinness. When all is said and done, your child will probably fulfill his genetic destiny, turning out to be about the same size as his parents. However, low-birth-weight babies (under five and a half pounds) born before 40 weeks may be smaller than average because they didn't grow enough during the pregnancy.

Safe at the Plate

Never withhold food from an infant because you think she's packing too much baby fat. You can cause serious nutrient deficiencies that will affect your baby now and much later in life. If you think she's eating too much or not enough, speak with your pediatrician or a registered dietitian (R.D.) for advice. Get a free referral to an R.D. in your area when you visit the American Dietetic Association's website at www.eatright.org. Local hospitals typically have outpatient dietitians who provide counseling, and you can also find an R.D. in private practice by searching the phone book.

Your Child's Choppers

You wouldn't know it from the toothless grin she flashes at you, but your baby already has a full set of pearly whites. She was born with all her "baby," or primary teeth. Primary teeth start peeking through a baby's gums around six months. Lower front teeth are most likely to show up first, one at a time, with upper front teeth following shortly thereafter. Other teeth appear in clusters until baby has "cut" all 20 primary teeth between her second and third birthday.

Primary teeth allow your child to move from puréed to chunkier foods that he can chew before swallowing. Teeth are for more than eating, however. They promote proper speech development, and help to shape your baby's face. Losing primary teeth to cavities or accidents shifts the remaining teeth and causes permanent teeth to come in crooked.

Teething may make for an irritable child who refuses food, sleeps fitfully, cries a lot, or does all the above. Chillable teether and gum massagers help soothe swollen gums. Some kids rub smooth or nubby toys against their gums, or suck their thumbs or pacifiers more when cutting teeth. Teething rings that can be cooled in the refrigerator or freezer might be preferable to baby. Don't mind him drooling like a St. Bernard—it's a normal part of teething even though babies drool when they're not expecting a tooth any time soon. Fever, diarrhea, and vomiting are not signs of teething, however. Talk to your doctor if your child has these symptoms.

Making the Cavity Connection

It doesn't take a math whiz to comprehend the cavity equation: Germs + Carbohydrates = Cavities

Safe at the Plate

Cavities can be contagious. Studies suggest cavity-causing bacteria are transmitted from mom's saliva to her baby from sharing cups, utensils, or food. Reduce your baby's cavity risk by brushing your teeth after meals and snacks and visiting the dentist regularly.

The mouth harbors acid-producing bacteria that erodes enamel, a tooth's hard, outer protection. Foods such as soft drinks, bread, crackers, and pasta provide food for these pesky bacteria. The longer carbohydrate lingers in the mouth, the greater the potential damage to teeth.

Foods commonly given to teething babies, including soft bread and pretzels, are stickier than other carbohydrate-containing foods and encourage cavities even more than sweet beverages, such as juice. Infant formula and breast milk do not get off so easily, however. These carbohydrate-rich beverages can also cause cavities when they are allowed to pool around teeth for long periods. Don't put your baby down for the night in his crib with a bottle of formula, and avoid nursing babies to sleep.

Older children should nosh on cheese instead of sweets for snacks and dessert. Hard-aged cheese, including cheddar, is an anti-cavity food. It's carbohydrate-free, so it doesn't supply a food source for mouth bacteria. And cheese appears to neutralize the acid that the germs produce, reducing the wear and tear on teeth.

Caring for Your Child's Teeth and Gums

The health and development of your baby's mouth is directly related to his well-being, now and later. Although it's hard to imagine brushing one or even two of your child's choppers, it's a good habit to begin. Before baby's teeth appear, rub his gums with a clean, damp washcloth or a small square of gauze after feeding to remove food that feeds mouth germs that make cavities. In addition to regular brushing and flossing (after teeth are touching), a balanced diet with few sugary foods is the best way to protect a child's teeth and gums.

The mineral fluoride goes a long way to curb cavities, working to strengthen tooth enamel and reduce the ability of mouth bacteria to produce damaging acid. Fluoride is most effective at fighting cavities after teeth have erupted. (See Chapter 11 for more on your baby's fluoride needs.) Talk with your pediatrician about starting fluoride supplements at six months of age if your baby is breastfed or drinking formula prepared with fluoride-free water. However, too much fluoride can be just as bad as too little. Excess fluoride causes cosmetic changes in teeth ranging from minor white lines that streak the tooth to a very chalky white appearance.

This might seem over the top to you, but pediatric dental health experts recommend a visit to the dentist after your child cuts his first tooth, which is usually between six and twelve months. If you can't imagine hauling your seven-month-old into a dentist's office, make sure you see a pediatric dentist before your child's first birthday at the latest.

The Least You Need to Know

- As long as your child is not allergic, it doesn't matter what order you introduce puréed fruits, vegetables, and meats.
- Babies grow differently, so avoid comparing your child to others. As long as your pediatrician says your child is healthy, that's what matters most.

- Children do not require juice for good health. However, it helps satisfy their requirement for fruit. Use juice sparingly, and choose only 100 percent juice with added nutrients.

- Your baby's first teeth are an important part of eating and overall development of speech; they also help shape your child's face and hold places for his permanent teeth.

Chapter 4

Feeding Your Baby: From 8 to 12 Months

In This Chapter

- Learning what foods to serve now, and how much
- Choking prevention
- Fostering self-feeding skills
- Talking candidly about bowel movements

Your baby can do more now with his body than he could when you first began feeding him solid foods. His newly acquired motor skills will bring major changes in what he eats, and how. By the end of these four months, puréed foods will be out and table foods will dominate your child's diet. And you can be sure his efforts at feeding himself will give new meaning to the term mess hall!

At this point, your baby is gaining a new feeling of control over her relationships with the adults who care for her. By her first birthday, she'll be more adept at communicating with you, too. Don't be surprised (or hurt) when your lovable little one shakes her head from side to side in a gesture that screams "no!" The so-called head shake is one of the earliest moves babies learn to make, but it's not necessarily a rejection of what you've prepared for dinner.

What Foods to Serve Now, and How Much

As your child gets closer to a year old, she might be eating more of the same foods you eat. That's okay, as long as you remember her special nutrient needs; pay attention to her developmental readiness for certain table foods; and are mindful of food allergy risks.

The following are suggested guidelines for what to feed your baby now.

Food	Suggested Amount
Infant formula	16–32 ounces in 2–3 feedings
Breastfeeding	3–4 feedings daily or on demand
Dry-fortified infant cereal	½ cup (mix with breast milk or infant formula)
Fruits and vegetables	1–2 cups total of puréed or mashed
Meat	1–4 ounces chopped, cooked, fresh, ground, or finely chopped poultry (remove all skin, bones, and fat) or ½ jar puréed meat

Your infant might also have …

● Full-fat yogurt and hard cheeses, such as cheddar and cottage cheese
● Cooked and mashed legumes, including lentils and garbanzo beans
● Cooked egg yolk
● Combinations such as macaroni and cheese or spaghetti and meat sauce (run through food processor to make chunky)

When children start eating table foods in earnest, choking risk goes up, largely because table foods are chunkier and harder to handle than their puréed counterparts. Read on for why children are prone to choking and ways to keep choking from happening.

Keep Your Child Choke-Free

When food or any other small object lodges in a child's throat and blocks his airway, it cuts off the supply of precious oxygen to his lungs and brain. If an oxygen shortage continues for more than four minutes, brain damage or death can result. Most victims who choke to death are under a year old.

Okay, enough scary stuff! There are plenty of ways to protect your child from choking. You may already be at it, going as far as cutting his Cheerios in half (no need, they easily dissolve in saliva, plus they have a whole in the middle!). Even the most conscientious adult can't conjure up every potential choking hazard, however. For example, letting children eat or drink while you're driving is a major mistake. There may be no way for you to help a youngster dislodge food from his throat during a car ride, especially if you are the only adult present.

A child could choke on food for any number of reasons, including …

- He lacks the skills. It's important to know where your child is developmentally. Do not rely on age. For example, just because your child is eight months old doesn't mean he's necessarily ready for thicker foods if it appears he can't handle them without difficulty.

- He lacks supervision. Keep a close watch over infants and other children at meal and snack times to prevent choking. Never leave a little one unattended when she's eating. Don't allow older children to feed an infant what they are eating, either.

- He's roughhousing. Kids can also choke when they overstuff their mouths, or when they laugh hard or run around with a mouth full of food. It's a good idea to establish early on that your child must be sitting to eat and drink.

The following foods pose a particular choking hazard and are dangerous to kids because they are hard, round, firm, or sticky. Some of them, including grapes and melon, are safe when cut into ¼- to ½-inch pieces. Some, such as hard candy, are not nutritionally worthy, so skip them for now.

- Whole nuts and seeds
- Popcorn
- Snack chips and puffs
- Pretzels
- Raw carrot and celery sticks
- Raw green beans
- Cherry or grape tomatoes (okay if cut into small pieces)
- Raisins, and other small dried fruit, such as cranberries, blueberries, and cherries
- Whole berries and grapes (okay if cut into small pieces)
- Melon balls (okay if cut into small pieces)
- Marshmallows
- Large chunks of cheese, meat, poultry, and hot dogs

- Peanut butter and other nut butters (okay to spread thinly on crackers or on bread, but break into small pieces)
- Hard candy and cough drops
- Chewing gum
- Gum drops and jelly beans

Many of the foods on this list are inappropriate for an older baby, too, so save it as a reference for years to come.

I Can Do It Myself, Mom!

At this age, your child's fine motor skills are developing at a rapid pace. One of his new moves will be the perfection of the pincer grasp—picking up food (and other objects) between his forefinger and thumb, which may have begun around his sixth month or so.

Until now, he may have tried to scoop up foods with his chubby little mitts, stuffing his fists into his mouth, without depositing very much food. Perfecting the pincer grasp opens up another eating horizon for your child because he is better able to feed himself. And believe it, he'll want a greater role at meal times.

Here are some safe choices for finger foods:

- Baby crackers
- Soft fruits
- Well-cooked vegetables
- Jarred or canned diced fruits and vegetables
- Small pieces of bread
- Small chunks of cheese
- Small chunks of firm tofu
- Dry cereals that dissolve easily in saliva
- Grain-based baby snacks, such as zwieback and teething biscuits

A Very Messy Affair

As he approaches his first birthday, he'll probably want to feed himself. Give him his own spoon, but hold off on the fork until after two. Sure, it may get ugly when he misses his mouth and applesauce lands in his hair or on the wall, but it's worth it in the long run. Playing with a spare spoon while you do the lion's share of feeding is fun for him. Plus, it fosters his muscle coordination. After all, you don't want to be spoon-feeding him forever!

Drinking from so-called sippy cups repre-sents another developmental hurdle for your child, one that kids relish because it's new and it's fun. Don't expect much fluid to make it into her mouth until around 10 months or even later, although some infants master the skill ear-lier. A two-handled plastic spill-proof cup allows your child to grab on with both hands while attempting to align the spout with her mouth. Fill the sippy cup with water at first. As she becomes better at using the cup, fill it with breast milk or infant formula.

Mother's Helper

Encouraging sippy cup use earlier rather than later in the first year is a plus for par-ents. Trying to convince a one-year-old to go from the breast or bottle to a cup is a lot harder than interesting an eight-month-old in the transition.

Thinking About Weaning

By his first birthday, your child will no longer require infant formula. Parents who are interested in taking steps toward weaning their infant from a bottle around 12 months or earlier should expose him to a sippy cup right about now. As he becomes more sure of his drinking skills, he can take more infant formula from a sippy cup. By 10 or 11 months, you can gradually cut back on bottle feedings if he is able to drink the same amount of infant formula from a cup.

As for breastfed babies, they will have received the bulk of the benefits of mother's milk by about 12 months. Of course, if you and your baby want to continue breast-feeding beyond one year, you should. Some babies discontinue nursing on their own by the end of the first year, while others show no signs of wanting that feeding part-nership to end. It's normal for a breastfeeding mother to feed sad when her child is ready to stop nursing and she herself is not.

Toilet Talk: The Scoop on Poop

When your child was drinking only breast milk or infant formula, his bowel move-ments, although never exactly pleasant, were fairly predictable. A breastfed baby's poop ranges in color from yellowish to tan and is mildly odorous. Bowel movements produced by formula-fed infants are stronger smelling, more solid, and medium to dark brown. You can stop counting on that kind of consistency. Adding solid foods means major changes in your child's pooping patterns.

He may go less often as more food is added that contain components that contribute to firmer, and fewer, bowel movements. The naturally occurring pigments in brightly colored vegetables, including beets, sweet potatoes, and carrots, often make an appearance in poop. Bowel movements will also stink more in the coming months, so get ready. Iron supplements can cause stools to darken and become less frequent, too. And until your child has molars, she'll "chew" with her gums which may leave small pieces of food in her diaper.

The bottom line on bowel movements is that it's hard to know what's normal when baby's food intake changes so often. The following signs in your baby's diaper may be cause for concern:

- Small, dry brown poop
- Blood-streaked bowel movements
- Solid black stools with what appears to resemble coffee-grounds
- Watery, loose and possibly explosive poop

If you have any questions about your child's bowel movements, call your pediatrician.

The Least You Need to Know

- As children go from puréed foods to mashed and diced, their risk of choking increases. Never leave a child unsupervised while eating and don't let children eat in the car while you are driving. Always chop food into very small pieces that are safe for baby.
- Your infant will want to feed herself more and more as she nears her first birthday. Foster self-feeding skills by giving her a child-friendly spoon during meals and safe finger foods.
- At one year, most children no longer require infant formula or breast milk. In preparation for that change, introduce a sippy cup with water during this stage of your child's life.
- Bowel movements will change drastically after your child is on a steady diet of solid foods.

Part 2

Feeding Your Toddler

The trick to feeding toddlers is understanding their point of view. Older toddlers in particular are suspicious of the unfamiliar, including new foods. Your child is also developing a sense of who she is and what she wants at the dinner table. Now's the time when you see glimpses of her emerging personality. Many children have already started "voicing" their opinions through gesturing, babbling, and practicing the few words they know over and over. By the end of the year, that will be par for the course. You're in "toddler territory" now. Read on for ways to meet the challenges of year two.

Chapter 5

Feeding Your Child: From 12 to 18 Months

In This Chapter

- Changing nutrient needs from infancy
- Making the move to cow's milk
- Handling your child's fear of new foods
- Explaining erratic eating

Your child might already be steady on his feet. Perhaps he's working on pulling himself up to standing in preparation for walking. Whatever the case, he'll be far more physically active this year than he was as a baby. Yet his calorie needs decline on a pound-for-pound basis. That's just one of the puzzling contradictions characteristic of "toddlerhood."

Here's another: one day, your child wants you to spoon-feed him like an infant; the next, he wants nothing to do with your help. And another: he's still attached to his baby bottle, something that he should be working on giving up in favor of sippy cups. There's no question that young toddlers are fickle. Find out how their contrarian nature affects how you feed them.

Calorie Needs

During infancy, your child may have packed on between 13 and 15 pounds and added 10 inches in length. There's no way he could continue to grow at that pace. A slower rate of growth means your child's calorie needs decrease pound for pound.

The following chart provides an example of the differences in calorie needs based on weight as your child gets older.

Example of Caloric Needs

Age	Weight	Calories per Pound	Calories per Day
3 months	15 lbs.	45	680
13 months	25 lbs.	37	925

Although your child's energy requirements go down based on weight once he's a toddler, as he grows and packs on more pounds his daily calorie needs will gradually increase. That's because calorie calculations for kids are based on per-pound energy needs; as a child increases his weight, his calorie needs go up.

"Mooving" to Milk

At 12 months, it's safe to give up infant formula or breast milk for cow's milk or other fortified beverages, including soy. By all means, continue nursing if you and baby want.

Why did you have to wait until now to start cow's milk? Cow's milk is low in iron and it may cause intestinal bleeding; both increase an infant's risk of iron deficiency anemia. Cow's milk also contains proteins that are difficult for babies to digest. Other dairy foods, such as cheese and yogurt, get the green light during infancy because they are consumed in small amounts.

In addition, when solid foods are a mainstay of a toddler's eating pattern, he no longer needs all the nutrition that infant formula or breast milk provides. Yet, he does require the nutrients found in 16 to 24 ounces a day of full-fat milk (and full-fat vegetarian options such as fortified soy beverages), including calories, fat, protein, B vitamins, vitamin D, and calcium.

To make a safe and effective transition from formula or breast milk, try mixing one-quarter cup infant formula or expressed breast milk in baby's bottle or sippy cup with full-fat cow's milk or fortified soy beverage. Gradually decrease formula or breast milk over the course of a week or two until you use none.

Good-bye Old Friend: How to Break the Bottle Habit

It might be difficult for your toddler to give up drinking from a baby bottle. The sooner you start trying to get him to break his bottle habit, the better. Your young toddler will become increasingly inflexible as the months go by, and you may find yourself locked in a battle of wills over the issue.

Many children take comfort in drinking from a bottle. But you never know. Weaning your child may be easier than you think. Perhaps you assume that your child won't easily give up the bottle. Or maybe you prefer the bottle because it makes less mess.

If your child is not already proficient with a spill-proof sippy cup, he can get up to snuff within weeks. Offer the cup more often and drop the bottle feedings that he cares least about. Make drinking from the bottle less appealing by restricting it to the kitchen or dining room.

What Foods to Serve Now

With the exception of reduced-fat milks, your one-year-old can eat just about anything you're having, as long as he's not allergic to it, and it's in kid-friendly form— either mashed or cut into small pieces.

Still, even with all those food options, feeding a one-year-old can be dicey. Here's the problem: a toddler's appetite typically drops off, putting more pressure on the food he eats to deliver the nutrients he needs. It's particularly important to offer your child the healthiest foods possible, and eliminate the treats that fill him up without providing anything but calories.

The following one-day menu for 12- to 18-month-olds is a suggestion for working in the foods your child needs. Do not panic if your child does not eat all the foods you offer, or wants more. The best you can do is serve small portions of a variety of foods at each meal and snack plus the recommended 16 to 24 ounces of milk throughout the day.

Breakfast
>   4 ounces full-fat milk or yogurt
>   ¼ cup whole grain ready-to-eat-cereal (iron-fortified)
>   ¼ medium banana, chopped

Snack

2 graham cracker squares

½ cup applesauce or 4 ounces 100 percent juice fortified with vitamins and calcium

Lunch

4 ounces full-fat milk

1 ounce cooked boneless, skinless chicken, chopped

1–2 tablespoons cooked carrots, diced

½ teaspoon butter, if desired

1 slice whole grain bread

Snack

1 ounce mild cheddar cheese, chopped into small pieces

2–3 whole grain crackers

4 ounces full-fat milk

Dinner

8 ounces full-fat milk

½ cup cooked noodles with 2 tablespoons marinara sauce with cooked, crumbled 100 percent ground turkey breast or lean beef

2 tablespoons cooked green beans, chopped

½ teaspoon butter, if desired

¼ cup fresh or canned pears, drained and chopped

Erratic Eating Explained

One day she eats nearly everything you give her for meals and snacks with great gusto; the next day she manages just a bite or two at each meal. What's up with the erratic eating habits? She's obeying her hunger, that's all. When you offer only nutritious foods to a toddler with topsy-turvy eating, you're doing all you can as a loving parent.

Her fluctuating appetite can be due to any one of the following:

- Growth spurts. Kids tend to grow out, then up. First they pack on a little weight, then, almost overnight, thin out by adding height. They will eat more in the weeks before they get taller.

- Teething. From about 13 to 19 months, children cut molars, which tend to be more painful than cutting smaller teeth. It may hurt to chew and your child may be more irritable because of inflamed gums.

- A fascination with the world. Young toddlers are often so taken with their surroundings and astonished by their own physical prowess that food plays second fiddle to having fun.

A decrease in appetite can also be the result of fever, fatigue, or an underlying chronic medical condition. Speak to your doctor if your child does not eat well after three or four days or is constantly out of sorts.

Give Grazing the Boot

Constant snacking is another reason for a poor appetite at meal time. You may think that when a child skimps on meals, he should have snacks. Sounds reasonable. Problem is, it can lead to a vicious cycle of grazing throughout the day, eating poorly at meals, and then more grazing. Remember, toddlers are smart and crafty. They learn quickly that if they don't want what's being served for breakfast, lunch, or dinner, all they have to do is wait for the foods they like later on.

Curb grazing by always feeding your child in a designated eating area (kitchen or dining room). When your child eats a very small meal, offer him leftovers a few hours later. This sends the message that he can eat what you offer when he's hungry for it.

No New Foods!

Food neophobia is a fancy term describing a person's rejection of new foods without even so much as a taste. Toddlers, highly suspicious beings that they are, suffer the most from food neophobia.

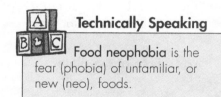

Technically Speaking

Food neophobia is the fear (phobia) of unfamiliar, or new (neo), foods.

Why all the fuss over new foods? It could be that because toddlers spend their days learning and mastering new skills—walking, running, climbing, and talking—and are so consumed by novel experiences and sensations, they don't want any surprises on their plates. It's also quite common for kids to latch on to favorite foods to the exclusion of new ones as a way of comforting themselves.

All you can do is ride out her rejection of new foods with good cheer and the following tactics, of course:

- Practice patience. A few deep breaths go a long way to reducing meal-time tension that toddlers easily pick up on (and exploit).
- Try the new food again in a few days. Feeding your child only his favorite foods because it's easy—including highly processed chicken nuggets and macaroni and cheese out of a box—will come back to haunt you when you want to expand his mealtime repertoire.

- Offer a new food at the same meal as familiar foods you know she likes. Some children get upset when foods touch, so be sure to keep the new food away from her favorites.
- Keep portions small. Give him about a teaspoonful of any new food. Big portions can be overwhelming, and you can always give him more if he wants.
- Keep new foods as similar to old favorites as possible.

It might take between 10 and 15 exposures to a new food before your child decides to give it a try. Look at it this way: He can't eat it if he's never seen it. Whatever you do, avoid overreacting when your toddler shows little interest in a meal, even when it contains his current favorite foods. Rejecting foods has nothing to do with you or your parenting skills.

Stealth Nutrition

A toddler's smaller appetite requires even greater attention to nutrition. You can use these covert techniques to stack the deck in favor of good nutrition without your little one being the wiser for it:

Safe at the Plate

It's okay to use mild herbs and spices in toddler food. Watch out for strongly favored seasonings, including garlic and onions. Some seasonings may still strike baby as too strong or be too harsh for her tummy, so go slow. There's no need to add salt to your child's food, now or in the future.

- Add puréed vegetables to meatloaf, meatballs, and pasta sauce.
- Allow him to dip cooked vegetables into a yogurt-based dip or cheese sauce.
- Make fruit more fun by topping small cubes (not balls) of melon or berries with sweetened yogurt sauce.
- Add wheat germ and orange juice to mashed sweet potatoes.
- Make mashed potatoes with condensed milk for twice the calcium.
- Prepare fruit and yogurt smoothies with added powdered milk.

There are numerous dip, topping, and smoothie recipes that you can try in Appendix A.

The Least You Need to Know

- After one year of age, a toddler's growth slows down and her calorie needs drop on a pound-per-pound basis. A reduced appetite may lead to erratic eating in young toddlers.
- Because your child's appetite can be up and down, it's important to offer nutrient-rich foods to maximize nutrition.
- Your child no longer requires infant formula, and should be making moves to give up drinking from a baby bottle. It's now safe for toddlers to drink full-fat milk and fortified soy beverages.
- New foods are highly suspect to a toddler. Don't let that discourage you from attempting to get her to eat them. It could take upward of 15 tries before she shows interest.

Chapter 6

Feeding Your Child: From 18 to 24 Months

In This Chapter

- How to avoid parental pitfalls
- Why family meals matter
- How to snack smartly
- What dietary supplements can do for your children

They say change is the one constant in life. Whoever came up with that one must have raised a toddler. By 18 months, your child may be struggling with both wanting to stay babylike and becoming more independent. Because he doesn't yet have a great command of the language, it's difficult for you to know what's going on in his head on any given day. That inner conflict can carry over to the dinner table where your otherwise charming and funny child tries your patience.

It might seem like you're going back to the drawing board every few weeks to revamp your feeding strategies during this stage. Hold tight. It will pass. Until it does, read on for how to handle the second half of your child's second year.

Time for a Reality Check

At this age, table food is the norm for toddlers, which means they are having what you are having. Is what you're eating as healthy as it could be? Perhaps it's time for a nutrition tune-up.

Toddlers today are showing signs of an unhealthy diet adopted by their parents. That's the conclusion of The Feeding Infants and Toddlers Study (FITS) published in the *Journal of the American Dietetic Association*. It surveyed the food and beverage consumption habits of more than 3,000 American infants and toddlers under the age of two. The following were among the findings:

- Nearly 25 percent of children ages 9 to 24 months don't eat any fruits or vegetables on a given day.

- Babies as young as 7 months swill soda and other sweetened beverages; 10 percent of 15- to 18-month-olds drink soda at least once a day.

- Parents use food to reward good behavior more often than they offer praise or a hug.

- French fries are the third most popular "vegetable" among 9- to 11-month-olds and the second most common one among 12- to 14-month-olds.

These findings are startling, largely because they are so far off from expert feeding recommendations. They also serve as a reminder that in order for children to eat a nutritious diet, adults must offer healthy foods.

Dining Together: Why It Matters

Family meals might seem like a thing of the past, but that doesn't make them any less important. All too often, hectic work schedules make eating together difficult, especially when it involves a toddler who is often tired by the end of the day and cannot wait for his dinner.

Even when it's just you and your child, dine together whenever you can. Don't fuss with cleaning the kitchen while your child eats. Sit and talk with him. And keep meals as free of distractions as possible. Turn off the television and turn on the answering machine. It may be the only time of day when you tune out the noise and talk directly with your family.

Young children are social beings who love to be included in any gathering, even one as simple as a meal. Encouraging toddlers to join in the mealtime conversation bolsters brain development and language skills. Facing your child when you feed him, talking directly to him, and making eye contact makes eating enjoyable and stimulating.

Children crave ritual. Family meals should be part of the routine he can count on to keep him feeling secure. Eating together not only brings family members together, it may increase your child's chances of eating healthy foods by exposing him to a wider array of choices.

Parent Traps

Parents are gatekeepers. Research suggests that moms rule when it comes to influencing the family diet (sorry, Dad!). With power comes responsibility, however. Alas, no parent is perfect, and at some point or another, you may find yourself falling into a few of the classic parent traps. Here are three to avoid.

Eat What I Serve, Not What I Eat

You're doing your best to keep sugar, saturated fat, and sodium to a minimum in your child's diet. So far, it's been a success. If you're not eating in the same healthy fashion as your child, ditch the double standard. You can't expect to nosh on a jelly-filled donut or snack chips in front of her without her clamoring for some of your food. Your actions speak louder than words.

Mom-as-Short-Order-Cook Syndrome

You don't run a restaurant, you run a family. So why is your toddler ordering what he wants to eat? Sure, a certain amount of choice is beneficial for toddlers because it encourages independence. Let your child decide between strawberries and a banana, not between snack chips and vegetables. When kids have these kinds of choices before them, you can't lose when both options are healthy. If she wants neither, she's probably not hungry.

There's nothing wrong with serving foods your child likes, especially because it cuts down on your aggravation. You can't constantly cater to his whims, however. If you did, processed chicken nuggets, French fries, and macaroni and cheese would become the mainstays of your family's diet. So go ahead and prepare a family meal, but do not make a separate meal for your toddler. Instead, try serving at least two healthy foods that are certain hits with your child at dinner, including bread, rice, potatoes, or pasta; fruit; and milk, cheese, and yogurt.

Food to the Rescue

Avoid using food as a reward or to help your child feel better. Don't soothe her agitation with a cup of juice or a lollipop, and refrain from bribing him with a bag of chips to munch on so that you can get things done around the house. It is a short-term solution that detracts from what we have been preaching all along: children should eat when they are hungry and for no other reason. Calorie-free and sugar-free bandages and hugs are much better for soothing frazzled nerves.

He Eats Like a Bird!

When you're faced with a toddler who seems to run on fumes in spite of the tempting meals and snacks you prepare, it's hard to keep your head. All the talk of daily nutrient requirements can have you in a spin when you realize your child hasn't touched milk, vegetables, or meat in a few days.

Here's a typical toddler eating pattern: he favors dairy foods for a few days, then shuns them for as many, and returns to them with great gusto. And another: he sticks to just one or two foods from each of the food groups. Such eating patterns seem inadequate, but upon closer examination they really aren't. What's really important is a child's intake over a few days, or even a week. In the end, most toddlers get what they need, much to their parents' surprise.

A typical toddler day may go something like this. Should you worry?

Breakfast

> 2 bites scrambled egg
> 4 ounces whole milk
> ¼ cup cubed cantaloupe
> ½ piece of whole grain toast

Lunch

> ¼ of a peanut butter and jelly sandwich on whole grain bread
> 3 bites of a banana
> 2 ounces whole milk
> Cooked, diced carrots, ¼ cup

Snack

> 1 ounce cheese stick
> 6 wheat crackers
> ½ apple, peeled and chopped

Dinner

> 1 to 2 ounces cooked chicken
> Few bites of rice with margarine
> 8 green beans
> 4 ounces of whole milk

Snack

> 4 ounces full-fat yogurt

How'd he do? Not bad for a finicky toddler. He came up a bit short for fruits and vegetables, really no surprise for a toddler. He met his protein and calcium goals without a problem and his hearty afternoon snack was a good choice, even if it appears to have taken the edge off his appetite at dinner.

Mother's Helper

Toddlers can be downright weird when it comes to food. Certain textures can turn off a young child to her meal. So can the way food is arranged on her plate, even when it's her favorite. Be careful. Your son or daughter could blow a gasket when foods touch each other; are mixed together; smell or look different; or have different seasonings in them.

Snacking Smarts

He's getting older, but his stomach is still small. That's why toddlers tend to eat small meals. Although some kids do fine on three meals a day, others have room for two or more snacks.

We are a nation of noshers, and the food industry has rushed to satisfy our urge to eat between meals with tempting crackers, chips, bars, cookies, candy, and dozens of other options designated as snack foods. These choices are not the best mini-meals for us or for our children. The most nutritious snacks are foods that you would typically serve at meals.

The following are among the most nutritious snack choices for toddlers and other family members:

- Natural cheese, such as cheddar, Havarti, or Swiss
- Milk (full-fat for up to two years old)
- Yogurt (full-fat for up to two years old)
- Hard-cooked eggs
- Cottage cheese (full-fat for up to two years old)
- Tuna

Mother's Helper

When should a toddler snack? When he's hungry, this could be about two to three hours after his last meal. Some children are not frequent snackers, especially if they eat well at meal times, so don't worry if your child isn't interested in between-meal noshing. Some children may not need a mid-morning snack, but require a mini-meal during the afternoon to bridge the gap between lunch and dinner.

- Whole grain breads and crackers
- Tortillas
- Fruit (with the exception of whole grapes)
- 100% fruit juice (limit to four ounces a day)
- Graham crackers
- Plain cookies, such as animal crackers
- Pudding (made with full-fat milk)
- Dry cereal or a small bowl of milk and cereal
- Vegetable juices
- Well-cooked vegetables, such as sliced, peeled sweet potatoes
- Tofu

Snacks should be big enough to take the edge off a child's hunger, but small enough to keep him hungry for his next meal. However, when you offer healthy snack foods, it's okay if he eats more than you had intended. Left to their own devices, kids naturally curb food intake at the next meal.

The Dish on Dietary Supplements for Kids

You take your daily multivitamin faithfully, and perhaps you pop some extra vitamin C or calcium. Should your child follow suit? Maybe. Daily multivitamins designed for young children provide insurance against a toddler's unpredictable eating. "Multis" are especially helpful when your child refuses foods from entire food groups for weeks on end. But how to pick the best one? Use these tips to guide your multivitamin choice:

- Choose liquid vitamins for children under three to limit choking risk.
- Avoid candylike supplements. Sugar-filled vitamin gumballs and gummy candies can cause choking in children under 4, and they encourage cavities. They also give children the idea that eating sweets is beneficial.
- Read labels carefully because dosages differ.
- Check the levels. Purchase supplements with about 100 percent of the Daily Value or less based on your child's age.
- Pick store brands. They are just as good as the more costly brands.

- Consider calcium. Kids who avoid dairy foods or consistently consume less than two servings daily might need a separate calcium supplement in addition to a multi.

- Store supplements in a cool, dry place well away from your toddler's reach.

Even when your child's multivitamin meets these criteria, it's no substitute for a balanced diet. Multivitamins lack calories, carbohydrates, protein, fiber, and fat; they typically don't contain enough calcium to make up for deficits in dairy food intake; and they don't provide phytonutrients, which are compounds in plant foods that fight disease.

Safe at the Plate

Herbal remedies and children are generally not a good combination. Although herbs and other botanicals are classified as dietary supplements, they are used as drugs. In effect, taking echinacea to ward off cold symptoms is the same as taking an antihistamine or a decongestant. Many people mistakenly think that because botanical products come from plants that they are safe for children. Not necessarily so. Because botanicals are dietary supplements, they do not have to undergo the same rigid regulatory scrutiny applied to over-the-counter and prescription medications before they go on the market.

The Least You Need to Know

- It's important for parents to avoid offering children low-nutrient foods that don't satisfy their nutrient needs and to include foods that do.

- Children learn by example. Family meals provide a sense of security and belonging; boost language skills; and help promote good eating habits when healthy foods are served.

- No parent is perfect. Keen toddlers pick up on a parent's foibles, so now's the time to take stock of your eating habits and improve what needs improving.

- Some kids need snacks more than others. Avoid so-called snack foods in favor of healthier choices that closely resemble meals.

- With the exception of a multivitamin for children and calcium supplements, dietary supplements and kids are not a good match.

Feeding Your Two-Year-Old

In This Chapter

- Making time for family meals
- Avoiding feeding pitfalls
- Recognizing portion distortion
- Knowing pyramid power
- Learning strategies for including nutritious foods

You've heard all about the "terrible twos," when everything from what toddlers wear to what they eat can become a daily battle of wills. Is that your lot in life? Not necessarily. Some older toddlers are much easier to live with than others, just gently asserting their autonomy and not always hitting you over the head with their need for independence.

Still, you may butt heads with your two-year-old, especially at the table, and especially because there are some changes in store.

Two is when your child begins to need less fat in his diet. It's also when portion sizes may become an issue. This chapter delves into what foods and how much a two-year-old eats and tackles the sticky issue of how to entice "selective" eaters.

Don't Supersize Me!

Americans suffer from a severe case of portion distortion. In the last few decades, we've gradually lost sight of reasonable serving sizes, in spite of clear definitions from health experts. We're not idiots, especially when it comes to weight control. We know that larger helpings means more calories, especially when the food is high fat. With childhood and adult obesity at an all-time high, calories count more than ever.

As a value-minded person, you might think bigger is better, but it would benefit you and your family to dispense with the notion right now. Supersized servings and value meals may seem like bargains, but it's only in the short-term. The long-term health complications of obesity, including heart disease and diabetes, are costly propositions.

Portion sizes of foods served at home and in restaurants have ballooned in the last 20 years. Take a look at some of the most dramatic changes.

Food	Then	Now	Calorie Difference
Bagel	140	350	210
Cheeseburger	330	590	260
Spaghetti and meatballs	500	1,025	525
French fries	210	610	400
Muffin	210	500	290

Source: National Heart, Lung, and Blood Institute - National High Blood Pressure Education Program.

Portion distortion can affect your child, especially because studies suggest children tend to eat what they are served as they get older. More food on their plate encourages overeating that could lead to obesity.

Pyramid Power

You're probably familiar with the Food Guide Pyramid, released in 1992 by the United States Department of Agriculture with the intent of helping Americans choose a balanced diet. Well, there's a new pyramid in town called MyPyramid. The shape is the same, but MyPyramid is an interactive food guidance program that personalizes eating recommendations. Why the change? To help motivate consumers to make healthier food choices that relate more to their needs, and to reflect the most recent nutrition research about what and how much to eat.

MyPyramid translates the 2005 Dietary Guidelines for Americans, which provides eating and exercise advice for people two years of age and older, into suggestions for everyday eating. The central message of MyPyramid, Steps to a Healthier You, promotes the idea of balancing nutrition and exercise for good health by making modest and gradual improvements in eating and physical activity habits.

MyPyramid helps parents make smart choices for children over the age of two. For now, the only way to use MyPyramid is by visiting the website at www.MyPyramid.org. When you use the MyPyramid Plan feature, you'll be prompted to key in your child's age, gender, and level of daily physical activity. From there, you'll receive the suggested number of servings from each food group.

The site also provides detailed lists of portion sizes for foods from each food group so you know exactly how much to offer your child. Be mindful that a child's appetite is variable, and the amounts and serving sizes that MyPyramid provides serve as guidelines, not absolute requirements on a daily basis.

The site has several other helpful features, including:

- MyPyramid Tracker, capable of comparing a day's worth of food your child has eaten against current nutrition guidance.
- Inside MyPyramid, which offers detailed information for every food group, including recommended daily amounts in commonly used measures, including cups and ounces. The section also includes suggestions for choosing healthy oils.
- Start Today, which provides tips and resources that include downloadable suggestions for eating foods from all of the food groups, and for physical activity, as well as a worksheet to track what your child is eating.

Phasing Out (Some) Fat

Turning two marks the point at which you can begin to pare some fat from your child's diet in the name of heart health and weight control. It's safe to serve 2 percent reduced-fat milk, 1 percent low-fat milk, or fat-free milk now because your child no longer relies heavily on milk to provide the nutrients he needs. By the way, your toddler should be baby-bottle free by this time, too. Allowing a baby bottle at this age is harmful to a child's teeth, and it may encourage excessive calorie intake.

See Chapter 9 for fat-trimming tricks to use after age two. Most children who are growing normally can begin to gradually decrease their fat intake for the sake of health. If you have questions about cutting back on fat in your child's diet, consult a registered dietitian or ask your pediatrician about it.

> **Safe at the Plate**
>
> Chubby kids are cute, but plump toddlers could be in for trouble. After age two, your child's doctor should calculate his Body Mass Index and plot it on the pediatric growth charts. A child with a BMI for his age that is higher than the eighty-fifth percentile is at risk for becoming overweight; measuring at the ninety-fifth percentile or above means he is overweight. See Chapter 13 for more on healthy weights for kids.

Tantrums and Little Tykes

Does your toddler seem to be compulsive about food? At this age, toddlers are not into variety. Their idea of changing things up may amount to demanding a crustless peanut butter and jelly sandwich one day, and one with crusts the next. Forget about serving her grilled cheese as a change from her two-month run with peanut butter and jelly. You might want to change, but don't push it. You could provoke a tantrum.

Eating jags and food strikes are more common at this age, much to a parent's chagrin. Keep in mind that kids crave attention, even when it's negative (for example, in the form of your angry reaction during mealtime). Older toddlers are fast learners. They remember that refusing to eat results in heavy scrutiny. Put on your poker face and pretend to ignore their mealtime antics. (We know! Easier said than done.)

> **Safe at the Plate**
>
> Does your toddler store food in her cheeks? Then she's probably pouching, which occurs when a child chews food and wads it up inside her mouth. Large wads of food could cause choking, but in general pouching is not dangerous. Always try to clear your child's cheeks of food before sleep. Pouching can be a phase, but speak with your doctor if it bothers you or if it persists.

My Child Doesn't Eat ...

You could probably fill in the blank with one or more of the following: fruit, vegetables, meat, or milk. Chances are you won't complain about his lack of affinity for the grain group. Kids tend to gravitate toward breads, cereals, and other grains. Nobody knows for sure why breads and cereals are so appealing. Perhaps children favor bread and pasta because these foods are relatively bland and don't overwhelm sensitive taste buds; cereals tend to be sweeter, which may be the source of their attraction. Plus, breads and cereals, as well as rice, pasta, and cooked cereal, are high-carbohydrate foods that children, and adults, find satisfying.

Now that you're clear on what your child be eating according to the Food Guide Pyramid, what if he doesn't eat what he should? These strategies can help make up for what's missing.

Vegetables

If your child does not gravitate toward vegetables, he's not alone. According to the Feeding Infants and Toddlers Study, nearly 25 percent of 19- to 24-year-olds do not eat a single fruit or vegetable on a given day. Increase the appeal of vegetables with these tips:

- Strong flavors and certain textures can turn toddlers off to certain vegetables, so forget about pushing broccoli and cauliflower for now. Stick with mild-tasting options, including potatoes, green beans, and cucumbers, to keep kids eating from this category until their taste buds mature.

- Children who balk at raw vegetables may do better with cooked ones (not too crunchy, though), and vice versa.

- Dips and dressings, including hummus, yogurt-based dips, Ranch dressing, and cheese and cream sauces increase the appeal of vegetables for some kids.

- Try grated cheeses, such as cheddar, havarti, or Parmesan, on top of vegetables to improve their palatability.

- Rely on vegetable juice to satisfy part or all of your child's vegetable requirements.

Fruit

Children are generally more accepting of fruit than vegetables, but may limit their favorites to two or three. Should you worry? No. Certain fruits may repel a toddler; she may not like the seeds, the texture, or the skin. Increase the appeal of fruit with these tips:

- Use puréed fruits or applesauce in place of maple syrup when you serve waffles or pancakes. Slice waffles into toddler-friendly slices to dip into fruit.

- Rely on 100 percent fruit juice to help satisfy your child's fruit requirements, but limit it to six ounces a day.

- Replace half the fat in recipes for muffins and other quick breads with applesauce or other puréed fruit.

- Serve fruit smoothies (refer to the Beverages section in the Recipes for the Early Years appendix).
- Offer frozen fruit, such as peaches and melon, in toddler-friendly pieces.

Meat

It's not the end of the world if your child doesn't like meat. Plenty of children are raised without eating meat and they are perfectly healthy. Meat and poultry pack protein, iron, and zinc, and many other nutrients beneficial to children so if you're child is meatless, make up for missing nutrients with eggs, milk and other dairy foods, fortified grains, and a daily multivitamin. Increase the appeal of meat with these tips:

> **Safe at the Plate**
>
> Stay away from cold cuts and overly processed meats. They contain too much sodium, nitrates, nitrites, and total and saturated fat.

- Keep it tender. Young children might reject tough, dry, overcooked meat. Braising is perfect for the lean cuts of meat. Long, gentle cooking in liquid softens meat.
- Use lean ground beef and ground 100 percent turkey or chicken breast in pasta sauce.

Milk

Maybe your child is allergic to milk and avoids dairy for health reasons, or she suddenly won't touch a glass of milk. Although plain milk is probably the food that packs the most calcium and vitamin D—two nutrients that work together for strong bones—avoiding plain milk does not a dietary disaster make. Increase the appeal of milk with these tips:

- Give it some flavor. Add a bit of chocolate syrup. A little extra sugar goes a long way to encouraging overall good nutrition.
- Offer cereal with milk or mix cereal with plain or vanilla yogurt.
- Serve pudding (refer to the Sweet Endings and Snacks section in the Recipes for the Early Years appendix) and smoothies for snacks.
- Offer foods with added calcium and vitamin D, such as orange juice and fortified soy and rice beverages.

Hopefully, you will find a few feeding strategies provided in this section to see you through your toddler's selective eating.

The Least You Need to Know

- Children are adopting some of their parents' bad habits, including eating low-nutrient foods. Serving up reasonable portions of healthy foods is the best strategy for you and your family.

- Larger portion sizes of restaurant foods and foods served at home encourage excess calories that can result in overweight children and adults.

- The Food Guide Pyramid for Children provides guidelines for what and how much your older toddler should eat.

- At two, your child should begin to make the transition to a lower-fat diet. Trim some, but not all, fat from his foods.

- Older toddlers can be finicky, so parents must employ strategies for getting children to accept alternative foods with the same nutrients.

Part 3

Nutrition Basics

Endless nutrition hype can leave you feeling like an idiot about healthy eating, especially when it comes to feeding your child. What's the best carbohydrate? How much fat should a child have? And how do you make sure your child is getting the protein, vitamins, and minerals he needs? You're unsure about nutrition basics. Not to worry. This part provides answers to your questions and presents the latest facts and kid-friendly recommendations for carbohydrates, fat, protein, and their partners in crime—vitamins, minerals, and water.

Counting on Carbohydrates

In This Chapter

- Avoiding simple carbohydrates
- Keeping kids (nearly) sugar-free
- Eating more complex carbohydrates
- Learning about low-calorie sweeteners and kids
- Finding fiber's role in your child's well-being

Carbohydrates have been taking it on the proverbial chin these last years. The popularity of high-protein diets has left people with the idea that carbohydrates cause excess pounds. You're smarter than that. You know that no single nutrient is completely culpable for an expanding waistline. Large portions of any food can put on pounds, not just carbohydrate-packed bagels weighing in at four ounces (equal to four slices of bread) or more; muffins the size of a small beach ball, and gigantic helpings of pasta, rice, and potatoes (fatty French fries, anyone?).

The truth is, carbohydrates rule when it comes to providing energy, especially for children. Still, some carbs are better than others. This chapter clears the air about carbs.

Clearing Up Carbohydrate Confusion

Carbohydrates, composed of carbon, hydrogen, and oxygen, are found primarily in plant foods, and in some animal products. The simple sugars found in foods are either single units of carbohydrate or two units linked together. Complex carbohydrates are bigger compounds with thousands of simple sugar units strung together.

> ### Technically Speaking
>
> **Glucose** is a basic single sugar unit that circulates in the blood and provides fuel for cells. With the exception of corn syrup, food does not supply glucose. Persons with diabetes have difficulty keeping the levels of blood glucose within a normal range.

After digestion, the body converts carbohydrates into the simple sugar *glucose*, which is the only carbohydrate that can energize cells. Carbohydrate's claim to fame is providing fuel for every cell in the body. With the exception of fiber, each gram of carbohydrate provides four calories.

Protein provides as much energy as carbohydrates. However, when the body goes after protein for its calories, it's incapable of carrying out its primary duties (see Chapter 10 for more on protein). Getting enough carbohydrates to eat prevents the body from using protein for fuel.

Short and Sweet: Simple Carbohydrates

The simple carbohydrates, such as table sugar, honey, and fructose, are sweeter than their complex counterparts, including starch. Simple carbohydrates are more rapidly absorbed into the bloodstream and deployed to cells.

The fact that simple carbohydrates can quickly reach cells is the proverbial thorn in your side. Sugary foods trigger energy surges in small children that are often followed by quick drops in blood glucose levels as the body attempts to get itself back on an even keel. Such sugar highs and lows can leave children irritable and parents exasperated.

A.K.A. Sugar

Sugar goes by many aliases. Even when you do your level best to keep sugar off your child's plate, it can easily creep in. Manufacturers add several types of sweeteners to the likes of ketchup, pasta sauce, and bread. Never mind the large amounts found in fruit-flavored yogurt and granola bars. Fruit-flavored beverages and other soft drinks supply a heap of sugar in some kids' diets.

Don't be fooled when a product says it's naturally sweetened. That does not mean it's lower in sugar. All the natural sweeteners listed here are actually other forms of sugar.

Sucrose	Corn syrup solids	High-fructose corn syrup
Fructose	Corn sweeteners	Sorghum syrup
Glucose	Honey	Maple syrup
Dextrose	Brown sugar	Corn syrup
Maltose	Raw sugar	Evaporated cane juice
Turbinado sugar	Crystal dextrose	

Sugar-Coated Kids

Most children prefer cakes, cookies, ice cream, and sweetened beverages to better-for-you foods featuring complex carbohydrates, such as whole wheat bread and vegetables. In fact, kids are born with an innate preference for sweetness, which only intensifies with a sugar-filled diet.

If your child never consumed another morsel of table sugar, corn syrup, or any other sweetener, she'd be no worse for the wear. But let's face it: no matter how much you hold off on the sugary foods, sooner or later, she'll get a taste. And she'll probably clamor for more.

Your job is helping her moderate her sugar intake. According to the World Health Organization, a child's daily added sugar intake should max out at 10 teaspoons—just about the amount found in 12 ounces of regular soda. Smaller children would do well with even less sugar.

As it turns out, many kids are getting much more than the recommended limit. A recent survey of what more than 5,000 children ages two through five ate over two days suggests an alarming trend. Penn State researchers found children ages two to three consumed an average of 14 teaspoons a day of added sugars, while four- and five-year-olds averaged 17 teaspoons. The study also found that more added sugar meant fewer grains, vegetables, fruits, and dairy foods. That's really no surprise given that children fill up on sweets and are not hungry for healthier foods.

Food Label Folly

It's great when parents can pick up a food product, scan the Nutrient Facts panel and decide whether it's right for their child. But food labeling can be misleading when it comes to sugar. You might be surprised by the amount of sugar listed on the labels of milk, plain yogurt, cottage cheese, and 100 percent fruit juice. What gives? It's not added sugar that drives the numbers up, it's the naturally occurring lactose—a simple sugar that's part of milk, plain yogurt, and cottage cheese. Milk wouldn't be milk without lactose. It's the same situation for fructose; it's found in fruit and 100 percent fruit juices. Fructose is a simple sugar that's present naturally.

Give the Sweet Life the Slip

As carbohydrates go, sugar is not high priority. Although not particularly harmful for most healthy children, every teaspoon adds 16 calories. And sugary treats are generally high in fat, too. They also contribute to cavities, crowd out healthier foods, and encourage a child's budding sweet tooth. Here's how to keep sugar at bay.

- Never serve soda to an infant or toddler. Offer only infant formula, breast milk, milk, water, or small amounts of 100 percent fruit juice mixed with water.

- Shy away from store-bought flavored milks. Cut sugar content by making your own with a teaspoon of chocolate, strawberry, or vanilla syrup for eight ounces of milk.

- Do not keep candy and other sweet treats in the house.

- Steer clear of pre-sweetened yogurt and "light" yogurts that contain artificial sweeteners. Serve plain yogurt mixed with a touch of sugar, jam, jelly, molasses, or honey (no honey for kids under age one). Or skip the added sweetener.

- Interest your child in healthier versions of cookies, including whole grain graham crackers and fig bars.

- Serve cereals with the least added sugar, including Cheerios and Chex.

- Use less sugar in quick bread and muffin recipes. Start with ¼ to ⅓ less sugar than the recipe calls for.

- Bake your own fruit-sweetened treats.

Safe at the Plate

You've curbed your carb consumption and whittled your waistline, so you think the same strategy will work for your little tyke. Not so fast. It's safe to slash sugar, but don't stop offering your infant and toddler foods rich in complex carbohydrates. They supply the calories, vitamins, minerals, and fiber that are crucial to a healthy child.

See the Recipes for the Early Years appendix for recipes that rely more on the natural sweetness of fruit instead of lots of added sweeteners.

Food and Behavior

Your child's had a few cookies and she's bonkers. She won't obey you and she's being really mean to the other kids. Sure, sugar surges are powerful, but they don't last. Unless your child is on a steady sugar diet, it's doubtful that sugar is the cause of any problems he has with learning or concentration.

However, if your child has Attention Deficit Disorder (ADD), he may need to limit sugar. Kids with ADD tend to be more sensitive to the highs and lows that sugar causes.

Caffeine, found in chocolate, sugary colas, and certain coffee-flavored foods, provides your child with an energy jolt, too. See Chapter 12 for more ways to keep kids away from caffeine.

The Low-Down on Low-Calorie Sweeteners

Your child loves sweets, and you'd like to give him more, but you don't want all that sugar in his diet. The U.S. Food and Drug Administration says saccharine, sorbitol and xylitol (sugar alcohols), aspartame (Equal, NutraSweet), acesulfame-K (found in Sweet One), and sucralose (Splenda) are safe. Are they any good for kids?

Most low-calorie sweeteners supply negligible energy and they don't contribute to tooth decay, so they sound like a good idea. Unless your child must restrict sugar for health reasons, low-calorie sweeteners are not for him on a daily basis. However, an occasional food with artificial sweeteners is harmless. Children require a balanced diet full of fresh and lightly processed foods for their nutrients and as an example of how to eat.

The Glycemic Index

You may have heard about the glycemic index (GI). It measures the effect of carbohydrate-containing foods on blood glucose levels. Several factors affect how the body responds to foods such as sweetened beverages, candy, fruit, rice, potatoes, and pasta, including whether a food is a whole grain, whether it's cooked or raw, and, in the case of fruit, what its ripeness is (the riper the fruit, the greater the simple sugar content). Eating foods with a high GI along with fat and protein slows down carbohydrate's capacity to get a rise out of blood glucose levels. Studies suggest a steady diet of low-glycemic foods helps with weight control.

Complex Carbs

Because they are more complicated compounds, the complex carbohydrates found in foods such as whole grain breads, cereals, rice, pasta, potatoes, corn, and legumes take longer to digest. That means their energy is released to the bloodstream and sent to cells on a slow and steady basis.

Complex carbs keep the right kind of company. Foods filled with starch and fiber typically supply vitamins, minerals, and phytonutrients (protective plant compounds).

You can get more nutrients from whole grain bread than in its highly refined cousin, white bread.

	1 oz. White Bread	1 oz. Whole Grain Bread
Calories	166	140
Carbohydrates	30 grams	26 grams
Fiber	1.4 grams	4 grams
Zinc	.38 milligrams	1.1 milligrams
Vitamin E	.14 milligrams	1.1 milligrams

Fiber: Complex, Yet Simple

Fiber is a special carbohydrate. Technically speaking, it's a complex carb without the calories. We humans can't digest fiber, so we can't get at the fuel it provides. That doesn't diminish its role in promoting good health, however. Like other complex carbohydrates, fiber is found in good-for-you foods, including grains, legumes, fruits, and vegetables.

Fiber and fluids work together to ward off constipation in children and adults. Fiber softens stools and adds bulk to bowel movements, stimulating the gut to pass waste with greater ease. Fiber is also filling. Foods packing highly refined carbohydrates, including white bread, potato chips, and corn flakes, are not as satisfying in the long run as their fiber-filled counterparts such as whole grain bread, baked potatoes, and bran flakes. It's much easier for a child to guzzle eight ounces of lemonade at 100 calories than to eat the same calories as two oranges. Fiber helps make the difference.

Safe at the Plate

Sure a little fiber is good for your little one. That doesn't mean more is better. The fact that fiber is filling is one of its failings when it comes to kids. Infants and toddlers have tiny tummies. Going overboard on high-fiber foods, which are typically lower in calories, fat, and protein, could jeopardize growth by filling him up before he can eat the calories and other nutrients he needs. Excess fiber in a child's diet can cause diarrhea, gas, and cramping, too.

Figuring Fiber

Experts differ on the amount of fiber young children should consume. The Institute of Medicine's Food and Nutrition Board's 2002 suggestions call for 19 grams a day for children between the ages of one and three. That's way off from the American Health Foundation's (AHF) recommendations. The AHF follows this equation for figuring fiber for children over the age of two:

Your child's age + 5 = Daily fiber need, in grams

Using the equation, your two-year-old's fiber quota is seven grams a day; a three-year-old's is 8, and so on. The American Academy of Pediatrics has endorsed the AHF's method, which seems closer to reality.

This list of foods and their fiber will help you provide your child with the right amount.

Food	Fiber (Grams)
Navy beans, ¼ cup, cooked	5
Bran cereal, ¾ cup	5
Lentils, ¼ cup, cooked	4
Black beans, ¼ cup, cooked	4
White beans, ¼ cup, cooked	3
Pear, 1 medium, with skin	3
Garbanzo beans, ¼ cup	3
Quinoa, ½ cup, cooked	3
Barley, ½ cup, cooked	3
Orange, 1 medium	3

continued

Food	Fiber (Grams)
Banana, 1 medium	3
Apple, 1 medium, no skin	2
Pumpernickel bread, 1 slice	2
Strawberries, ½ cup	2
Lentils, ¼ cup	2
Whole wheat English muffin, ½	2
Carrots, ½ cup, cooked	2
Potato, ½ medium, baked with skin	2
Sweet potato, ½ medium, baked with skin	2
Whole wheat bread, 1 slice	2–3
Broccoli, ½ cup, cooked	2
Peas, ½ cup, cooked	2
Brown rice, ½ cup, cooked	2
Wheat germ, 2 TB.	2
Millet, ½ cup, cooked	1

Source: USDA; manufacturer data.

The Least You Need to Know

- Carbohydrates are considered simple or complex. Simple sugars are sweeter and more quickly digested.
- All carbohydrates are converted to glucose, the fuel the body uses to energize cells.
- Processed foods with added natural sweeteners introduce sugar to a child's diet that may contribute to weight gain and cavities.
- Foods that are rich in fiber are filling and they help to fend off constipation.
- Fiber, a complex carbohydrate, can't provide calories but is useful for promoting good health. Fiber-rich foods are also packed with vitamins and minerals.

Chapter 9

Figuring Fat (and Cholesterol)

In This Chapter

- Understanding the different types of fat
- Providing the best fats for infants and toddlers
- Knowing when to begin trimming fat intake
- Deciphering kids and cholesterol

If you're like so many adults, your love of dietary fat is equal only to your scorn for it. You adore the way fat makes food so appealing. What's egg salad minus the mayonnaise or croissants prepared without butter? Hardly worth eating. Taste isn't the only way fat satisfies. By slowing digestion, fat keeps you feeling full longer.

Despite favoring fat, you abhor the way it can wreak havoc on your weight and heart health, and for its connection to certain cancers affecting adults, such as cancer of the breast, colon, lung, prostate, and uterus. Ironically, although you pare dietary fat in the name of good health and good looks, your young son or daughter thrives because of it. Getting enough of the best fats early in life is vital to a child's well-being. This chapter clears up fat phobias.

Meet the Lipids

Fat is far more complicated than carbohydrates and protein, so let's get the technical stuff out of the way first.

Chemically speaking, fat belongs to the lipid family (*lipo* means "fat"), which also includes cholesterol. The main form of fat found in foods is called triglycerides, which include fatty acids. Fatty acids are chains of carbon atoms strung together like beads on a bracelet. Hydrogen hangs from the carbons in different configurations, depending on the fatty acid.

Fatty acid composition determines whether fat is classified as saturated or unsaturated. Saturated fat is denser and more solid at room temperature. That's why you can't pour butter or lard unless it's melted, and why the visible fat in meat is solid. There are exceptions to this rule, however. The so-called tropical oils: palm, palm kernel, and coconut, contain high levels of saturated fats, but are pourable at room temperature.

Unsaturated fats include the polyunsaturated and monounsaturated varieties. These lighter and less dense fats, found in foods such as olive and canola oils, are liquid at room temperature.

> **Nutrition Nugget**
>
> Triglycerides are also stored in the body, serving as calorie reserves; insulation to keep body temperature constant; protection for nerve cells; and a cushion for internal organs.

Why Your Child Needs Fat

Phew! I bet you're glad the chemistry lesson is over. Now, let's get down to the details. Your infant and toddler needs fat, and lots of it at an early age. Until age two, about half the calories your child consumes every day should be derived from fat. The sections that follow detail the many reasons why.

For the Calories

At nine calories per gram, fat provides more than twice the calories of carbohydrates or protein. That kind of concentrated calorie source is perfect for infants and toddlers because their energy needs are high and their tummies are tiny. In fact, it would be impossible to meet a baby or toddler's daily calorie quotas without dietary fat.

For the Essential Fatty Acids

Dietary fat supplies Essential Fatty Acids (EFAs), compounds critical to your child's development and overall health. The body can't make the EFAs it needs, so your child (and you) must obtain them from food. Linoleic acid, found in foods such as corn oil and chicken, and alpha-linolenic acid, found in foods such as wheat germ and canola oil, are the two EFAs essential to life. Breast milk and infant formula supply the necessary EFAs; later on, food steps in.

To Ferry Vitamins

Fat is a vehicle for vitamins A, D, E, and K. These fat-soluble vitamins can't dissolve in water, and require fat for their absorption, transport through the bloodstream, and storage in the body.

For Brain Development

Your kid is a fat head, and we mean that in a good way: Fat is a huge component of brain tissue.

Upward of 60 percent of the brain is fat. Along with protein, fat is part of cell membranes, the thin layers encasing the millions (and counting!) of cells in your child's brain. It is also a component of myelin, the nerve cells' protective coating. Docosahexaenoic acid (DHA) is the dominant fatty acid in the brain.

> **Mother's Helper**
>
> Topping vegetables with cheese sauce, salad dressing, butter, olive oil, or other fats is a great way to get kids interested in eating them. Fat also improves the body's absorption of carotenoids, the plant form of vitamin A.

For Good Eyesight

Fat, particularly DHA, is also a component of the cells of the retina, located at the back of each of your child's eyes. The retina is lined with millions of light-sensitive cells called rods and cones. It registers pictures and converts the images into information that's sent to the brain for processing. Your baby "sees" when the brain interprets messages the retina passes along.

Green Light, Red Light Fats

Now that you're a whiz at the technical side of fat, you might be wondering how all that information translates into what to feed your baby or toddler every day. This section spells it out for you.

Green Light: Polyunsaturated Fats

Polyunsaturated fats are considered heart-healthy because they help curb blood cholesterol levels when substituted for saturated fats, reducing the risk of clogged arteries that lead to heart disease.

Polyunsaturated fats are good for you. That's simple enough. But just when you thought fat was getting easy to understand, there are two categories of polyunsaturated fats—omega-6 and omega-3, to consider. Omega-6 fats dominate the typical American diet. Vegetables oils such as soybean, corn, safflower, and sunflower supply most of the omega-6 fats we consume. Alpha-linolenic acid, also present in soybean and canola oils, green leafy vegetables, walnuts, and flaxseed, is the parent compound of the omega-3 family.

Your body can make DHA and other omega-3 fats such as eicosapentaenoic acid (EPA) from alpha-linolenic acid, but in limited amounts. Mother's milk and certain infant formulas provide DHA, but after your child stops those, food must supply the lion's share. See Chapter 1 for more DHA details.

Green Light: Monounsaturated Fat

Monounsaturated fat is most prevalent in canola, olive, and peanut oils, avocados, nuts, and nut butters. Monounsaturated fats are considered heart-healthy because they help avoid blocked arteries that choke off blood to vital organs such as the heart and brain.

Red Light: Saturated Fat

Saturated fat is found in varying levels in animal and plant foods, including high-fat meats and dairy foods. Coconut, palm, palm kernel oil, and cocoa butter, used in packaged foods such as cookies, crackers, and candy, are also rich in saturated fat.

The body might need fat, but it does not require one bit of saturated fat from foods. Your child (and you) produces all the saturated fat he needs to strengthen cell walls, among other functions, on an as-needed basis. And because he manufactures what he needs, there is no minimum daily saturated fat requirement from government health organizations, or other reputable health groups.

In fact, experts recommend putting a lid on saturated fat intake, because too much over time could be a health hazard. Eating excessive amounts of saturated fat year after year is related to an increased risk for *atherosclerosis*, a condition that can lead to a heart attack or stroke.

> **Technically Speaking**
>
> **Atherosclerosis** chokes off blood supply by encouraging deposits of fatty substances, cholesterol, and other junk in arteries to the point of narrowing them significantly or completely blocking them.

Should your child avoid foods because of saturated fat? That depends. Many foods packing saturated fat are also rich in the calories, protein, vitamins, and minerals that young children thrive on. For example, milk and cheese provide much-needed protein, calcium, and B vitamins. And meat is an excellent source of protein, iron, and zinc, all necessary for growth. Sweet treats and other foods harboring saturated fats should be doled out in limited quantities, however.

Foods contain a mixture of saturated and unsaturated fats, but one always prevails.

All Mixed Up

Polyunsaturated	Monounsaturated	Saturated
Corn oil	Canola oil	Fatty meats
Cottonseed oil	Olive oil	Butter
Safflower oil	Peanut oil	Full-fat dairy foods
Soybean oil	Sesame oil	Coconut oil
Sunflower oil	Most nuts and oils	Cocoa butter
Margarine (tub)	Avocados	Palm oil
Seafood	Peanut butter	Palm kernel oil
Flaxseed		

Red Light: Trans Fat

Trans fat, the product of *hydrogenation*, is found primarily in processed foods such as margarine, shortening, fast-food French fries, pastries, microwave popcorn, cookies, crackers, granola bars, and even bean dip.

Although fattier cuts of meat and full-fat dairy products naturally contain tiny amounts of trans fat, it's the man-made version that's cause for concern. Like saturated fat, there is no biological need for trans fat. And in the case of trans fat, there is more harm than good in consuming them.

Technically Speaking

Hydrogenation forces hydrogen atoms into vegetable oils, transforming unsaturated fats into trans fatty acids. Hydrogenation creates tastier, firmer fats with a longer shelf life that are ideal for processed foods.

Trans fats block the removal of cholesterol from the bloodstream, contributing to heart disease risk by plugging up arteries, and they also may be linked to certain cancers.

The Institute of Medicine, a group of scientists that advises on health issues, recommends eating as little as possible of trans fatty acids.

That recommendation could leave margarine lovers in a quandary. Does it mean butter is better? As long as you use either of them sparingly, margarine and butter are fine choices for children. Tub margarine contains less trans fat than the stick variety, so go for the softer fats. Better yet, prepare foods with canola or olive oils. Both are rich sources of unsaturated fats.

Details, Please

Although trans fat should not be a regular part of anyone's diet, it's virtually impossible to completely avoid. You can limit trans fat intake with a smidgen of supermarket smarts.

Beginning in 2006, food labels will sport trans fat content as part of the Nutrition Facts panel. Until then, track trans fat by looking for the words "hydrogenated" or "partially hydrogenated" on the label. If either of those terms fall within the first four ingredients, put the item back on the shelf—that food is packing trans fats.

Striking a Fat Balance

Too little total dietary fat typically results in poor growth and development because it robs kids of the calories they need. Coming up short on the essential fatty acids could result in scaly skin, as well as visual and neurological abnormalities.

On the other hand, too much fat over time might increase a child's obesity risk, and may set the stage for eating habits that encourage heart disease later in life.

When to Trim the Fat

There is a happy medium between too little and too much dietary fat, but don't try to find it until your child is at least two years old. That's when The National Cholesterol Education Program (NCEP), set forth by the National Heart, Lung, and Blood Institute of the National Institutes of Health, suggests parents begin the transition to a diet plan with a maximum of about 30 percent of calories coming from total fat, and no less than 20 percent total fat calories, averaged out over several days.

How to Cut Back on Dietary Fat

As much as you want to head off heart disease and obesity in your little tyke, there is no rush to reach the 30 percent fat goal. Experts say it's okay to gradually decrease dietary fat intake, the goal being a lower-fat diet by the age of five.

The NCEP guidelines stress balance. That means it's okay for a child to have one or two days filled with higher-fat foods as long as they are balanced out by a few days of lower-fat eating.

Achieving a 30 percent fat calorie diet does not mean every food your child eats must be low-fat or fat-free, either.

You don't have to slash all the fat in his diet, just some. Here are tried-and-true tricks of the trade.

Instead Of ...	Try
Full-fat milk	2 percent reduced-fat or 1 percent low-fat milk
Beef or hot dog	100 percent ground turkey breast
French fries	Mashed potatoes with reduced-fat milk
Chocolate chip cookies	Fig bars and graham crackers
Store-bought muffin or donut	Whole grain bagel
Fast-food chicken nuggets	Make your own (see the Recipes for the Early Years appendix)
Premium ice cream	Frozen yogurt
Bacon	Canadian bacon
Stuffed-crust cheese pizza	Thin-crust cheese pizza

Chewing the Fat

What does a 30 percent fat diet mean anyway? It's meant to convey that no more than about a third of your child's calories should come from fat. Here's how to figure it in grams, which will help you put daily fat quotas into perspective when reading food labels.

Here's an example:

1. Daily calorie needs of 1,400.
2. $1,400 \times .30 = 420$ calories from fat are allowed.

   To translate this into grams of fat in food, divide the number of calories from fat (420 calories) by the 9 calories in each gram of fat. You get about 47 grams of fat per day.

To figure your fat allowance, repeat the calculation using the number of calories you need to achieve and maintain a healthy weight.

Standing In for Fat

There is an old nutrition saw that says all foods fit in a balanced diet. It's simply not true when it comes to very young children. There are foods that contain ingredients that need not be part of your child's diet.

Olestra, which goes by the brand name Olean, is one of them. It's a man-made sucrose (table sugar) with up to eight fatty acids attached. Olestra offers a way to replace fat to produce fat-free or low-fat foods. Olestra can even be used to fry foods. Olestra is approved for use in savory snacks such as chips, crackers, and tortilla chips.

Problem is, olestra molecules are so large and fatty that they can't be metabolized by enzymes and bacteria in the gut. So olestra is neither absorbed nor digested, and that means your child reaps no benefits from it. Plus, olestra can give your child gas, diarrhea, and anal leakage.

Because olestra is fatty, it can bind cholesterol, vitamins, and other fat-soluble molecules. That's another problem.

Despite the Food and Drug's approval, foods containing olestra must carry a label that states:

> *This Product Contains Olestra. Olestra may cause abdominal cramping and loose stools. Olestra inhibits the absorption of some vitamins and other nutrients. Vitamins A, D, E, and K have been added.*

Kids and Cholesterol

Cholesterol gets a bad rap, but life would be impossible without it. Cholesterol is part of every cell. It serves as the building block for hormones including estrogen (the primary female sex hormone) and testosterone (the primary male hormone); the bile acids that aid digestion; and vitamin D, critical for calcium absorption and bone strength. Myelin, the sheath that surrounds nerve cells and protects them for peak function, contains cholesterol, too.

Cholesterol is similar to saturated fat in that there is no daily minimum requirement for it. Your child's body balances cholesterol production with his consumption, so if he eats more than he needs, production is trimmed for a time.

Adults might be down on cholesterol because of its potential for blocking blood vessels that lead to the heart and brain. True, a diet rich in saturated fat and cholesterol may result in elevated blood cholesterol levels that lead to heart disease and stroke. But experts say saturated fat is by far the greater culprit in high blood cholesterol concentrations. Many foods rich in saturated fat also contain cholesterol, such as meat and full-fat dairy products, so cholesterol is often guilty by association.

Although they have their differences, fat and cholesterol are often discussed in the same breath, largely because of their connection to heart disease.

There's no need to limit cholesterol intake to the recommended 300 milligrams a day until a child reaches the age of two. In fact, curbing a child's cholesterol consumption is difficult without limiting his calories and fat. That's because many high-cholesterol foods, including eggs and cheese, are among the most nutrient-packed foods that tend to be kid favorites.

All animal foods contain some cholesterol, but concentrations vary.

Countdown to Cholesterol: Food Sources

Food	Portion	Cholesterol (Milligrams)
Beef liver	3 oz.	324
Whole egg, medium	1	186
Egg white, medium	1	0
Fast-food chili	1 cup	170
Beef, bottom round, cooked	3 oz.	84
Danish pastry (fruit)	1	81
Soft-serve ice cream, vanilla	½ cup	81
Pork chop	3 oz.	78
Ground beef, 20 percent fat, cooked	3 oz.	77
Chicken breast, skinless, cooked	3 oz.	73
Turkey breast, skinless, cooked	3 oz.	72
Haddock, cooked	3 oz.	66
Salmon, cooked	3 oz.	60
Whole milk ricotta cheese	½ cup	63
Part skim ricotta cheese	½ cup	38
Scallops, cooked	3 oz.	45
Yogurt, whole milk, plain	1 cup	32
Yogurt, low-fat, plain	1 cup	15
Butter	1 TB.	31
Cheddar cheese	1 oz.	30

Countdown to Cholesterol: Food Sources *(continued)*

Food	Portion	Cholesterol (Milligrams)
Whole milk	1 cup	24
2 percent reduced-fat milk	1 cup	20
Cream cheese	1 TB.	16
Mayonnaise, regular	1 TB.	4
Mayonnaise, low-fat	1 TB.	4

The Least You Need to Know

- Fat is vital to your child's growth, now and well into the future. Fat plays an integral role in brain development and eyesight.

- Some fats are better than others when it comes to feeding kids. Focus on unsaturated fats, but don't limit nutrient-rich foods that contain saturated fats. Limit trans fat as much as possible by avoiding processed and fast foods.

- Although there's no dietary need for cholesterol, there's no reason to limit it during the first two years of life. Foods rich in cholesterol tend to be packed with kid-friendly nutrients.

- It's safe to begin trimming some fat from your child's diet at age two, but remember to balance high- and low-fat foods to encourage a nutritious and delicious eating pattern.

Chapter 10

Powerful Protein

In This Chapter

- Understanding protein's role in your child's diet
- Getting the real explanation of amino acids
- Determining how much protein your child needs
- Learning what food sources contain protein

Dietary protein makes life possible. It's the fundamental structural material of every cell. Protein is not only the basis for life, it's responsible for growth and the repair of worn-out or damaged tissue. Protein differs from carbohydrates and protein in one very significant way: it contains nitrogen as part of amino acids. Read on to find out more about how nitrogen fosters your child's growth and development.

Protein Is Paramount

Protein provides four calories per gram, but it is prized less for its energy content than for its nitrogen and *amino acids*. In fact, nitrogen is protein's defining characteristic. The body needs nitrogen to build new cells and tissues. And it requires amino acids for the raw materials needed to build body proteins.

A
B C

Technically Speaking

Amino refers to compounds containing nitrogen, including the **amino acids** in protein. Nitrogen is necessary for building body proteins. The protein in food provides nitrogen; carbohydrates and fat don't contain any.

All About Amino Acids

The proteins in food are a series of amino acids strung together in unique sequences. Digestion breaks up food protein into amino acids. Your child's body supplies those amino acids to construct cells, skin, fingernails, hair, muscle, neurotransmitters, and the hormones and enzymes that drive bodily functions, among other compounds.

Each body protein also contains amino acids connected in a specific order. When the body builds a protein, no amino acid substitutions are allowed. A shortage of just one amino acid grinds protein construction to a halt.

The body does not store amino acids to any great extent, although it can break down body tissues to get at the amino acids it needs (don't worry, they get built right back up). Because he is in a state of constant growth, your young child requires a steady protein supply from food.

Essential and Nonessential Amino Acids

Amino acids are not created equal. The body produces 11 of the amino acids critical for good health, but they are called nonessential amino acids. What gives? It seems strange to call important nutrients nonessential, but experts have dubbed them as such because the body can make them on its own. Nine of the amino acids fall into the category of essential amino acids (EAA) that must come from food because the body can't produce them.

Amino Acids

Essential (Body Cannot Make)	Nonessential (Body Can Make)
Valine	Glycine
Tryptophan	Glutamic acid
Phenylalanine	Arginine
Methionine	Aspartic acid
Histidine	Proline
Isoleucine	Alanine

Essential (Body Cannot Make)	Nonessential (Body Can Make)
Lysine	Serine
Leucine	Asparagine
Threonine	Cysteine
	Tyrosine
	Glutamine

A Question of Quality

Animal and plant foods supply amino acids, but there's a catch. Protein in eggs, meat, poultry, seafood, milk, cheese, and yogurt provide all the nine EAA your child needs. Plant foods, including legumes and grains, contain fewer EAA. In fact, no single plant food contains every essential amino acid. That does not diminish the role of plant protein in a balanced diet, nor does it disparage the many forms of vegetarianism. Rather, children who avoid animal products should aim to eat an array of plant foods to get the right amount of essential and nonessential amino acids. See Chapter 15 for more on vegetarianism.

Nutrition Nugget

When it comes to protein quality, eggs rule. Eggs have a biological value of 100 percent because they contain all the essential amino acids necessary to promote growth and sustain life. The amino acid pattern in eggs is the basic standard against which all other foods are measured.

How Much Protein Do Children Need?

When it comes to children, quality counts, but so does the quantity of amino acids they consume. A diet deficient in protein will come up short for EAA as well as nonessential amino acids. In trying to produce nonessential amino acids, a child's body uses energy that would otherwise be directed toward his growth and development.

Protein requirements are based on ideal body weight and periods of growth. It doesn't look like it from the following chart, but infants have the highest per-pound protein needs because they are growing so quickly. In fact, an adult's per-pound protein quota is about half that of an infant's.

Protein Quota

Age	Daily Protein Needs
0–6 months	9 grams
7–12 months	10 grams
1–3 years	13 grams
19–50 years	
Female	46 grams
Male	56 grams

In order to get the calories they need, formula-fed infants typically consume more protein each day than stated in this chart. However, that's no reason to cut back on baby's formula to meet these quotas because they serve as a guideline for the minimum amount of protein your child needs daily, not the maximum. Reducing formula intake can threaten your child's growth.

There's little chance of protein deficiency in healthy infants and toddlers who are offered adequate portions of nutritious foods as part of a balanced diet. As children move on to table food toward the end of their first year, and away from breast milk or formula as their dominant protein source, you should offer protein-packed foods at each meal. Even the erratic eating habits of toddlers probably won't lead to a protein shortfall: Less than 16 ounces of milk satisfies a toddler's daily protein requirement.

Getting enough protein is fairly easy, so don't go overboard. Any protein not used for energy will be converted to body fat. Use this chart to be sure your child reaches his daily protein quota.

Packing Protein

Food	Protein (Grams)
Chicken, 3 ounces, roasted	26
Canned tuna, white, 3 ounces, drained	20
Beef, 95 percent lean, 3 ounces, cooked	22
Follow-up formula, 1 liter (33 ounces)	17
Infant formula, 1 liter (33 ounces)	14
Breast milk, 1 liter (33 ounces)	10
Peanut butter, 2 tablespoons	9
Cheddar cheese, 1 ounce	7

Food	Protein (Grams)
Cottage cheese, ¼ cup	7
Egg, 1 large, whole	6
Almond butter, 2 tablespoons	5
Pizza, cheese, 2 ounces, from frozen	5
Tofu, ¼ cup, raw	5
Pasta, enriched, ½ cup, cooked	4
Lentils, ¼ cup, cooked	4
Milk, 4 ounces	
Whole	4
1 percent low-fat	4
Yogurt, 4 ounces	
Whole milk, plain	4
Low-fat, fruited	4
Bread, whole wheat, 1 ounce	3
Bulgur, ¼ cup, cooked	3
Garbanzo beans, ¼ cup, cooked	3
Quinoa, ¼ cup, cooked	2

The Least You Need to Know

- Although protein can provide calories to a growing child, it is prized for its capacity to promote growth. Protein supplies nitrogen and the amino acids necessary for making new tissue.

- Protein quality counts. It's important for your child to get enough dietary protein, but he must also consume the essential amino acids in amounts that spur development and tissue repair.

- The body does not store protein, so your infant and toddler (and you) should eat the protein he needs every day to supply his body with the essential amino acids.

- Without enough dietary carbohydrates in your child's diet, her body will break down protein for its calories, diverting it from its primary duties.

- Protein is found in plant and animal foods, but animal foods contain all the amino acids that drive growth and development. However, an array of plant foods can supply the essential and nonessential amino acids your child needs to thrive.

Chapter 11

Vital Vitamins and Mighty Minerals

In This Chapter

- Finding fat-soluble vitamins
- Finding water-soluble vitamins
- Knowing the mightiest minerals
- Learning which foods are rich in vitamins and minerals

Carbohydrates, proteins, and fats grab most nutrition headlines, probably because they contain calories that contribute to adults' battle of the bulge. In reality, carbohydrates, proteins, and fats are essentially useless without an entourage of vitamins and minerals working together to back them up, often in amounts that could fit on the head of a pin.

Although vitamins and minerals are calorie-free, they are instrumental in harnessing the energy that carbohydrates, fats, and proteins have to offer. That's not all they can do, however. These mighty nutrients lend strength and provide structure to body parts, including bones, teeth, and red blood cells, and are basically responsible for keeping your child's body in top form.

Valuable Vitamins

There are many different vitamins, but just two categories: *fat-* and *water-soluble*.

Fat-soluble vitamins—A, D, E, and K—need to travel into and around the body in fat. And they are stored in fat tissue, so your child always has some on board. That's not the case for the water-soluble variety—vitamin C and the B vitamins. They are not retained by the body in any significant amounts, which means a daily source is required.

Vitamin A

Vitamin A garners a lot of attention for fostering good eyesight, but that shortchanges its other roles in health promotion. In addition to keeping your peepers in top form, vitamin A bolsters the immune system, and keeps all cells and tissues running smoothly.

The vitamin A found in animal foods, particularly organ meats, is the form called retinol. Retinol is ready for the body to use. Plant foods contain carotenoids, raw materials that the body converts to active vitamin A, as needed. Vitamin A is also added to milk, infant formula, and certain grains. Because your child is unlikely to dine very often on liver and kidney, he'll most likely rely on these foods rich in vitamin A to get what he needs:

- Sweet potatoes
- Carrots
- Winter squash
- Cantaloupe
- Fortified cereals

Vitamin D

Vitamin D boosts calcium absorption from foods, and helps calcium move in and out of bones. In children, vitamin D prevents rickets (soft and malformed bones).

Vitamin D has been dubbed the sunshine vitamin, and with good reason. Strong summer sunlight initiates the production of vitamin D in the skin. The body stores finished vitamin D for future use.

Infant formulas provide adequate vitamin D, but breastfed babies need extra. The American Academy of Pediatrics suggests starting breastfed babies on 200 International

Units of daily supplemental vitamin D within the first two months of life. Most likely, your pediatrician will prescribe a multivitamin in liquid form that includes the recommended amount of vitamin D for nursing infants.

Few foods are good natural sources of vitamin D, so children must rely on fortified products to get the bulk of what they need:

- Fortified milk and yogurt
- Fortified margarine, cereals, breads, yogurt, and orange juice
- Egg yolks

Vitamin E

Your child is young, so it's hard to think of his cells as damaged. Truth is, his body does constant battle with free radicals, those naughty forms of oxygen looking to start trouble by tampering with your kid's DNA. Vitamin E heads off potential cell damage. It also prevents a form of anemia while preserving nerve tissue.

Vitamin E and fat are typically found in the same foods. Common cooking oils, including olive and canola oils, contain concentrated amounts of vitamin E. Other vitamin E sources include the following:

- Almonds and almond butter (do not give infants and toddlers whole nuts)
- Wheat germ cereals
- Fortified ready-to-eat cereals
- Sunflower (high linoleic) and safflower oils (high oleic)
- Avocadoes
- Peanut butter

Vitamin K

K is for klotting, er, clotting. The spelling is incorrect, but it's an easy way to recall vitamin K's claim to fame. Soon after your baby arrived in the delivery room, he received vitamin K by injection to prevent a common bleeding disorder in newborns.

Vitamin K also contributes to bone health. It just so happens that foods rich in vitamin K also provide potassium, magnesium, and calcium, which contribute to strong bones. Like vitamin D, the body can make vitamin K; it's produced by the good bacteria in the intestine.

Here are some top vitamin K picks:

- Romaine lettuce
- Broccoli
- Spinach
- Egg yolks

B Vitamins

The B vitamins are a tight group. With similar and interrelated functions, they often work together for good health. Many of the B vitamins are sensitive to heat and light, so they are easily destroyed by overcooking and light exposure.

Riboflavin (B2) plays a role in energy metabolism, vision, and skin health. Food sources include dairy foods, whole and enriched grains, whole eggs, and broccoli.

Pyridoxine (B6) is essential for new cell growth and energy metabolism. It fosters brain-cell communication by playing a role in the production of the neurotransmitter serotonin. Pyridoxine also helps prevent a type of anemia by participating in red blood cell production, and it boosts the immune system. Pyridoxine is found in meat, poultry, fish, bananas, soy, and garbanzo beans.

Folate/folic acid is required for robust red and white blood cells; repairing cell damage; and preventing neural tube defects and cleft lip and palate during pregnancy. Folic acid is the synthetic form added to foods. Folate is found in orange juice, legumes, spinach, broccoli, strawberries, peas, enriched cereals, breads, rice, pasta, and other grains. Folic acid during early pregnancy reduces the risk of neural tube defects that occur within the first thirty days after conception, a time when women often do not realize they are pregnant. For that reason, the March of Dimes and other health experts recommend 400 micrograms of folic acid daily for all women capable of becoming pregnant.

Thiamin aids in the metabolism of carbohydrate, fat, and protein. Thiamin-rich foods include legumes, pork, enriched and fortified whole grain cereals, breads, and other grains.

Pantothenic acid fosters the production of amino acids, hormones, vitamins A and D, and neurotransmitters. Pantothenic acid is found in foods including potatoes, broccoli, tomatoes, whole grains, egg yolks, and poultry.

Niacin (B3) helps convert food energy to energy your body can use. Niacin can be found in meat, milk, fish, poultry, potatoes, corn, fortified whole grains, breads and cereals, and legumes.

Vitamin B12 (cobalamin) is critical for proper red blood cell formation and a healthy central nervous system. It's found naturally only in animal foods, so vegans require supplemental vitamin B12 or fortified foods. Find B12 in meat, tuna, salmon, milk, whole eggs, and fortified items such as soy beverages, cereals, and nutritional yeast.

Nutrition Nugget

It's neither vitamin nor mineral, but it's important. Choline plays a role in memory function in fetal brain development and possibly heads off certain birth defects during pregnancy. It's involved with insulating nerve fibers, too. Choline requirements increase during pregnancy and lactation to facilitate brain development.

Eggs are an excellent source of choline. Other sources include beef, breast milk, cauliflower, and peanut butter.

Vitamin C

You might think of it as the ultimate immunity booster, but you'd be underestimating vitamin C's involvement in your child's developing body. In addition to helping the body mount a defense to germs as part of a balanced diet and healthy lifestyle, vitamin C promotes the production of collagen, a connective tissue that holds together bones, skin, and tissue. Vitamin C is also involved in tissue health and wound healing. And it's particularly beneficial for young children because it boosts the body's absorption of iron.

Vitamin C-rich foods include the following:

- Citrus fruits and their juices, such as orange and grapefruit
- Tomatoes and tomato juice
- Frozen peaches
- Strawberries
- Mangoes
- Raw, sweet red and green bell peppers
- Broccoli
- Kiwi

Offering your child a variety of foods is the best way for him to meet his vitamin and mineral needs. Read on to find out more about the many minerals required for good health, some of which work together with each other and with the vitamins mentioned here.

Mighty Minerals

Your child's body requires a minimum of 22 minerals for optimum health. The sections that follow detail the six you really need to know about.

Iron

A child's growth and development depend on iron. As part of red blood cells, iron transports oxygen to every cell. It also plays a role in brain development and function by fostering communication between nerve cells.

Iron deficiency is the most common nutritional deficiency in America, affecting older infants, young children, and women in the childbearing years. Infants and toddlers are at particular risk because they grow so fast. Most babies are born with iron reserves to last them for about six months. Infants born prematurely or who did not grow properly during pregnancy and children of moms with diabetes run an even greater risk for iron deficiency, largely because of their lower-than-normal iron reserves at birth.

Iron deficiency can cause iron deficient anemia. One of the symptoms is fatigue. However, an iron shortfall can be more subtle than that, and is possible in children who appear well nourished. The problem is that inadequate iron in infants and toddlers can have long-term consequences on learning and attention span.

Breast milk and fortified infant formula supply iron. The American Academy of Pediatrics disagrees with the use of low-iron formula. After your child begins cutting back on liquid nutrition, he must rely on iron from other food sources. Iron-fortified cereals and other grains and meats help your child avoid iron deficiency.

Animal products and plant foods supply iron in different forms. Heme iron, the dominant type in animal foods, is best absorbed by the body. Nonheme iron is the only type of iron in plant foods. It's also the type that's added to processed foods, such as grains. Combining a source of vitamin C (orange juice) or heme iron (meat) with foods containing nonheme iron (fortified bread) improves your child's chances of absorbing nonheme iron.

The table that follows lists some foods containing heme and nonheme iron.

Heme Iron	Nonheme Iron
Clams	Iron-fortified infant formulas
Oysters	Iron-fortified infant cereals
Meat	Spinach

Heme Iron	Nonheme Iron
Poultry	White beans
Pork	Raisins
Egg yolks	Lentils
	Fortified breads, rice, cereals, pasta, and other grains

Zinc

Zinc is vastly underestimated, considering its job description: participate in making DNA, the cell's blueprint for reproduction and the very essence of growth; help body break down and use carbohydrates, fats, and proteins for energy; be a part of insulin, the hormone that regulates blood glucose levels; and boost immunity and wound healing.

Animal and plant foods supply zinc. As with iron, zinc is better absorbed from meat, seafood, and other animal products.

Here are some zinc-rich foods:

- Pork
- Poultry, particularly dark meat
- Lamb
- Yogurt (plain contains the most)
- Milk
- Fortified breakfast cereals
- Wheat germ cereals
- Legumes (including peas) and tofu

Calcium

Calcium, the most abundant mineral in your child's body, builds bones and teeth. Starting in childhood, the body accumulates calcium in bones to keep them strong. Bones also serve as a reserve for calcium which is needed for a regular heartbeat, normal blood clotting, muscle contraction, and relaxation.

Dairy foods top the list for calcium; certain fortified plant foods are good or excellent calcium sources, too. Here is a list:

- Milk
- Yogurt

- Cheese
- Calcium-fortified soy beverages
- Tofu processed with calcium sulfate
- Calcium-fortified grains, such as cereals
- Almonds and legumes

Fluoride

Fluoride is best known for protecting teeth. After a child's primary teeth show up, fluoride goes to work shoring up enamel to deflect damage from cavity-causing bacteria.

Fluoridated municipal water is how most little ones get their fluoride. Formula-fed infants can benefit from fluoride when powdered or liquid-concentrate infant formula is prepared with fluoridated water. If you're unsure whether your tap water contains fluoride, ask at your town or city hall.

Using bottled water without fluoride may mean your child isn't getting enough. Check the label to be sure the water has fluoride or call the bottler to get fluoride levels of the brand you buy. According to the U.S. Public Health Service, the optimum concentration of fluoride in drinking water ranges from .7 to 1.2 parts per million (ppm). Some home distillation systems rob tap water of its fluoride.

Breastfed babies don't need fluoride supplements for the first six months of life, but may need some after that. Ask your pediatrician about supplements.

Sodium

Sodium catches a lot of flak. Some of it is well-deserved, because sodium is linked to high blood pressure in many adults. Sodium has its upside, too. It's necessary for fluid balance, muscle contraction, nerve conduction, and ferrying nutrients into and waste out of cells.

Sodium's not the problem, the amount we eat is. Sodium is found naturally in every food to some degree, so you'll never completely avoid it. Nor should you. Focus on *curbing* the following processed foods to save on sodium:

- Canned soups
- Hot dogs
- Boxed and microwavable macaroni and cheese
- Canned vegetables
- Snack chips
- Cold cuts

Potassium

Potassium is everywhere. It's found in every single cell in your body. It's also in foods in varying amounts. Potassium works with sodium to promote fluid balance. It's also necessary for normal blood pressure, muscle activity and nerve impulses, and strong bones.

The following are potassium-packed:

- Avocadoes
- Sweet and white potatoes
- Lentils
- Winter squash
- Milk
- Yogurt
- Orange juice
- Meat
- Bananas

The Least You Need to Know

- Vitamins and minerals are calorie-free.
- Providing your child with a varied diet will help him get the vitamins and minerals he needs for growth and development.
- Carbohydrates, fats, and proteins are useless to the body without the help of vitamins and minerals.
- No single vitamin or mineral is a superstar. They all work together as a team to promote good health.
- Water-soluble vitamins (B vitamins and vitamin C) are not stored by the body. Fat-soluble vitamins (A, D, E, and K) are stored in tissues.

Fluid Facts

In This Chapter

- Discovering how water works in the body
- Figuring fluid requirements
- Finding water sources
- Learning bottled and tap water facts

There's no such thing as a most vital nutrient, but if there were, water would be it. Without water, you'd be a goner in just days. Water is the basis of life, after all.

Small children are loaded with fluid. An infant's body is close to 75 percent water. With facts like that, water's importance to life becomes crystal clear. This chapter spells out the facts about how water works for your child's well-being.

Water Works

You might take water for granted. You shouldn't. Water is constantly performing functions that keep your body, and your child's, running smoothly. Water …

- is a solvent. Every life-giving bodily process takes place in an aqueous (watery) environment. Water dissolves certain nutrients (the B vitamins and vitamin C, for example) to help them get to cells, where they are in great demand.

- is a mediator. The body is always trying to achieve balance. Water helps maintain a normal internal temperature of around 98.6°F, because that's the most favorable environment for life.

- is a lubricant. Joints require water to keep them moving. Water also cushions and protects joints and internal organs, and lubricates the digestive tract to keep it in top form.

- is a transporter. Nutrients, most importantly glucose for cellular energy, and other compounds are carried about the body in the water found in blood and other bodily fluids.

- is a filler. Water lends form to the body as it fills in spaces within and between cells and body tissues, such as muscle.

- is a maintainer. Water keeps the body's blood volume in check, affecting circulation and overall health.

- is a way out. You need water to make the urine that rids your body of the waste products from everyday *metabolism*.

Technically Speaking

Metabolism refers to all the body functions that together provide energy, build tissue, and regulate bodily processes.

How Much Water Your Child Needs

Babies require water, but they do not need plain water in addition to the fluid they receive in breast milk or infant formula, according to the American Academy of Pediatrics. Surprised? There's more. The AAP also says even hot, dry weather and fever do not increase an infant's water needs. Providing infants with bottles of water instead of formula or breast milk and solid foods encourages nutrient deficiencies.

Toddlers need about 40 ounces of fluid daily. Don't worry. That does not mean your child must drink five glasses of water. Water is found in the juice and milk kids like, so that counts toward his daily water quota. It's better to satisfy thirst with plain water than constantly offering juice or soft drinks, because water is calorie- and sugar-free. Physically active toddlers might need more water when they are running around in warm weather or whenever they tell you they are thirsty.

Water In, Water Out

The body requires a daily fluid influx of water to run smoothly because it loses water through sweating, urination, and breathing. A fever with prolonged sweating, vomiting, and diarrhea can also cause excessive body water loss, especially in infants and young children who more readily lose body water. When vomiting is severe or prolonged, your child may lose *electrolytes*, crucial minerals that play a role in health. Your pediatrician may recommend a commercial electrolyte solution to prevent serious loss in a child with prolonged diarrhea or vomiting. Sports drinks with electrolytes, such as Gatorade, do not supply the correct balance of electrolytes to replenish an infant's losses.

> **Technically Speaking**
>
> Sodium, potassium, and chloride are all **electrolytes.** These three minerals play an important role in regulating the body's fluid balance, muscle contraction, and transmission of nerve impulses.

Don't Dry Out!

Infants have more water on board, and that's a good thing. Because of the way water is stored in an infant's body, children are also capable of losing body water faster than adults. Watch for these signs of dehydration in small children (there's usually more than one):

- Restlessness
- Irritability
- Reduced tears
- Dry mouth and tongue
- Reduced urination
- Fewer wet diapers
- Hard, dry, small bowel movements
- Headache or confusion
- Dizziness and weakness

> **Mother's Helper**
>
> If your child can't seem to get enough to drink and she pees frequently, call your doctor. Excessive thirst plus excessive urination *may* be a sign of diabetes.

Water Sources

Water is the most beneficial fluid when you need fluid fast because it's rapidly absorbed into the bloodstream from the digestive tract. Other beverages such as infant formula, breast milk, milk, and juice help provide a steady fluid supply to meet your child's needs. Fruits and vegetables are also excellent fluid sources while fatty foods, such as cooking oils, contain nearly no fluid. Use the chart that follows to see how much water certain fruits and vegetables supply.

Food	Percent Water by Weight
Water	100
Lettuce	95
Watermelon	92
Broccoli	91
Grapefruit	91
Milk	89
Orange juice	88
Carrot	87
Yogurt	85
Apple	84

Source: American Dietetic Association, United States Department of Agriculture.

The Caffeine Conundrum

Fluids provide the bulk of the water children need. They can also contain caffeine. Health experts have changed their minds about caffeine's link to water loss: they say there really is no connection. When it comes to kids and caffeine, water balance isn't the issue, however. Caffeine causes kids to go bonkers and interferes with sleep. Small amounts of caffeine can provide a major jolt in children for two main reasons: because they are so small and because they don't regularly consume caffeine.

Curbing Caffeine

You know that caffeine is not good for children, but it's getting harder to figure out which foods contain caffeine. For one, there is no requirement for listing caffeine on food labels. And caffeine is being added to beverages including orange soda and water. What's the recommended caffeine intake for children? Try zero. The table that follows will help you carve caffeine out of your child's life.

Food	Caffeine (Milligrams)
Red Bull, 8.2 oz.	80
Java Water, 8 oz.	63
Mountain Dew, 12 oz.	55
Surge, 12 oz.	51
Krank20, 8 oz.	50
Snapple Iced Tea, all varieties, 16 oz.	48
Diet Coke, 12 oz.	47
Coca-Cola, 12 oz.	45
Dannon Coffee Yogurt, 8 oz.	45
Ben & Jerry's No Fat Coffee Fudge Frozen Yogurt, ½ cup	43
Sunkist Orange Soda, 12 oz.	40
Pepsi Cola, 12 oz.	37
Hershey's Special Dark Chocolate Bar, 1.5 oz.	31
Haagen-Dazs Coffee Ice Cream, ½ cup	29
Barq's Root Beer, 12 oz.	23
Hershey Bar, 1.5 oz.	10
Yoplait Cafe Au Lait Yogurt, 6 oz.	5
7-UP, 12 oz.	0
Minute Maid Orange Soda, 12 oz.	0
Mug Root Beer, 12 oz.	0
Sprite or Diet Sprite, 12 oz.	0
Stonyfield Farm Mocha Latte Yogurt, 6 oz.	0

Source: Center for Science in the Public Interest.

Get the Lead Out

As a rule, water from municipal supplies is lead-free when it leaves the water treatment plant. The water that comes out of your tap is another matter. Lead from pipe and solder in your home can leach into water. Lead is dangerous to children and adults. Just a small amount of lead, which builds up in the body over time, can have long-term effects on a child, causing irreversible developmental problems and learning disabilities.

If you have any doubt about the lead levels in the tap water your child drinks, contact the Environmental Protection Agency (EPA) to get the names of certified labs in your state that can test tap water for lead. Until you're sure lead levels are acceptable, let the cold water run through your pipes for a minute or more before using tap water for drinking or for cooking. How does that help? It flushes out water that's been sitting in pipes and collecting lead.

Safe at the Plate

You probably take your municipal water supply for granted. You can easily learn what's in your water by reading the Consumer Confidence Report (CCR) that comes to your house annually. CCRs provide key information about those contaminants that could be present at higher than normal levels. If you tossed yours, call your town or city hall to get the latest copy. They are not difficult to read, and they provide a wealth of information.

Is Bottled Water Better?

What comes to mind when you think of bottled water? Purity? Great taste? Excessive cost? Here are some pointers for filtering hype from fact:

- Bottled water is regulated, but only if it is imported or sold interstate. The Food and Drug Administration (FDA) oversees bottled water; the Environmental Protection Agency (EPA) monitors tap water.

- Certification of bottled water is voluntary. The FDA requires bottlers to monitor their own water, but they are not required to also submit to independent evaluation. Choose a brand that's certified to be sure you're getting a purer product.

- Bottled water is not always from a pristine spring located high up in the mountaintops. Sometimes it's tap water in a bottle!

- It's not guaranteed lead-free. The FDA allows up to about a third of the lead permitted in tap water. Contact the bottler to get the most recent results of their analysis for lead levels.

- It may lack fluoride. Most brands do not contain fluoride, necessary for strong, cavity-resistant teeth. Check the label. Switch to a brand with fluoride if bottled water is your child's main beverage, and if you mix your own infant formula.

- It's usually free of chlorine. Municipalities and private water utilities most often employ chlorine to kill germs in water that can make you and your child sick. Many bottled water producers choose ozone or ultraviolet disinfection instead.

The Least You Need to Know

- Because kids are smaller than adults, body water is lost more readily. That's why children run a greater risk of dehydration.

- Water is the essence of life. The body must balance its losses with its gains for overall well-being.

- A thriving infant drinking breast milk or infant formula does not require extra water. Avoid giving water because it displaces more nutritious formula or breast milk, or solid foods.

- Tap water might contain some harmful contaminants, but bottled water isn't always as pristine as you think. Do your homework when it comes to the water you drink.

Part 4 Special Nutrition Concerns

When you were a kid, there's a good chance your parents didn't have to deal with the issues covered in this part of the book. Vegetarian children? Few and far between. Peanut allergy? Rare or nonexistent in their circle of friends. Overweight toddlers? Maybe there were one or two, but hardly common. Times have changed. This part goes beyond basic nutrition to explore three major issues facing many American children and their parents. So if you'd like to know how to head off obesity, prevent food allergies, and feed a vegetarian child to the best of your ability, read on.

13

Healthy Weight for Kids

In This Chapter

- Knowing the hazards of extra body fat for kids
- Learning how family health habits affect body weight
- Getting active with your child
- Discovering television's role in a child's weight

You've probably heard that more American adults and children are overweight than ever before. And it seems that young children are not immune to the trend toward chubbiness: more than 10 percent of two to five year-olds are carrying around too much body fat. Childhood obesity has become so serious that this may be the first generation of American kids to not outlive their parents because of the health problems related to extra weight.

There is good news, however. You can help turn the tide in your very own home. No matter your child's age, working toward a healthier lifestyle is a crucial part of keeping your son or daughter from becoming a statistic in the battle of the bulge.

What's Wrong with Kids Packing On Extra Pounds

Children need to gain weight to grow. The problem comes when they pack on too much body fat. Too often, kids don't shed their "baby fat." Studies show that children who weigh more than they should at age three are much more likely to become overweight adults.

As compared to their normal-weight counterparts, overweight children are prone to the following:

- Higher blood pressure; higher blood cholesterol, and lower levels of beneficial high-density lipoprotein (HDL) cholesterol, all risk factors for later heart disease and stroke

- Elevated blood glucose levels (a warning sign for type 2 diabetes)
- Elevated liver enzymes (a warning sign for liver damage caused by the accumulation of fat in liver cells)
- Type 2 diabetes
- Breathing problems
- Joint problems
- Depression and low self-esteem

Mother's Helper

"An ounce of prevention is worth a pound of cure" has never rung truer than when applied to healthy weight for kids. Research suggests it's much harder for a child and his parents to reverse the trend toward heaviness than it is to prevent it.

Our Overweight Children: Who Is to Blame?

It's ironic. For all the pressure to be trim and healthy, our society actually encourages adults and children to become overweight and stay that way.

For example, high-calorie, high-fat foods are cheaper and more readily available than healthier options, including fresh fruits and dairy products. Food is just part of the problem. Because we value saving time, we rely on using calorie-saving remote controls, and using the drive-thru to do our banking, and, even worse, pick up fast food. Furthermore, new housing subdivisions are often designed without sidewalks or play areas, so children end up having restricted activity. It doesn't take a genius to understand that too many calories consumed plus too few burned by moving around equals an unhealthy weight in most kids.

Is body weight genetic fate? According to the American Academy of Pediatrics, when one parent is overweight, a young child is about three times more likely to weigh too much; when both parents are carrying around excess fat, he's more than 10 times as likely as a child without two overweight parents. An overweight child is not raised in a vacuum. Although everyone in the family may have trouble controlling their weight because they are genetically prone to being heavier, chances are all family members are consuming too much of the wrong types of foods because they don't know what to eat for weight control; in addition, parents and their children are probably not exercising enough.

It Takes a Family

You know that saying "It takes a village to raise a child"? Well, it takes the family to keep him trim and healthy.

Even when the genetic odds are stacked against your child, a home environment conducive to healthy lifestyle habits can override a predisposition to becoming overweight. Your job as a parent is to promote healthy eating and regular physical activity. You can't control whether there's a fast-food joint on every block, but you can control whether you serve French fries or a healthier baked potato; offer cookies in place of fruit; and allow your child to sip soft drinks instead of water or milk.

It won't be easy, but investing in healthier habits now provides a huge payoff. Children are highly suggestible, and they can be taught to like nutritious foods and exercise. Up until your child goes to elementary school, you're basically in control of what he eats, how much, and when. Priming children early on to make healthy choices can mean they learn to make better choices when you're not around.

> **Nutrition Nugget**
>
> Eating more is linked to a lower weight in children. More fresh fruit, that is. Research shows children who munch on fruit have a lower Body Mass Index. What's the connection? Fruit is full of fiber and water, two elements that keep kids fuller longer. Eating fruit may also crowd out other higher-calorie, low-nutrient foods.

Is Your Child Overweight?

He may be plump, but that doesn't mean your child has a weight problem. Starting at age two, your doctor should determine whether your child has excess fat by calculating his Body Mass Index and plotting it on the pediatric growth chart. See Chapter 3 for more on the growth charts.

When you have a concern about your infant or toddler's weight, talk it over with your pediatrician. You and your doctor might be able to identify easy changes to make in your family's lifestyle that will promote a healthier weight. Change doesn't happen overnight, however. It takes time and effort to make new habits part of your daily routine.

If your doctor confirms your concerns, here are some helpful hints for handling the information:

- Don't put your child on a diet unless you have been advised to by your pediatrician or a registered dietitian who has provided the specifics about what to eat.
- Consider weight control a lifelong effort for the entire family.
- Let your child know he or she is loved and appreciated whatever his weight.
- Focus on your child's health and positive qualities, not your child's weight.
- Be a good role model for your child. If your child sees you enjoying healthy foods and physical activity, he or she is more likely to do the same now and for the rest of his or her life.

Nutrition Nugget

Your mother was almost right. If there is a most important meal, it's breakfast, if only for its contribution to weight control. Among the nearly 3,000 men and women enrolled in the National Weight Control Registry (NWCR) who shed at least 30 pounds and kept it off for a year or more, 78 percent of them ate breakfast every day. Because the brain doesn't store energy, a healthy breakfast revs up kids for the day while providing an opportunity for good nutrition.

Get a Move On

American children today are less physically active overall than previous generations of kids, and it's figuring into the increased prevalence of overweight children. Aside from weighing more, sedentary kids have higher blood pressure and lower levels of HDL than their active counterparts. Even worse, sedentary tater tots tend to grow into adult couch potatoes.

Physical activity is a way for kids to develop motor skills and coordination; reduce stress; and burn calories. It's important for parents to make time for free play. Have toddlers fetch toys you've scattered about the room; play airplane with your tot; and put on music and dance around the room with your youngster. At the playground, let your child chase you on the grass to practice running, and help him climb on age-appropriate playground toys.

Here are some activities for older toddlers:

- Gathering leaves and jumping in them
- Playing in the snow
- Playing in the pool with parents or other adults
- Walking around the neighborhood with family
- Kicking a soccer ball in the backyard
- Going sledding
- Playing tag
- Playing hide and go seek
- Flying a kite
- Learning to hula hoop

Turn Off the TV

You've probably parked your child in front of the television to get a few things done around the house or to grab a few moments of peace. Should you feel guilty? No, as long as it doesn't become a habit.

Watching TV, or sitting idle in front of any screen for that matter, is linked to unhealthy weight. It doesn't take a rocket scientist to figure out that the more time your child spends on the couch, the less time he spends burning calories in play and other movement. What's worse is that children who are allowed to eat while watching TV consume extra calories, perhaps because they are not focused on fullness. Watching television during mealtimes is related to eating fewer fruits and vegetables.

Television ads have a profound effect on a child's food choices, too. According to research publicized in *The Lancet*, U.S. children see about 10 food commercials for every hour of TV they watch; most ads are for—you guessed it—fast food, soft drinks, sweets, and sugar-sweetened breakfast cereals. That kind of exposure increases the likelihood that a group of three- to five-year-olds would select an advertised food when presented with the chance after watching the commercials.

The American Academy of Pediatrics is adamant about no television for children under the age of two. That may sound harsh, but it's for a purpose. Television watching is a strong habit that's difficult to break as children get older. Clearly, parents are not taking the AAP's advice to heart. According to a report released by the Henry J. Kaiser Family Foundation, 43 percent of kids under two watch TV on a daily basis; 26 percent have a TV in their room; and 9 percent have a TV remote control specially designed for children. For more information about the effects of television on your child's health, visit the American Academy of Pediatrics website at www.aap.org.

Follow My Lead

When the entire family participates in healthier eating, no single member feels singled out or punished for being overweight. With time, eating healthy foods and regular physical activity becomes second nature to the group.

Before you make any changes in your child's life, you may need to deal with some of your less-than-stellar lifestyle habits. Take heart. Nobody eats an exemplary diet every day, least of all busy parents. And becoming a parent doesn't automatically erase the issues you might have with overeating or underexercising, or your poor body image.

Even when you want the best for your child, you may be unwittingly undermining your own good intentions. Mothers who are overly concerned with their own body image and weight tend to have daughters who obsess about the same issues, as early as age five. Is it a genetic trait? Probably not. When you openly voice your displeasure with your "fat thighs," or "sagging butt," you influence your daughter's developing weight issues and body satisfaction. Bottom line: Watch your waistline in private and keep your thoughts to yourself. Taking a vow of silence about your feelings helps.

Allowing your child to eat according to her hunger cues fosters a healthy relationship with food, too. When mothers severely restrict what and how much their children can eat, it may backfire. Studies show that when left to their own devices, these same kids tend to overeat. The more you curb a child's intake, the more likely she will develop a preoccupation with food.

The Least You Need to Know

- The earlier a child becomes overweight, the greater the health risks. Overweight children have health problems that usually appear in adults who are decades older.
- Both parents should adopt healthier lifestyle habits, including eating nutritious foods and getting regular exercise, so that they become second nature for their child.
- Limit television time to encourage more free play for helping kids stay trim and healthy. Don't allow a child under the age of two to watch TV.
- Severely restricting how much a child eats can be counterproductive, because it can result in eating past the point of hunger when parents aren't around to direct.

Chapter 14

Foiling Asthma and Food Allergies

In This Chapter

- Learning who's at risk for food allergies and asthma
- Heading off food allergies and asthma
- Knowing what the food allergy symptoms are
- Determining what to do if your child is allergic to food

Food allergies and asthma are on the rise in young children. The common denominator appears to be a hypervigilant immune system that senses danger when there is none. To make matters worse, children with asthma are more likely to develop food allergies. This chapter explains food allergies and asthma in detail, highlighting who is at risk and how best to protect your child during infancy and beyond.

Food Allergy in Perspective

A food allergy is an overreaction of the immune system to an *allergen*, a food substance the allergic person's body interprets as harmful. In searching out and destroying so-called "invaders," your child's immune system is acting on his best behalf. Unfortunately, it also means his immune system is over-protective.

Technically Speaking

Allergens are proteins found in foods not broken down during cooking or digestion that trigger the body's immune response.

About four percent (11 million) of Americans suffer from food allergies; one to two percent are children, according to the Food Allergy and Anaphylaxis Association. Although the number of children truly allergic to food is relatively small, the stakes are high. Food allergy reactions can land a child in the hospital, or worse.

The Worst Offenders

Any food can cause an allergic reaction, but a mere eight foods are responsible for about 90 percent of food allergy reactions. They are: milk, soy, eggs, wheat, peanuts (actually a legume), tree nuts (including walnuts and almonds), fish, and shellfish. Severe, life-threatening reactions are most common in people allergic to peanuts, tree nuts, shellfish, fish, and eggs; these reactions are likely in people who also have asthma. Infants and toddlers tend to be most allergic to eggs, milk, and peanuts.

Some raw fruits and vegetables, seeds, and nuts can cause allergies, particularly in people with hay fever. So-called Oral Allergy Syndrome (OAS) is the result of a cross-reaction of allergens in the pollen of birch, alder, hazel, grass, ragweed, mugwort, and certain foods. OAS is typically more annoying than dangerous, as symptoms are confined to itchy or swollen lips, tongue, throat, or mouth. OAS symptoms disappear without treatment. These foods are largely responsible for OAS: apples, apricots, bananas, carrots, cantaloupe, celery, cherries, fennel seed, hazelnut (filbert), honeydew, oranges, parsley, peaches, pears, potatoes, sunflower seeds, tomatoes, and watermelon. Cooking them can destroy allergens.

Food additives may trigger allergy in some children, but it's uncommon. Sulfites are particularly problematic because they can cause life-threatening symptoms in people with asthma. Refer to Chapter 16 for more on sulfites and other food additives.

Seeing the Signs of Food Allergy

The first time an infant or toddler eats food with an allergen he is sensitive to, there will be no outward symptoms. It's a different story on the inside, where his body is gearing up to repel the next allergen "attack" by producing *antibodies*. From then on, every time he eats food with the allergen, antibodies will spring into action, triggering a cascade of events leading to symptoms that appear within minutes to hours. Sometimes, it's a day or two before it's apparent your child is allergic to food.

Call your pediatrician if your child experiences any of the following food allergy symptoms:

- Swelling of the lips, mouth, tongue, face, or throat
- Hives
- Itchy eyes
- Rashes (eczema)
- Sneezing
- Nasal congestion or runny nose
- Chronic coughing
- Itching and/or tightness in the throat
- Shortness of breath
- Asthma or wheezing
- Nausea
- Abdominal pain and bloating
- Vomiting
- Diarrhea
- Cramping

Dial 911 if your child or any adult shows the signs of *anaphylaxis* or anaphylactic shock, which includes an array of reactions to food, most often from peanuts, tree nuts, fish, shellfish, and eggs.

Is it food allergy or indigestion? It's not always easy to tell, especially in infants. Foods can produce many of the same symptoms without involving the immune system. For example, foodborne illness may lead to diarrhea and vomiting, which are also signs of food allergy. When in doubt, call the doctor.

> **Technically Speaking**
>
> **Antibodies** are proteins produced by the immune system to defend the body against allergens.

> **Technically Speaking**
>
> **Anaphylaxis**, the most dangerous and life-threatening result of a food allergy, causes blood vessels to widen to the point of pushing blood pressure to precariously low levels. Anaphylaxis can result in an abnormal heartbeat that can be fatal if not treated promptly.

Foiling Food Allergy in Your Child

He's got your nose. Maybe she has your eyes. Your child may also have your allergies, because they are often passed down from generation to generation. Two allergic parents further increase a child's allergy risk.

Food allergies can develop at any age, but people who are prone are more likely to discover one or more food allergies during early childhood. Why? A child's less-developed immune and digestive systems make it harder for them to do battle with allergens.

No parent can be sure if their infant or toddler will develop food allergies. That's why it pays to introduce a single food at a time and wait three to five days before trying another, whether allergy runs in the family or not. Keeping a diary allows you to pin down an offending food. Encourage your sitter to do the same. Save labels from processed foods, because they could contain ingredients that trigger food allergies.

Parents who have food allergies need to take extra steps to reduce their child's overall food allergy risk and to keep their child allergy-free for as long as possible. When mom and dad are allergic or one parent and a child's sibling have allergies, follow these guidelines from the American Academy of Pediatrics to keep food allergies at bay:

- Breastfeed baby for a year or more. Breastfeeding boosts the immune system, possibly providing an edge on avoiding allergies. Studies suggest infants who are breastfed exclusively during their first 6 to 12 months of life develop fewer allergies by age one or two than infants fed with formula. Don't worry if you and your baby don't nurse for a full year; any amount of breastfeeding benefits your baby's immune system.

- Nursing moms should eliminate peanuts and tree nuts and consider eliminating eggs, cow's milk, fish, and perhaps other foods from their diets while nursing. To avoid nutrient deficiencies, speak with a registered dietitian to design a personal eating plan.

- Wait until six months to start solid foods.

- Put off serving your child dairy products until age one; wait until at least age two to serve eggs; and do not offer peanuts, nuts, and fish until three years old.

For more information on reducing food allergy risk in children, visit the American Academy of Pediatrics' website at www.aap.org.

Will Your Child Get Over His Food Allergy?

As a child's digestive tract matures, he absorbs fewer allergens into his bloodstream and his immune system becomes stronger, allowing him to prevent allergens from wreaking havoc on his body. So he could outgrow food allergies, but it's not a certainty.

Milk, soy, and egg allergies may disappear by age four. Allergies to peanuts, tree nuts, and shellfish probably won't go away, although there is some promising scientific evidence suggesting about 20 percent of children outgrow peanut allergies. Never take it upon yourself to test whether your child is over a food allergy, particularly a peanut allergy. Discuss the possibilities of reintroduction with your pediatrician or allergist.

Food Allergy or Intolerance: Sorting It Out

Food allergy is often confused with food intolerance. Mistaking a food allergy for a food intolerance can mean withholding foods from your child that you think are dangerous.

Lactose intolerance, the inability to digest some or all lactose, the carbohydrate in milk, is often mistaken for milk allergy. A child who has lactose intolerance will probably become uncomfortable due to gas, diarrhea, and bloating soon after consuming milk products.

The symptoms of lactose intolerance are uncomfortable, but they are fleeting. Still, a lactose intolerance may last for life. The good news is that lactose-reduced dairy foods, such as Lactaid brand milk, cottage cheese, and ice cream, are real milk products with all the same nutrition. Many people with lactose intolerance can tolerate small amounts of milk products, particularly yogurt, with no or minimal effects.

Because milk allergy involves the immune system, the only solution is complete avoidance of milk, milk products, and ingredients derived from milk, including casein, milk solids, whey, and whey protein concentrate often added to processed foods.

Feeding Your Allergic Child

If your child has been diagnosed with food allergy, work closely with your health-care providers, especially a registered dietitian, to design a diet that will prevent allergic reactions while avoid nutrient deficiencies. Discuss formula options with your pediatrician and follow his recommendations for an allergic infant.

Steer clear of foods your child is allergic to. That means keeping foods that trigger his allergy out of the house. Some children are so sensitive to allergens that getting a whiff of an offending food, or getting a kiss from someone who ate the food, can

Mother's Helper

The Food Allergy and Ana-phylaxis Network provides excellent resources for parents of allergic children, including how to scan labels for allergens. Reach them at www.foodallergy.org.

cause trouble. Processed foods may contain ingredi-ents that your child must avoid. Study ingredient lists with every purchase; ingredients can change without warning. Food companies often display a warning on food packages alerting consumers to the fact that the product was manufactured in the same plant as nuts or other allergens. This is done as a precaution be-cause of the potential for cross-contamination.

Eat Bugs to Boost Immunity?

Germs are scary, but they are not all bad. The friendly bacteria that live in the intes-tinal tract, known as probiotics, may enhance the immune system and help to reduce allergies and asthma. Certain probiotics produce the enzyme lactase needed to digest lactose, the carbohydrate in milk and milk products, particularly yogurt. That could be why people with lactose intolerance can eat yogurt without consequence.

Probiotics are added to some cultured dairy products including kefir, fermented milk, and yogurt. Prebiotics are food for probiotics; prebiotics may also increase the absorption of minerals, such as calcium, from the foods they are in.

In general, the greater the variety of probiotics in a product, the better. Reap the most benefit by including probiotics in your child's diet every day. The most likely choices for children are Stonyfield Farm yogurt and DanActive cultured probiotic dairy drinks because they contain high levels of several types of beneficial live active cultures. Stonyfield Farm yogurt also contains inulin. Inulin supplies food for pro-biotics to thrive on.

About Asthma

Asthma is a constant inflammation of the airways. When a person with asthma has an "attack," his airways swell up even more and the muscles outside the airways tighten, further restricting airflow and making breathing difficult. To make matters worse, swollen airways are flooded with mucus.

According to the American Lung Association, an estimated six million children under 18 years of age have asthma. Asthma is the leading cause of chronic illness among children. At least half of children with asthma show some sign of it before the age of five. Most children have mild to moderate problems. Like food allergy, child-hood asthma has a genetic component, and upward of 80 percent of kids with asthma have significant allergies.

Preventing Asthma: How Diet Helps

No one is sure what causes asthma or how best to prevent it. Certain aspects including respiratory infections, such as colds; stress and excitement; and allergic reactions to allergens, such as pollen, mold, animal dander, dust, and food, are only some of the potential asthma triggers. Youngsters with asthma and food allergies run a greater risk of anaphylactic reactions.

If your child is at risk for asthma, or already has it, you'll want to do what you can to prevent or manage the condition. Diet may make a difference.

- Help your child achieve and maintain a healthy weight. Research suggests a link between excess body weight in children and asthma risk.

- Pile on the produce. Children who consume the most vitamin C and other antioxidant nutrients found in fruits and vegetables have better lung function. Researchers at Cornell University report that children with higher blood levels of vitamin C, beta-carotene, and selenium were 10 to 20 percent less likely to have asthma than children with lower levels of these nutrients. Why? Antioxidants may protect against inflamed airways.

- Give your child a daily dose of multivitamins to insure he's getting the nutrients he needs to keep his immune system in top form.

- Offer omega-3s. Omega-3 fats fight inflammation. Fatty fish, including salmon and trout, are among the fish harboring the most omega-3s, and are good for children with asthma as long as they are not allergic to fish and seafood. Walnuts, flaxseed oil, canola oil, and green leafy vegetables also contain omega-3 fats.

Asthma is a growing problem among children. Offering your child the healthiest diet that includes the elements mentioned above is one way of combating the condition.

Can Children Outgrow Asthma?

As a child's airway matures, he is able to handle airway inflammation and irritants better, so his asthma symptoms may notably decrease. About half of children with asthma appear to outgrow the condition by their teenage years. However, after kids develop sensitive airways, they remain that way for life. Some children will have recurring asthma symptoms in their late thirties or early forties. New triggers may set off symptoms at any time in people who have asthma.

The Least You Need to Know

- Asthma and allergy of any type have a strong genetic component. There is no cure for food allergy or asthma, but there are many ways to manage the conditions.

- Any one of the many symptoms of food allergy can appear within minutes or days of eating an allergen. When starting solids, keep a detailed food diet to track potential allergens.

- Children at high risk of food allergies should be fed in a conservative manner for the first three years of life to help them avoid developing food allergies and to keep them allergy-free for longer. Consider breastfeeding for as long as possible to boost your child's immunity.

- Lactose intolerance does not involve the immune system. Although it's typically a lifelong condition, there is no reason why children should avoid lactose-free dairy foods.

- Maintaining a healthy weight and eating a balanced diet that contains lots of produce and omega-3 fats can bolster a child's immune system, possibly heading off asthma.

15

Feeding Your Vegetarian Child

In This Chapter

- Discovering the many forms of vegetarianism
- Learning why plant-based diets may be better for you
- Knowing which nutrients to be mindful of
- Finding fabulous phytonutrients

Let's face it. Once upon a time, vegetarians were regarded as weird. Not any more. When soy milk and veggie burgers pop up on supermarket shelves and in fast food restaurants, you know vegetarianism has gone mainstream.

Avoiding or reducing animal food consumption is growing in appeal thanks to concerns about personal health and the environment, and ethical reasons. You may already be enamored with vegetarianism. Or maybe you're considering going cold turkey and giving up animal foods for good. Either way, you're probably wondering how a vegetarian diet affects your child's well-being. This chapter spells it out.

What Is a Vegetarian?

The meaning of "vegetarian" seems crystal clear, only it's not. Taken literally, the term implies eating vegetables exclusively. However, even the most ardent meat-lover knows vegetarians eat more than vegetables. How much more depends on the type of vegetarianism you're talking about.

- Vegans avoid all animal products, including honey and gelatin.
- Ovo-vegetarians eat eggs, but no dairy, meat, seafood, or poultry.
- Lacto-ovo vegetarians eat dairy products and eggs, but avoid meat, poultry, and seafood. (Most American vegetarians are lacto-ovo.)
- Whew! As if that wasn't enough, enter the flexitarian, a person who eats a mostly vegetarian diet, but who is also willing to eat meat or fish occasionally.

Vegetarians May Be Healthier Than Meat Eaters

As a group, studies show vegetarians' risk for heart disease, high blood pressure, and certain cancers are lower than that of meat-eating carnivores. Why? Lower levels of total and saturated fat and cholesterol in plant-based diets may be responsible for keeping artery-clogging cholesterol in check. Vegetarians eat plants that are typically richer in nutrients, such as fiber, vitamins, minerals, and phytonutrients—protective plant compounds—that prevent chronic conditions such as high blood pressure and cancer in adults.

Do the benefits of eating more plant foods extend to children? Research on vegetarian children is lacking. Yet it makes sense to think that children who follow a plant-based diet starting early in life will reap the benefits later on. As an added benefit, plant-based diets help reduce the risk of foodborne illness in children. That's because grains and fresh fruits and vegetables that have been thoroughly washed harbor far fewer germs that make you sick than meat, poultry, and seafood.

That does not mean vegetarianism is automatically synonymous with wellness. The healthfulness of a vegetarian diet depends on food choices and eating patterns. Depending on what a vegetarian eats, he could be worse off healthwise than a meat-eater. For example, French fries, white bread, and sugar are technically permissible under vegetarianism, but are not as healthy as lean meat, grilled chicken, or low-fat milk.

Smart Food Choices for Vegetarian Children

Whether you include animal products in your child's diet or not, offering healthy foods matter to his growth and development. You know enough to understand that you can't just ditch an entire food group or two without nutritional consequences. Infants and toddlers grow so fast that consistently missing out on one or more nutrients could cause irreparable harm.

According to the American Dietetic Association, a bit of planning goes a long way to providing vegetarian children with the nutrients they need to thrive. For peace of mind, speak with a registered dietitian about your child's vegetarian eating plan. For now, watch out for these potential problem areas:

- **Calories.** Children on a plant-based eating plan may consume large amounts of fiber from whole grains, fruits, and vegetables. Fiber is healthy, but too much can thwart adequate weight gain by filling up your child's tiny tummy before she consumes enough energy.

- **Protein.** When calories are inadequate, a low protein intake might be right behind. Plant foods, including soy products, legumes, rice, and grains, contain all the essential amino acids (EAAs) your child needs to grow, but no single plant food provides all the essential amino acids (see Chapter 10 for more on protein).

- **Iron.** Meat, poultry, and seafood are natural sources of the form of iron most readily absorbed by the body. That's not to say vegetarian children are always iron deficient. As long as they eat enough fortified grains, such as infant cereal and other cooked cereals, ready-to-eat breakfast cereal, rice, and pasta, and plant foods with iron, they will probably get the iron they require (see Chapter 11 for more on iron).

- **Calcium and Vitamin D.** Milk is an excellent source of protein, calcium, and vitamin D; other dairy foods don't supply vitamin D, however. Vegans must make up for missing milk. Soy and rice beverages fortified with vitamin D and calcium help. However, rice beverages contain a tiny fraction of the protein of cow's milk (see Chapter 11 for more on vegetarian sources of calcium).

- **Vitamin B12.** Vitamin B12 is necessary for your child's nervous system; without it, irreversible nerve damage is possible. Vitamin B12 is unique to animal foods, so vegans are particularly vulnerable to B12 deficiencies. For supplemental vitamin B12, look to fortified foods such as breakfast cereals and soy products. Read the label before purchasing.

- **Zinc.** Children require zinc for a number of bodily functions, the least of which is cell growth and repair and energy production. (Zinc is described in detail in

Chapter 11.) Because meat, poultry, and seafood are superior sources of zinc, avoiding them may lead to a shortfall. To boot, the absorption of zinc from plant foods is not as good as from animal foods. However, manufacturers often fortify plant foods with large amounts of zinc to offset any absorption deficiencies. Legumes, peanut butter, wheat germ, fortified grains, yogurt, and cheese make fine zinc choices for vegetarian kids.

- **Docosahexanoic Acid (DHA).** Avoiding fish means a shortage of DHA, a form of omega-3 fat that's critical to peak eyesight and brain function. Read more about DHA in Chapter 9.

If food does not satisfy your child's nutrient needs on a regular basis, it's wise to give him a multivitamin with iron to fill in potential nutrient gaps beginning after his first birthday. Kids who don't eat at least two servings of dairy foods daily (see Chapter 7 for more on serving sizes) may come up short for calcium and may need a calcium supplement in addition to a daily multivitamin.

Nutrition Nugget

Vegetarians, especially vegans, should include refined grains, such as white bread and cornflakes, in their diets. Nutritionists typically champion whole grains for good health, but refined flour serves a two-fold purpose in vegetarianism. It fosters the body's zinc absorption, and its lower-fiber content helps children consume the calories they need before filling up.

Those Fabulous Phytonutrients

Phytonutrients are among the benefits everybody reaps from eating produce. Phytonutrients, a.k.a. phytochemicals, are plant compounds that technically include carbohydrates, proteins, vitamins, minerals, and fiber. However, most nutrition experts use the term to describe the other substances in plants. Phytonutrients represent an exciting frontier in nutrition research. The list of phytonutrients and their benefits seems to get longer every day.

A single plant food, such as a fruit, may contain hundreds of phytonutrients. Some phytonutrients, such as the lycopene that makes tomatoes crimson and watermelon bright pink, are pigments that provide plants with their bright hue; others have less obvious functions, such as defending plants against pesky germs, that may translate into protecting humans from cell damage.

The Least You Need to Know

- There are many different forms of vegetarianism: vegan, ovo-vegetarians, lacto-ovo vegetarians, and flexitarians.
- It is possible to raise a healthy vegan child with no nutrient deficiencies, as long as you choose foods wisely, and he eats what you give him. Lacto-ovo vegetarians run less of a risk of nutrient deficiencies.
- Vegetarianism doesn't guarantee good health. You must offer your child options to offset the omission of animal products from one or more food groups.
- Fruits and vegetables are brimming with phytonutrients that bolster a child's health. Plant products may have hundreds of different protective phytonutrients.

Part 5

Let's Make a Meal!

The next step is pairing nutrition knowledge with your culinary skills to bring good health to the table. In this part, you find out how to make savvy supermarket choices and why you should forego certain convenience foods, such as salad dressings and pasta sauces, in favor of easy-to-prepare homemade versions. You also learn about the best techniques for keeping food safe at home. And because Americans love to dine out, and do so often, you find a chapter that includes surviving restaurant meals with an infant or toddler in tow, as well as the best ways to transport your child's food when on the go.

Chapter 16

Supermarket Savvy

In This Chapter

- Picking the best produce
- Hunting down whole grains in the grocery
- Finding the best bets for meat, poultry, and seafood
- Understanding food additives
- Learning simple recipes for everyday foods

Remember when, BK (Before Kid), you ate what you wanted when you wanted and shopped for food on the fly? You can still live that way, but it won't get you very far in making healthy meals and snacks for your youngster.

Let's face it: when you must choose between trudging to the market with a cranky newborn or tired toddler for one or two ingredients and ordering out for dinner, the latter usually wins. Shopping on a regular basis for kitchen staples puts you ahead of the game. This chapter highlights how to choose the ingredients you need for nutritious kid cuisine.

About Fruits and Vegetables

Your mother said fruits and vegetables were good for you, and boy, was she ever right. Produce is brimming with nutrients that children thrive on. The latest government recommendations for fruits and vegetables are the highest ever, and they include an emphasis on deeply colored produce that offers more nutrients, as well as legumes (see Chapter 7 for more on feeding your two-year-old).

Picking Produce

Fruits and vegetables aren't cheap, so you'll want to get the most for your money. In-season fresh produce is lower in price and may provide more nutrition. Purchase only what you need and use fresh fruits and vegetables within a few days to prevent throwing your money down the drain. When your favorite fruits are in season, buy extra, and cut up and freeze them in labeled, sealed plastic bags or plastic containers.

The time it takes to peel and prepare fruits and vegetables can be a roadblock to serving them. Purchase pre-washed, pre-cut vegetables and stock up on frozen fruits and vegetables. They save time and money because you can take what you need out of the package. Canned fruits are a suitable substitute for fresh, especially when they are packed in their own juices. Steer clear of high-sodium canned vegetables, however.

Minimize your child's pesticide exposure by choosing organic fruits and vegetables when you can. If your budget doesn't allow for organic produce, don't worry. What's important is serving your family a variety of fruits and vegetables. So far as we know, the nutritional benefits of conventionally grown fruits and vegetables far outweigh the risk. Washing fresh produce helps reduce pesticide residues and lowers the risk of food-borne illness from germs. Wash produce thoroughly before eating with warm running water, including fruits and vegetables with rinds and skins, such as melons, avocadoes, and oranges; gently remove any dirt or other debris with your hands. Do not use soap or any other cleaning agent on produce. Use a clean vegetable scrub brush on hardier produce such as potatoes and sweet potatoes. Peel fruits, such as peaches, nectarines, pears, and apples, to cut back on pesticide residues and prevent choking in tiny tots.

Choose your own produce, such as apples and oranges, over prepackaged, to get the best quality. Go early in the day to farmers markets for the freshest produce. Here are some helpful hints for choosing fruits and vegetables.

Fruit/Vegetable	Should Be ...
Apples	Firm, with clean, smooth skin free of bruises or decay.
Asparagus	Firm with tightly closed tips. Entire piece should be light green. Thinner spears are more tender.
Bananas	Unblemished and nearly all yellow (a sign of ripeness).
Beans	Slender, crisp, bright, and free of blemishes.

Fruit/Vegetable	Should Be ...
Blueberries	Plump, firm, and bright.
Broccoli	Uniform dark green color; firm; bud clusters closed.
Carrots	Firm, clean, and bright orange-gold.
Cantaloupe	Rough skin without blemishes. Should be slightly soft.
Cauliflower	Firm, clean, compact, and creamy white.
Celery	Rigid and crisp with uniform light green color.
Oranges	Thin, brightly colored skin.
Peaches	Bruise-free; creamy yellowish pink; slightly soft but not mushy.
Pears	Firm with no wrinkles or distinct bruising.
Peas	Small, plump, bright-green pods.
Potatoes	Firm and smooth with no wrinkles, sprouts, cracks, bruises, or green areas (on white potatoes).
Raspberries	Firm and without mold.
Strawberries	Uniform in color and firm.
Tomatoes	Smooth and well formed. Firm but not hard.
Watermelon	Cut: firm flesh with bright red hue. Uncut: bruise-free surface with pale green color.

Produce: Handle with Care

Produce is perishable and should be treated accordingly. As soon as you get home from the store, refrigerate the fruits and vegetables that require it, which is nearly everything. Refrigeration slows down ripening and preserves quality. No need to refrigerate bananas, tomatoes, onions, or potatoes, however. Tomatoes taste better when stored at room temperature. Onions and potatoes keep longer in cool, dry, dark places (such as a closet). Remove onions and potatoes from plastic bags and store in a bin or bowl.

Refrigerate fresh produce within two hours of peeling or cutting; throw it away after two hours at room temperature.

Mother's Helper

When you don't want fresh vegetables to go to waste, blanch them by immersing them in boiling water for a minute or two, rinse them immediately with ice cold water, and then transfer them to an airtight container and freeze for future use.

Go with the Grain

Grains, such as breads, cereals, and pasta, provide energy primarily as carbohydrates. They also supply protein and some fat. In their natural state, grains are cholesterol-free.

Whole grains supply more B vitamins, vitamin E, selenium, fiber, and other beneficial plant substances than refined grains, such as white bread. In the refining process, grains lose nutrients. Many of the refined grains we eat are *fortified* or *enriched* with nutrients, helping to reduce the risk of nutrient deficiencies.

> **Technically Speaking**
>
> **Fortified** grains supply nutrients not originally present in the grain, such as iron and the B vitamin folic acid. **Enriched** grains contain the nutrients lost during the refining process.

Hunting for Whole Grains

Think grains and you probably conjure up bread, pasta, and rice. The newest grain recommendations emphasize whole grains over refined, suggesting everyone, including small children, consume whole grains to satisfy at least half of their daily grain quota.

A whole grain is more than whole wheat bread or brown rice. Barley, bulgur, and quinoa are examples of whole grains that are easy to prepare and are good for you. (Also look to the recipes in the Recipes for the Early Years appendix for more examples.) Whole grain cereals for meals and snacks can easily contribute to your child's whole grain quota (see the section that follows to help you choose whole grain cereals).

When buying whole grains in bulk, look for clean grains free of debris. Be sure the store has a quick turnover rate to guarantee the freshest product. Supermarkets, such as Whole Foods, and smaller specialty stores tend to have a more rapid turnover rate.

Cruising the Cereal Aisle

Cereal is a kid-worthy food. When you choose right, cereal can boost a child's intake of whole grains, and a slew of nutrients, including fiber, carbohydrates, B vitamins, and iron, as well as those found in milk. Studies suggest young children who eat breakfast cereal at least every other day do better at maintaining a healthy body weight.

You know cereal is good for you, but you may feel like avoiding the cereal aisle because it's crammed with colorful boxes designed to grab a child's attention and influence his parent's buying habits. You must literally look high and low to find cereals with more fiber and less added sugar, because the upper and lower supermarket shelves showcase the healthier choices.

To choose a healthy cereal, scan the label for whole grain, high-fiber prompts. For example, all General Mills cereals are now whole grain, so that makes it easier on parents. Other ways to identify whole-grain cereals include a "good" or "excellent" source label statement on the front of the package. When in doubt, scan the ingredient list for "whole" before the name of the grain in any grain product.

Check to see whether cereal is fortified with vitamins and minerals, including iron (most are). Put it back if it contains palm or coconut oils or partially hydrogenated fat. The least convenient cooked cereals tend to be the best choices. For example, the oats that take five minutes to cook are better for you than the ones in the individual packets.

Get Fresh with Meat and Poultry

Meat and poultry provide protein, varying amounts of fat, and other nutrients vital to your child's growth and development, including B vitamins, iron, and zinc. To be safe and get the greatest nutrition, you must choose the freshest meat and poultry. Here's how:

- Always look for the Safe Food Handling label on packages. It indicates the meat has been processed safely and provides tips for proper food handling and cooking.

- If today is the "sell by" date, you'll need to cook meat or poultry within a day or two to be safe. Never purchase meat that is past the sell-by date.

- Use ground meat and poultry within one to two days of purchasing, or freeze. Opt for 100 percent ground turkey or chicken breast to get the leanest meat.

Nutrition Nugget

There are many lean cuts of meat to choose from, including the following: eye round roast, top round steak, bottom round roast, top sirloin steak, 95% lean ground beef, chuck shoulder roast, top loin (strip or New York steak), flank steak, ribeye steak, tenderloin steak; white meat chicken and turkey (skinless) and ground 100 percent chicken or turkey breast); pork tenderloin; lamb fore shank; and veal shoulder (blade, arm or whole).

- Small whole turkeys or roaster chickens are a great idea for busy parents because they require a minimum of preparation and provide more than one meal. Pick whole frozen turkeys that are hard to the touch, and be sure the protective wrapping is intact.

- Be sure meat and poultry packaging is tightly sealed and is cold to the touch.

- Avoid packages with pinkish ice; it's a sure sign meat has been refrozen, reducing its quality. Packaged chicken parts should look pink, never gray or yellow, and poultry or meat should not smell.

- Pick up meat and poultry last and bag it separately from other groceries. Meat and poultry are perishable and should be kept refrigerated for as long as possible before purchasing.

Following these few simple rules will help to ensure the best-tasting and safest meat and poultry for you and your child.

Mother's Helper

Family packs of chicken, pork, or other cuts of meat aren't always a bargain. They may actually cost as much per pound as smaller packages of meat, so always check the per-pound price before purchasing. Likewise, scan the unit pricing on prepared foods to get the best deal. Warehouse clubs seem to offer bargains, but the prices aren't always what they seem. You must figure in the cost of your yearly membership; when the dues don't pay for themselves within a year, warehouse clubs aren't worth it.

Searching for Seafood

Seafood supplies protein, vitamins, minerals, and omega-3 fatty acids. It's also relatively low in cholesterol. At this point in your child's life, he probably won't be eating seafood very often. However, it pays to introduce him to fish as soon as possible because of its many health benefits. Mild-tasting white fish such as cod, catfish, and haddock are more acceptable to children than stronger tasting fish with more fat, including bluefish and trout.

On the whole, fish is good for kids, but certain species are so contaminated with chemicals that children should avoid them or limit them. See Chapter 17 for more on seafood safety.

Choose seafood from places where it's displayed on ice in a closed refrigerated case. The freshest fish has only a mild scent. Whole fish should be firm to the touch with scales that cling tightly to shiny skin. Eyes should be clear, bright, and protruding.

Examining Eggs

Protein-packed foods tend to be on the pricey side. Not so for eggs. Eggs offer a low-cost source of high-quality protein, along with more than a dozen vitamins and minerals. Best of all, kids love eggs prepared in a number of ways. Eggs are versatile and convenient, and can serve as the basis for fast and healthy meals and snacks.

To get the best buy, scan the outside of an egg carton. Cartons from plants where eggs are inspected by the United States Department of Agriculture must display a packing date. Although not required, they may also have an expiration date; don't buy expired eggs. Open the carton and check out each egg. Shells should be clean and whole. Buy only eggs that have been refrigerated; get them home quickly and refrigerate them for safety and top quality. Eggs are generally good for four to five weeks beyond the packing date listed on the carton. Store eggs in their carton and place them on a shelf in the refrigerator to maintain freshness. Do not store eggs on the refrigerator door; the temperature fluctuates too much there.

Shell color has nothing to do with nutrition or egg quality. But does size matter? You're most likely to see extra large, large, and medium eggs in the stores. Because of the varying sizes, nutrition differs, but only slightly.

When you have too many eggs on your hands, freeze them for future use. The easiest way is to beat whole eggs until just blended and pour into sturdy containers with airtight covers. Seal and label with the date and the number of eggs inside. Thaw overnight in the refrigerator and use as soon as they defrost. Defrosted eggs should be used only in dishes that are thoroughly cooked, such as scrambled eggs or custard.

Nutrition Nugget

Once upon a time, an egg was an egg. Now you can choose between regular eggs and those with added nutrients. Should you bite? It wouldn't hurt. Eggs with extra omega-3 fats and vitamin E can only benefit a child's development, particularly if he doesn't eat seafood on a regular basis. You'll pay a bit more for so-called designer eggs, but they are worth it.

Delving Into Dairy

When it comes to dairy foods, the trick is to purchase products that fit your child's stage of life. Youngsters under the age of two need full-fat dairy. In general, reduced-fat foods are most appropriate for kids over two. The beauty of most dairy products is that even when the calories, fat, and cholesterol differ, there's no real difference between other important nutrients, such as protein, calcium, and vitamins A and D.

Choose yogurts with live active cultures. Purchasing plain to make your own fruited yogurt at home cuts down on sugar. Avoid yogurt with artificial sweeteners.

Consider adding cottage cheese and ricotta cheese to your supermarket cart. They are relatively low-cost protein sources that work well in a number of dishes and snacks. See the recipes in the Recipes for the Early Years appendix for ways to use cottage cheese and ricotta cheese.

Mozzarella cheese, and hard aged cheese, including cheddar, havarti, and Gouda, contain more calcium than processed American cheese. That means limited eaters will get a bigger bang for their nutritional buck when they eat hard cheese.

Keep nonfat dry milk around to use in kid-friendly recipes. Evaporated milk packs twice the calcium of regular milk and works well in dishes such as mashed potatoes or puréed cauliflower.

Learning to Love Legumes

If your childhood impression of legumes includes choking down lima beans your mother served and the little ditty that begins "Beans, beans, the musical fruit …" what you know about legumes amounts to a hill of beans.

Whether it's garbanzo beans (chickpeas), black beans, or the white variety, legumes are inexpensive, versatile, and full of carbohydrates, fiber, protein, vitamins, and minerals. And they're cholesterol-free. Technically speaking, peanuts are legumes. So are soybeans—often found as tofu, tempeh, and soy.

Beans are the perfect food to keep on kitchen shelves. Cooked canned beans are a good way to get familiar with legumes because they are so easy to use. Or purchase dried beans with a uniform appearance and a deep glossy color to cook from scratch. Do not buy beans that are cracked or dried-looking, because they are probably old and less tasty.

Now, back to the gas issue. That tune you'll recall is true to form, but only to a point. Beans can cause gas in some people. Ironically, people who eat the most beans tend to have the least flatulence from them. The trick to preparing lower-gas legumes is by changing the water several times during the soaking process and by simmering beans slowly until tender. Soaking makes beans more digestible.

Food Additives

Processors add any number of substances to foods for different reasons. Food additives prevent spoilage; preserve and enhance color and taste; and boost nutrition. Some food additives are not as safe as others, so be careful when buying. Use this table to determine what additives are in your food and why.

Common Name	Function
Ascorbic acid, sodium Ascorbate (vitamin C)	Antioxidant; nutrition
Pyridoxine hydrochloride	B vitamin; adds nutrition
Niacinamide	B vitamin; adds nutrition
Thiamin mononitrate	B vitamin; adds nutrition
Sodium chloride (salt)	Taste, preservative
Ferrous gluconate (iron)	Adds nutrition
Corn syrup, high-fructose corn syrup	Sweetener
Beta-carotene	Natural pigment; improves nutrition
Alpha-tocopherol (vitamin E)	Preservative; improves nutrition
Inulin (fiber)	Increases fiber content
Sodium nitrate, sodium nitrite*	Provides hot dogs and other cured meats with pink color and protects against food-borne illness
BHA,* BHT*	Preservatives found in fats and oil and baked goods made with lard; used to preserve color and flavor and to prevent spoilage
Monosodium glutamate (MSG)	High-sodium flavor enhancer

* Considered unhealthy

Sulfites are used to preserve dried fruits, white grape juice, frozen potatoes, maraschino cherries, fresh shrimp, and certain jams and jellies. They may elicit symptoms in some people with asthma. Sulfites go under the names sulfur dioxide, sodium or potassium sulfite, bisulfite, or metabisulfite in ingredient lists.

How to Keep Kids (Nearly) Additive-Free

The more processed foods your child eats, the more additives he consumes. That's not all bad. Fortunately, most additives, such as calcium and vitamin C, improve nutrition. But sugar and salt are food additives, too, and they are not associated with good health.

Stick with products labeled "preservative-free." "No added preservatives" on a label may mean the product contains ingredients that were already preserved prior to inclusion in the final product.

Avoid any food with sodium nitrite or sodium nitrate (typically hot dogs, bologna, and other cured meats); saccharin; caffeine; olestra; artificial sweeteners; and artificial colors. These additives may pose the greatest health risks to a child. More to the point, they are typically found in foods with little more to offer than calories.

The Convenience Conundrum

Busy parents crave convenience but may curse the price. Convenience foods, such as pre-cut vegetables and takeout pizza, cost more; others, including chicken nuggets and boxed macaroni and cheese, are more expensive, higher-fat versions of what you'd make at home. What's a time-starved parent to do? Use convenience foods in a pinch, and in ways that benefit you and your family. The table that follows explains how to improve upon packaged fare.

The Food	The Fix
Packet of instant oatmeal	Add finely chopped apple or pear to dry oatmeal and prepare according to directions. Microwave with milk instead of water. Stir in ¼ cup applesauce and ⅛ teaspoon ground cinnamon after cooking.
Frozen pizza	Top with grated cheese and vegetables.
Store-bought roasted chicken	Add quick-cooking brown rice, cooked vegetables, fruit, and milk for a complete meal.
Macaroni and cheese	Toss cooked diced carrots and broccoli with cooked macaroni.
Take-out pizza	Add fruit and cooked vegetables to make a complete meal.
Condensed tomato soup	Make with evaporated milk and mix in shredded cheese; top with homemade croutons.
Condensed potato soup	Add puréed cauliflower.
Stuffing mix	Prepare with apple juice and add chopped raisins and diced celery.
Canned alphabet soup	Add cooked, puréed beans.

The Food	The Fix
Refrigerated cookie dough	Unwrap and allow to soften; stir in 1 cup instant oatmeal or ½ cup wheat germ. Roll into balls and bake as directed.
Brownie mix	Replace half the fat with equal amounts of puréed prunes or low-fat plain or vanilla yogurt.

The Least You Need to Know

- You can't make healthy snacks and meals without having the ingredients on hand. Shop with meals in mind to make sure you stock your kitchen with the staples you need.

- In the store, fill your shopping cart with produce, fresh meats, vegetables, seafood, and whole grains. They are the basis of nutritious kid cuisine.

- Children need whole grains to satisfy at least half of their daily grain requirement. Search the ingredient list for "whole grain" or "whole" in front of the name of the grain.

- You don't have to make every food from scratch to be healthy. There are plenty of ways to improve upon convenience foods, including adding fruits and vegetables.

Better-Than-Store-Bought Recipes

So many times you find yourself reaching for convenience foods that you could make at home in minutes and for a lot less money. These homemade versions are more nutritious for your child.

Better-Than-Boxed Rice

2 cups low-sodium chicken or beef broth

½ tsp. dried parsley, cilantro, or basil

1 cup white or brown rice

1. In a medium saucepan, bring broth and parsley to a boil.
2. Add rice. Reduce heat to low. Cover and simmer until done.

Makes 3 cups
Great-tasting grain, minus the sodium of processed varieties.
Prep Time: 0
Cook Time: 20–30 minutes
Total: 20–30 minutes

Breakfast Bars

Makes 16 bars
These breakfast bars supply more fiber, vitamins, and minerals than store-bought.
Prep Time: 10 minutes **Cook Time:** 30 minutes **Total:** 40 minutes

⅓ cup margarine

¾ cup packed light brown sugar, divided into ½ cup and ¼ cup

½ cup quick-cooking oats

⅓ cup all-purpose flour

⅓ cup whole-wheat flour

2 TB. wheat germ

2 eggs, beaten

½ cup slivered almonds, chopped

¼ cup dried apricots, chopped

1. Preheat oven to 350°F. Grease a 9-inch baking pan.
2. In a medium mixing bowl, beat margarine and ½ cup brown sugar until light and fluffy.
3. Stir in oats, flours, and wheat germ.
4. Press mixture into the baking pan. Bake for 10 minutes.
5. Meanwhile, in a medium bowl, stir together beaten eggs and ¼ cup brown sugar; stir in almonds and apricots.
6. Spread the brown sugar mixture evenly over the baked layer.
7. Return to the oven for 20 minutes, or until browned.
8. Remove from oven and score bars into 16 pieces while still warm. Allow to cool before serving.

Cranberry Orange Sauce

Makes about 2 cups
You won't look twice at canned cranberry sauce after making this vitamin-C packed version that's ready in minutes.
Prep Time: 0 **Cook Time:** 15–20 minutes **Total:** 15–20 minutes

1 cup orange juice

1 cup water

1 cup sugar

2 cups fresh or frozen cranberries

1. Place cranberries in a colander. Rinse with cool water, and remove any damaged berries.
2. In a medium saucepan combine orange juice, water, and sugar. Heat fluids and sugar to boiling, stirring occasionally.
3. Add cranberries to the pan. Heat to boiling over medium heat, stirring occasionally. Continue boiling, until cranberries pop, about 5 minutes.
4. Allow to cool completely before serving.

Creamy Avocado Dressing

2 ripe avocadoes, peeled, cut in half, and pits removed

¾ cup buttermilk

2 TB. yogurt or sour cream

¼ cup mayonnaise

1 TB. lemon juice

Makes about 2¼ cups
Avocadoes are sodium- and cholesterol-free and are a good source of fiber for your little one.
Prep Time: 5 minutes **Cook Time:** 0 **Total:** 5 minutes

1. Place avocadoes in a blender or food processor and purée.
2. Add buttermilk, yogurt, mayonnaise, and lemon juice and blend. Use immediately as a dressing for salad or cooked chicken or as a dip.

Crunchy Croutons

¼ cup butter or margarine

6 cups crust-free day-old whole-grain bread, cut into ½-inch cubes

6 TB. Parmesan cheese, finely grated

⅛ tsp. garlic or onion powder, if desired

Makes about 2½ cups
Do it yourself cheesy croutons avoid bread waste and provide your little one with a high-fiber snack.
Prep Time: 10 minutes **Cook Time:** 15 minutes **Total:** 25 minutes

1. Preheat oven to 350°F.
2. In a large skillet over moderate heat, melt butter. Remove from heat.
3. Add bread cubes and toss to coat with the butter. Add cheese and garlic or onion powder and toss.
4. Transfer bread cubes to a baking sheet. Arrange in single layer.
5. Bake for 10 minutes, then stir. Bake for an additional 5 minutes or until bread cubes are dry and crisp.
6. Let cool. Store in an airtight container.

Cucumber Mint Dressing or Dip

1 cup yogurt

½ cup peeled and seeded cucumber, chopped very fine

2 TB. minced fresh mint

3 TB. rice wine vinegar

Salt and pepper, to taste

Makes about 1½ cups
So good, your child won't even notice he's eating a vegetable.
Prep Time: 5 minutes **Cook Time:** 0 **Total:** 5 minutes

1. In a medium bowl, whisk together ingredients. Refrigerate until ready to use.

Fruit Yogurt

Makes 1 cup
Low-sugar preserves curb the sugar in fruit yogurt.
Prep Time: 2 minutes **Cook Time:** 0 **Total:** 2 minutes

1 cup plain yogurt　　　　　**1 TB. low-sugar preserves**

1. In a serving bowl, mix yogurt and preserves, and serve.

Fruity Yogurt Pops

Makes 6 to 12, depending on size of mold
These frozen treats have far more calcium and far less sugar than store-bought.
Prep Time: 5 minutes **Cook Time:** 0 **Total:** 5 minutes

8 oz. plain or vanilla yogurt

1 (6-oz.) can orange fruit juice concentrate

Small paper cups and wooden "popsicle" sticks or freezer pop molds

1. In a medium bowl, combine yogurt and fruit juice concentrate. Mix well.
2. Pour mixture into molds or paper cups and place in the freezer.
3. When partially frozen, insert sticks into cups for handles. Cover with plastic wrap and freeze. Or pour into larger plastic freezer pop molds.

Laura's Fresh Tomato Sauce

Makes about 4 cups
This sauce is brimming with lycopene, a tomato compound that protects against cell damage.
Prep Time: 10 minutes **Cook Time:** 10–15 minutes **Total:** 20–25 minutes

2 TB. olive oil

½ medium onion, diced

2 cloves garlic, peeled and minced (optional)

1 (20-oz.) can ground, peeled tomatoes

1 TB. sugar

1 tsp. salt (optional)

1 tsp. chopped fresh basil or 1 tsp. dried basil

1. In a medium skillet, heat olive oil.
2. Add onion and garlic and sauté until tender.
3. Add tomatoes, sugar, and salt.
4. Simmer, uncovered, for 10 minutes, stirring frequently. Add basil and stir. Cook 2 to 3 minutes more. Remove from heat.

Make Your Own Peanut Butter

1½ cups unsalted roasted   1 TB. peanut oil
peanuts, shelled, with skins
removed

Makes about 1½ cups
Commercial peanut butter contains sugar and some added saturated fat that you won't find in this recipe.
Prep Time: 20 minutes **Cook Time:** 0 **Total:** 20 minutes

1. Place peanuts and peanut oil in a food processor. Process until very creamy.
2. Transfer to a sealed container. Refrigerate up to 2 weeks.

Orange Fizz

4 oz. 100 percent orange   4 oz. sparkling water or
juice   club soda

Makes 8 ounces
Use calcium-added orange juice in this soft drink stand-in.
Prep Time: 1 minute **Cook Time:** 0 **Total:** 1 minute

1. Mix together.
2. Serve immediately.

Peanut Butter Pudding

⅔ cup sugar   1 tsp. vanilla extract
¼ cup cornstarch   ½ cup creamy peanut butter
3 cups milk

Makes 5 cups
You won't go back to instant after preparing this tasty pudding that provides healthy doses of calcium and vitamin D.
Prep Time: 0 **Cook Time:** 10 minutes **Total:** 10 minutes

1. In a medium saucepan, combine sugar and cornstarch. Gradually whisk in milk.
2. Place pan over medium heat and bring to simmer while whisking.
3. Reduce heat and simmer until thickened, for about 2 minutes. Whisk frequently.
4. Remove from heat and stir in vanilla and peanut butter. Stir until peanut butter melts.
5. Divide among four serving bowls, or pour into a 2-quart casserole dish and refrigerate until firm.

Pudding Pops

Makes 4 to 8, depending on the size of the mold
A frozen pop with protein? You got it, along with calcium, vitamin D, and B vitamins.
Prep Time: 0 Cook Time: 10 minutes Total: 10 minutes

1 (4-oz.) pkg. regular pudding mix, any flavor (or 2 cups homemade pudding)

Small paper cups and wooden "popsicle" sticks or freezer pop molds.

1. Prepare pudding according to package directions, if necessary.
2. Pour pudding into molds or paper cups and place in the freezer. When partially frozen, insert sticks into cups for handles. Cover with plastic wrap and freeze. Or pour mixture into larger plastic freezer pop molds.

Rich Chocolate Pudding

Makes 2½ cups
A creamy chocolate treat that packs protein, too.
Prep Time: 0 Cook Time: 15 minutes Total: 15 minutes

¼ cup sugar
2 TB. cornstarch
2 cups milk

4 oz. semisweet chocolate chips
1 tsp. vanilla extract

1. In a medium saucepan, combine sugar and cornstarch. Gradually add milk and stir until well mixed.
2. Over medium heat, stir constantly until sugar dissolves and mixture begins to boil and thicken, about 10 minutes.
3. Add chocolate and continue cooking and stirring over medium-low heat until chocolate is melted and mixture thickens, about 5 minutes.
4. Remove from heat. Cool for 5 minutes. Add vanilla extract and stir well.
5. Pour into small custard cups or a shallow serving bowl.

Tartar Sauce

⅔ cup light mayonnaise
(or make your own)

¼ cup sweet or dill pickle
relish, drained well

⅓ cup plain yogurt

1 tsp. lemon juice

Makes 1¼ cups
Yogurt and reduced-fat mayonnaise lower the fat and boost the nutrition in this homemade version.
Prep Time: 5 minutes **Cook Time:** 0 **Total:** 5 minutes

1. In a medium bowl, combine mayonnaise, yogurt, relish, and lemon juice and mix well.
2. Best when allowed to sit covered in the refrigerator.

Tomato Salsa

3 cups chopped tomatoes

2 TB. olive oil

½ cup fresh cilantro

2 TB. fresh lime juice

1 red pepper, chopped

Salt and fresh ground black
pepper to taste, if desired

1 yellow pepper, chopped

Makes about 4 cups
This kid-friendly version of salsa packs more flavor and far less sodium than store-bought.
Prep Time: 15 minutes **Cook Time:** 0 **Total:** 15 minutes

1. Place tomatoes, cilantro, peppers, olive oil, lime juice, salt, and pepper in a food processor and pulse until you get the desired consistency.
2. Store covered in the refrigerator for at least an hour for more flavor or serve immediately.

Kitchen Safety

In This Chapter

- Discovering why germs love food
- Heading off food-borne illness
- Washing some foods and not others
- Learning meat and seafood safety

Food-borne illness grabs headlines. Outbreaks of illness caused by germs such as Salmonella and Escherichia coli (E. coli) in undercooked and raw foods are big news, especially when they involve children.

If you consider how many times a day humans eat, the risk of becoming ill from food is relatively low. That does not dismiss the seriousness of foodborne illness, especially in small children. Infants and toddlers have immature immune systems. That means their ability to repel the bacteria and viruses in food is still developing. When confronted with germs, a youngster's body may not be able to mount a strong enough defense to knock them off before they amount to trouble.

This chapter is full of food safety commandments to live by. Read on to see how to keep your family as safe from food-borne illness as possible.

Food: Treat It Right

Germs love food because it provides the water, nutrients, and right temperature they need to reproduce. You can't see, taste, or smell the elements of food that can make you ill. Because no food is completely sterile, you should always treat it carefully when handling it and storing it. Here are some rules to live by to keep food as safe as possible.

Wash This, Not That

Nearly half the cases of food-borne illness could be prevented if people would wash their hands more often before preparing and handling food. Americans tend to multi-task while preparing meals. That's according to a survey by the American Dietetic Association and the ConAgra Foods Foundation as part of their joint Home Food Safety … It's In Your Hands program. The program communicates the role consumers play in keeping foods safe in their own homes. The result of this particular survey: about a third of home cooks do not consistently wash their hands during food prep.

You should wash your hands after using the bathroom, blowing your nose, sneezing, or coughing; before eating or handling food; after handling raw meat, poultry, or seafood; after taking out the trash; after changing a diaper; after handling dirty laundry; and after petting an animal—at the very least. When in doubt, wash up with warm soapy water while singing the Happy Birthday song to yourself (or out loud) twice, the amount of time it takes to wipe out most germs. Dry hands with disposable towels or a clean cloth, or air dry completely. Stress the importance of clean hands from infancy.

Don't bother washing meat and poultry in an effort to make it safer. Recent studies show there is no significant benefit to giving meat a hot water bath. On the contrary. Washing meat may spread bacteria to other foods that are ready-to-eat (that's called cross-contamination). Washing produce is a good idea, however (see Chapter 16 for more on this).

Details, Please

If you favor sponges for cleaning up, you may be surprised to hear they do just the opposite. Sponges spread germs throughout your kitchen that can get into food. Change sponges frequently and place them daily in the dishwasher to kill the germs they harbor. Better yet, use a fresh paper towel to sop up meat, poultry, and seafood debris from countertops. Launder all kitchen towels and other cloths used to clean in the hot cycle of your washing machine and add bleach for certain germ death.

Separate Foods

Keep raw meat, poultry, and seafood apart from ready-to-eat foods, such as bread, fruits, and vegetables. Raw animal foods can spread germs to other foods that will not be killed off because they aren't exposed to heat. Separate cutting boards for each type of food makes it easier to avoid "cross-contamination."

Heat It Right

Bacteria and viruses in foods thrive between 40°F and 140°F; animal foods, such as meat and poultry, are particularly prone to germs. Cooking decimates most germs, but only when it's done right. With the possible exception of seafood and eggs, food safety experts say that you can't determine doneness by a food's appearance. Invest in a reliable meat thermometer for peace of mind. Here is a listing of certain foods and the temperature to cook the food to (at least):

Whole turkey or chicken	180°F (in the thigh)
Poultry breast and well-done meats	170°F
Medium meats, eggs and egg dishes, pork, and ground poultry and meats, such as ground beef	160°F
Medium-rare beef steaks, roasts, veal, and lamb	160°F
Egg dishes, such as quiche or strata	160°F
Leftovers	165°F
Egg yolks and egg whites	Until both are firm
Fish	Until the flesh is opaque and flakes easily with a fork

Keep Cool

Never leave food sitting out for more than two hours at room temperature (70°F). The higher the mercury goes, the less leeway you have for not refrigerating or freezing foods. For example, when it's 90°F, refrigerate food after one hour.

Be sure your refrigerator temperature registers 40°F or below for optimum cooling; freezers should be operating at 0°F or lower. Invest in a reliable refrigerator thermometer to accurately gauge temperature. Don't overpack a refrigerator or freezer; cold air must be able to circulate freely to squelch germ reproduction.

> **Mother's Helper**
>
> Store leftovers in airtight, shallow containers (two inches or less) to prevent the buildup of bacteria. Larger containers do not allow for rapid cooling, and they may give germs a chance to grow to the point of causing trouble for you or your little one. Do not allow leftovers to cool to room temperature before refrigerating them.

Temperature also comes into play when thawing food. Do not defrost food on the counter. As the food warms up at room temperature, any germs that are present can double in number every 20 minutes. Even when you cook the thawed food to the recommended temperature, there is a possibility the heat will not kill enough of the bacteria or the toxins they produce to prevent food-borne illness. Here are some better ways to defrost: use the refrigerator; a cold-water bath (wrap food well in plastic and change water frequently, refrigerating as soon as food is thawed); or the microwave oven.

In the Interest of Safety

Unless you've been living under a rock, you've probably heard about so-called Mad Cow disease and the controversy surrounding seafood. A less familiar topic in the news of late is acrylamide, found in certain foods. Here's the lowdown on each.

All About Acrylamide

Acrylamide is a potentially harmful compound formed in foods processed at high temperatures. Acrylamide is known to cause cancer in animals and may be toxic to the nervous systems of animals and humans. In April 2002, the Swedish National Food Authority caused concern when they announced elevated levels of acrylamide in certain foods.

Acrylamide has been found in a range of cooked and processed foods in other countries, including the United States. The highest levels found so far were in starchy foods cooked at high temperatures, including French fries. The information available on acrylamide so far reinforces the recommendations to limit fried and fatty foods.

How Now, Mad Cow?

You love beef, but you're apprehensive about serving it because of so-called Mad Cow disease. It is possible to get the human form of Mad Cow disease known as bovine spongiform encephalopathy (BSE), by eating contaminated beef. Although the risk of BSE is low, you can reduce it even further by purchasing 100 percent certified organic beef. Organically raised livestock cannot be fed anything but certified organic grain. Avoid ground beef, making your own from whole cuts of beef in a food processor or meat grinder.

Navigating Seafood Safety

Seafood (fish and shellfish) is a good food for kids, to a point. The primary problem with seafood is methylmercury, a contaminant that concentrates in fish, especially larger species. Mercury accumulates in the bloodstream and can harm an unborn baby's or young child's developing nervous system. That's why the Food and Drug Administration (FDA) and the Environmental Protection Agency (EPA) advise women who may become pregnant; pregnant women; nursing mothers; and young children to avoid shark, swordfish, king mackerel, and tilefish.

Canned light tuna, salmon, pollock, catfish, and shrimp are among fish low in mercury. Albacore or "white" tuna harbors more mercury than canned light tuna, so limit consumption to six ounces a week. Fish sticks and fast-food sandwiches are commonly made from fish that are low in mercury, such as farmed catfish, and are a safe choice for children.

Here's what it boils down to: it's okay to eat up to 12 ounces weekly of a variety of fish that is lower in mercury. Eating seafood that you or someone else caught requires a certain amount of vigilance. Always check whether there is an advisory against eating that type of seafood by contacting your state department of health.

Do Not Eat This

There is no doubt that young children should always avoid the following: raw or undercooked animal foods, including meat, seafood, and eggs; soft cheeses made with unpasteurized milk, such as Brie, Camembert, feta, and blue-veined varieties of cheese made from unpasteurized milk; unpasteurized juice and milk; honey, if under age one; alfalfa, clover, radish, and mung sprouts.

A Safer Kitchen

You and your child spend a lot of time in the kitchen. Unfortunately, it can be one of the most dangerous places for curious infants and toddlers. Let these tips guide you in making your kitchen safer.

- Keep small appliances, such as toasters, food processors, and coffee makers, away from counter edges. Roll up extra cords and tie off with a rubber band so little hands can't pull appliances down on themselves.

- Use the back burners to cook whenever possible; rotate pot and pan handles to the back if you must use the front burners.

- Invest in safety locks for drawers that hold all your sharp knives and other hazardous tools, including corkscrews; and for cabinets that little hands can open, including those that contain cleaning supplies.

- Store trash and recyclables in a locked cabinet or closet, if possible.

- Turn down your hot water heater to 120°F. It will save money, as well as help prevent burns.

Microwave Safety

If you're like most people, you rely on your microwave oven daily to defrost and warm foods. And you probably take the safety of your microwave oven for granted. Not a good idea. Older or damaged microwave ovens may leak radiation.

You should always follow instructions for microwave oven use and maintenance found in the owner's manual (you have it handy, right?). Regularly clean the oven cavity, the outer edge of the cavity, and the door seals with water and a mild detergent to prevent dirt buildup that allows microwaves to escape. Don't operate the oven if the door does not close securely.

Always stand at least two feet away from in-use microwave ovens to decrease potential radiation exposure. Consider buying a new microwave if you have ever dropped yours. Contact the manufacturer, a microwave oven service organization, your state health department, or the nearest FDA office if you suspect you have a leaky microwave oven. Do not rely on microwave testing devices marketed to consumers.

To prevent burns, stir and rotate food once or twice during cooking to reduce uneven heating, which is common in food heated in microwave ovens. Food that's warm to the touch on the surface can be scalding at the center, so take care. Always follow manufacturers' directions for microwaving processed foods. Use lower power and shorter cooking times for liquids, and poke holes in potatoes to reduce steam buildup.

Plastics, including wraps used to cover food during microwave cooking, may contain plasticizers. Plasticizers are chemicals some experts regard as *endocrine disrupters*, chemicals that are dangerous to health, especially a child's.

Whether preparing foods or heating leftovers in a microwave oven, you should choose glass cookware. Do not use containers such as margarine tubs and Styrofoam take-out containers, because chemicals can easily leach into the food when heated. Sturdy plastic cookware labeled microwave-safe runs a close second.

Avoid plastic wraps in favor of paper towels, wax paper, or specially made hard plastic microwave covers. Never allow plastic wraps to touch food during microwaving or after it's hot. Cover containers loosely with plastic wrap, leaving one inch or more of space between the plastic and the food; pull back a corner to vent. Discard plastic film after a single use. Opt for plasticizer-free Glad Cling Wrap and Saran Cling Plus Clear. Avoid Saran Original Premium Wrap (contains trace levels of a plasticizer other than DEHA) and DEHA-containing Reynolds Premium Plastic Wrap.

> **Technically Speaking**
>
> **Endocrine disrupters** are compounds that mimic or block the body's natural hormones. Endocrine disrupters have been implicated in birth defects, developmental or growth problems, low sperm counts in men and early puberty in girls, and an increased risk for certain hormone-dependent cancers.

The Least You Need to Know

- Handle food with care at home, and you can greatly reduce the risk of food-borne illness in family members. Young children are most vulnerable to the effects of contaminated food.

- Proper handwashing could wipe out half the cases of food-borne illness in the United States. Be sure to lather up with soap before handling food, as well as during food preparation if you have stopped to do another activity. Remember, two verses of Happy Birthday plus warm soapy water is a good way to kill germs.

- Heat destroys most germs, but don't rely on it to keep food completely safe. You must also store and handle foods properly.

- You don't have to avoid feeding seafood to children, you just need to make wise choices.

- Always choose glass when cooking or heating food in a microwave oven. If you use plastic film as a cover, do not let it touch the warm food.

Chapter **18**

Baby, Let's Hit
the Road!

In This Chapter

- Dining out with a baby or toddler
- Finding healthy restaurant fare for kids
- Knowing when and where to bring baby out to eat
- Managing daycare cuisine

Picture this: a quiet, leisurely dinner in a fine restaurant where you and your loved one have adult conversation over delicious food and wine, then linger while enjoying dessert and coffee. Wouldn't that be nice? Okay, you can wake up! Intimate dinners at expensive establishments are history, unless you're willing to fork over some serious dough for a sitter *and* a meal. Dining out with kids is a whole different ball of wax. Steakhouses and pizza joints may be on the menu now. You can still enjoy yourself, as long as you adhere to a few simple guidelines to keep you, your child, and your fellow diners happy.

Dining Out with a Youngster in Tow

When is the best time to start bringing baby to restaurants? Go as soon as you can bundle him up and you feel comfortable taking him out—usually between six weeks and two months of age. Don't wait until your child is at a so-called "good age" to dine out with him. Dining out early on is good for you (gets you out of the house); easy (if you time it right, an infant will sleep while you're eating); and skill-building (you are teaching your child how to feel comfortable in a restaurant setting). Here's what to do to make it work out well:

Pick a Place. The first rule of taking children to restaurants is to go where you are welcome. Many of the large chains, such as Outback Steakhouse and Olive Garden, are kid-friendly and affordable for families. Even smaller, independent establishments are hospitable to younger diners. If you're in doubt about a restaurant's child policy, call ahead to ask if children are welcome, and find out if they supply highchairs and booster seats.

Time It Just Right. Go out early when restaurants are the least crowded. If possible, make reservations. There's nothing worse for you and other diners than listening to a whining child who has to wait for 45 minutes to get a table. Chinese, Thai, and Japanese restaurants tend to serve food quickly after you order, so consider Asian cuisine, or any other quick meal, when you're pressed for time.

Avoid taking your child out when he is overly fussy from hunger. Try to order your child's food first, then take the time to ponder your own. When the waiter returns, order appetizers, salads, and entrées all at once to cut down on the wait for your food. If it's mealtime for baby, too, feed him while waiting for your food to arrive. Tote your child's food in a refrigerated bag, and don't forget the bib, bowl, spoon, baby bottle with breast milk or infant formula, and a cloth to wipe up spills.

Location, Location, Location. Request a booth or out-of-the-way table, but don't settle for seats near a crowded serving station or the kitchen doors just because you have a child that might (oh, no!) fuss at some point during the meal. Nursing moms may feel more comfortable in a booth when baby demands to eat while you are, too.

Mother's Helper

Babies are most energetic and less fussy in the early part of the day (aren't we all!). Consider dining out for breakfast, brunch, or lunch for a more enjoyable meal. Eating earlier in the day can also cut dining costs.

Order Up!

As a rule, restaurant fare is higher in calories, fat, and sodium and lower in fiber, vitamins, and minerals than what you make at home. When it comes to the kid cuisine offered by fast-food joints and leading restaurant chains, the situation is often worse. Although your menu offers healthy choices such as broiled chicken or shrimp and an array of luscious salads, your child's choices may be confined to chicken nuggets, burgers, macaroni and cheese, French fries, and soft drinks. Sometimes, dessert is thrown in as part of a kid's meal deal.

Patronize places you know offer healthy options. For example, Cracker Barrel restaurants allow children to choose between fried and grilled chicken; they also serve a variety of vegetable side dishes with kids' meals. Go where you know you can get pasta with tomato sauce, a meal where the nutrient-rich sauce counts as a vegetable, or pizza, which is generally a wise selection. Red Lobster recently overhauled their children's menu to offer more grilled fish and chicken, and vegetables. You can order smaller portions of adult food for older infants and young toddlers, including half portions, appetizers, and side dishes.

Here are some best bets for kids at various types of restaurants.

Chinese

- Plain rice instead of fried rice and high-fat noodle dishes
- Stir-fried entrées featuring chicken, beef, pork, or tofu; pick out what your child can eat

Italian

- Pasta with marinara and meatballs or pasta with meat sauce
- Grilled chicken or seafood
- Fresh vegetables
- Milk or 100 percent juice

Fast Food

- Grilled chicken sandwich
- Baked potato
- Bowl of chili topped with cheese
- Frozen yogurt and fruit desserts
- Fruit cup or fruit bowl with yogurt (available at Wendy's)
- Milk or 100 percent juice

Mexican

- Guacamole and salsa
- Bean soups
- Cheese, chicken, or bean enchiladas
- Bean burritos
- Chicken and rice
- Soft chicken taco
- Milk or 100 percent juice

American

- Grilled chicken sandwich
- Grilled cheese
- Grilled chicken or fish
- Pasta with marinara sauce or meat sauce
- Side order of cooked vegetables
- Baked potato
- Milk or 100 percent juice

Pizza Place

- Thin-crust cheese or vegetable pizza
- Side order of cooked vegetables
- Milk or 100 percent juice

Safe at the Plate

Restaurants can be treacherous for children who know how to grab objects close to them, including the waiter. Get rid of forks, knives, plates, and anything else nearby that they can get their tiny mitts around. Occupy a child with cereal from home or her favorite toys.

Dealing with a Cranky Child

After they are mobile, little ones tend to be fidgety—especially if they have to sit for long periods in a restaurant or any other public place. Older infants often need a change of pace during the meal, so you and another adult may have to take turns walking your child around to keep the peace. Don't let a toddler wander. It could cause serious harm to himself, the waitstaff, or both.

During your child's fidgety phase, his behavior in public places can be trying. Don't forget about the other diners who are paying for a meal, too. If you can't placate your child, you may need to leave. Doggy bag, anyone?

Daycare Dining

You may have a sitter watch your child for one day a week or five. The more time your little one's away from home, the more important your daycare provider's attitude and knowledge about his nutrition.

Never assume your daycare provider is giving your child what he needs in terms of nutrition. You need to spell out your expectations as far as food goes. Relay your feelings about rewarding good behavior with treats (please don't), keeping sugar- and fat-laden foods to a minimum, and serving balanced meals and snacks every three hours or so. Also, talk about any other requests you have, such as no juice or soft drinks for your child. If you've hired someone to care for your child in your home, it may be easier to prepare simple meals ahead of time for the sitter to serve, including infant formula. Nursing moms should have expressed breast milk in bottles and ready for feeding.

When bringing your own baby food to the sitter's, be sure to tote it in an insulated tote bag with a freezer pack. To make things easier in the morning, pack the bag with baby food and fill baby bottles the night before. If you rely on frozen, homemade baby food, select what your infant needs for the next day's meals. Allow frozen cubes or food blobs to defrost overnight in the refrigerator in a portable, airtight container. Put your child's name and the type of food on the container.

When you arrive at the sitter's or daycare center, transfer your child's food to the refrigerator. Don't forget to pack spoons, bibs, bowls, infant cereal, and infant formula or expressed breast milk if necessary.

The Least You Need to Know

- After you have a child, dining out is different, but it's not impossible. You probably won't be eating at four-star establishments too often, but you can still enjoy restaurant meals.

- For the least aggravation, pick kid-friendly places with healthier fare. Go out to eat on the early side for a more enjoyable meal.

- Trips to restaurants at an early age teach a child to be comfortable in public places. Plus, it's fun for them, and it may expose them to different types of food.

- Discuss your views about feeding your child with anyone who cares for them. Be sure sitters have all the food they need to feed your child the way you would like.

Recipes for the Early Years

Berry Banana Smoothie

½ cup milk or soy beverage (more for thinner consistency)

¼ medium banana

¼ cup fresh or frozen berries

¼ cup crushed ice or 2 ice cubes (not necessary if using frozen berries)

Makes about 1 cup
Berries make this drink pretty while providing fiber and phytonutrients, protective plant compounds.
Prep Time: 5 minutes **Cook Time:** 0 **Total:** 5 minutes

1. Combine milk, banana, berries, and ice in a blender or food processor.

2. Whip on high speed for 2 to 3 minutes, or until frothy.

3. Serve immediately.

Cherry Vanilla Freeze

1 medium frozen banana

½ cup frozen sweet cherries

¾ cup vanilla yogurt

Makes about 1½ cups
Cherries supply vitamin C and phytonutrients.
Prep Time: 5 minutes **Cook Time:** 0 **Total:** 5 minutes

1. In a food processor or blender, process banana until smooth.

2. Add cherries and yogurt. Process until well blended.

3. Serve immediately.

Lemon Limeade

4 cups boiling water

½ cup sugar

2 lemons, washed, then thinly sliced

1 lime, washed, then thinly sliced

1. Bring water to a boil in a large saucepan.

2. Stir in sugar and dissolve.

3. Pour mixture into large heat-safe pitcher.

4. Add lemon and lime.

5. Stir well. Refrigerate to chill.

Makes 4 cups
Homemade lemonade has many more times the limonene, a plant substance that protects against cell damage, than store-bought.
Prep Time: 5 minutes **Cook Time:** 5 minutes **Total:** 1 hour (for chilling)

Orange Cranberry Spritzer

2 oz. calcium-added orange juice

2 oz. cranberry juice

4 oz. calorie-free seltzer water or club soda

1. In tall glass, combine orange juice, cranberry juice, and seltzer.

2. Serve immediately.

Makes 1 cup
A high-potassium, low-sodium beverage.
Prep Time: 2 minutes **Cook Time:** 0 **Total:** 2 minutes

Orange Cream

½ cup milk

½ cup orange juice

1. In a tall glass, combine milk and orange juice.

2. Stir and serve.

Makes 1 cup
Another way to work in fruit and milk at the same time.
Prep Time: 1 minute **Cook Time:** 0 **Total:** 1 minute

Beverages

Peachy Pineapple Cooler

¼ **cup frozen peaches**

¼ **cup crushed pineapple**

¼ **cup vanilla low-fat frozen yogurt**

1. Combine peaches, pineapple, and yogurt in a blender or food processor.

2. Whip on high speed for 2 to 3 minutes, or until frothy.

3. Serve immediately.

Makes about 1 cup
Frozen peaches are a surprisingly good source of vitamin C.
Prep Time: 5 minutes
Cook Time: 0
Total: 5 minutes

Peanut Butter Smoothie

½ **cup plain yogurt**

½ **medium banana**

1 **TB. peanut butter**

2 **ice cubes**

1. Combine yogurt, banana, peanut butter, and ice cubes in a blender or food processor.

2. Whip on high speed for 2 to 3 minutes, or until frothy.

3. Serve immediately.

Makes about 1 cup
A fun source of protein for kids who don't like meat.
Prep Time: 5 minutes
Cook Time: 5 minutes
Total: 10 minutes

Beverages

Pumpkin Pie Smoothie

½ cup canned pumpkin   Pinch nutmeg

½ cup milk   2 tsp. sugar

Pinch cinnamon

Makes 1 cup
Canned pumpkin is a source of fiber.
Prep Time: 5 minutes
Cook Time: 0
Total: 5 minutes

1. Combine pumpkin, milk, cinnamon, nutmeg, and sugar in a blender or food processor.

2. Whip on high speed for 2 to 3 minutes, or until frothy.

3. Serve immediately.

Mother's Helper

Use the remaining canned pumpkin from this recipe to make pumpkin pancakes.

Purple Cow

½ cup milk   ½ cup purple grape juice

Makes 1 cup
Grape juice contains antioxidant nutrients that protect cells.
Prep Time: 1 minute
Cook Time: 0
Total: 1 minute

1. In a tall glass, combine milk and grape juice.

2. Stir and serve.

Raspberry Almond Smoothie

1 cup almond milk*

6 oz. frozen raspberries

1 medium banana, cut into chunks

¼ cup slivered almonds

Makes about 2½ cups
Almonds are rich in vitamin E and fiber.
Prep Time: 5 minutes
Cook Time: 0
Total: 5 minutes

1. Combine milk, raspberries, banana, and almonds in a blender or food processor.

2. Whip on high speed for 2 to 3 minutes, or until frothy and almonds are broken down.

3. Serve immediately.

*Almond milk is available in most supermarkets in a sealed, unrefrigerated box near the soy beverages.

Tropical Fruit Cooler

¼ cup sliced strawberries

¼ cup pineapple

½ cup orange juice (more for thinner consistency)

¼ cup crushed ice or 2 ice cubes

Makes about 1 cup
Use orange juice with added calcium for even more nutrition.
Prep Time: 5 minutes
Cook Time: 0
Total: 5 minutes

1. Combine strawberries, pineapple, orange juice, and ice in a blender or food processor.

2. Whip on high speed for 2 to 3 minutes, or until frothy.

3. Serve immediately.

Baked Cinnamon Orange French Toast

6 eggs

½ cup orange juice

¼ cup milk

⅓ cup sugar

1 TB. grated orange peel

½ tsp. vanilla extract

8 slices day-old cinnamon bread

Makes 8 slices
Eggs and milk provide the protein your child thrives on.

Prep Time: 5 minutes
Cook Time: 30 minutes
Total: 35 minutes

1. Preheat oven to 375°F. Grease one large baking sheet.

2. In a medium bowl, beat together eggs, juice, milk, sugar, peel, and vanilla until well blended.

3. Place bread in single layer in 13×9×2-inch pan. Pour egg mixture over bread. Let soak for 5 minutes or until liquid is absorbed.

4. Place bread slices in single layer on buttered baking sheet.

5. Bake for 12 to 15 minutes. Turn slices. Continue baking until browned, about 10 to 12 minutes.

Breads

Blueberry Buttermilk Mini Muffins

1⅓ cups all-purpose flour

⅔ cup cornmeal

½ cup sugar

1 TB. baking powder

1 tsp. baking soda

½ tsp. salt

1⅓ cups buttermilk

⅓ cup canola oil

1 egg, slightly beaten

1 cup fresh or frozen blueberries

Makes 24 muffins
Calcium-packed buttermilk only seems rich. It's actually low-fat.
Prep Time: 10 minutes   Cook Time: 15 minutes   Total: 25 minutes

1. Preheat oven to 350°F. Coat mini muffin pans with nonstick cooking spray.

2. In large bowl, stir together flour, cornmeal, sugar, baking powder, baking soda, and salt.

3. In a medium bowl, stir together buttermilk, oil, and egg.

4. Pour liquid mixture into dry ingredient bowl; add blueberries and stir just enough to moisten ingredients.

5. Spoon dough into prepared muffin pans.

6. Bake for 10 to 12 minutes or until toothpick inserted in middle comes out clean. Remove from pan and allow to cool completely before serving.

Blueberry Oat Flapjacks

1 cup all-purpose flour

½ quick-cooking or old-fashioned oats, uncooked

1 TB. baking powder

½ tsp. ground cinnamon

1 cup milk

1 egg, lightly beaten

3 TB. canola oil plus oil for cooking

¼ cup fresh blueberries

Makes 12 pancakes
Blueberries, packed with fiber, vitamin C, and other phytonutrients, make these healthy pancakes sweet enough to eat without syrup.
Prep Time: 5 minutes **Cook Time:** 15 minutes **Total:** 20 minutes

1. In large bowl, combine flour, oats, baking powder, and cinnamon. Mix well.

2. In medium bowl, combine milk, egg, and oil; blend well. Add to dry ingredients all at once; mix just until dry ingredients are moistened. (Do not overmix.)

3. Heat a skillet or griddle over medium-high heat. Lightly grease griddle with canola oil.

4. For each pancake, pour scant ¼ cup batter into hot pan to form a 4-inch pancake. Top with 1 TB. fresh blueberries, pressing each into batter.

5. Turn pancakes when tops are covered with bubbles and edges look cooked.

Breadsticks

1 lb. frozen purchased bread dough, thawed

2 TB. olive oil

Makes 12 (6-inch) breadsticks
An easy source of energy for hungry kids.
Prep Time: 10 minutes **Cook Time:** 12 minutes **Total:** 22 minutes

1. Coat 2 baking sheets with cooking spray.

2. Divide bread dough into 12 equal pieces. Form each into a 6-inch rope.

3. Place breadsticks on baking sheets and brush with olive oil.

4. Allow to rise in a warm area free of drafts for about 1 hour.

5. Preheat oven to 350°F. Bake 12 minutes or until golden brown. Remove from baking sheets to cool.

Breads

Carrot Zucchini Bread

2 cups all-purpose flour

1 cup rolled oats

¾ cup firmly packed brown sugar

1 tsp. ground cinnamon

¼ tsp. salt

⅔ cup milk

⅔ cup canola oil

1 egg

¾ cup finely shredded carrots

¾ cup finely shredded unpeeled zucchini

½ cup finely chopped walnuts

Makes 2 loaves
Walnuts and canola oil provide the healthy fats children need.
Prep Time: 15 minutes Cook Time: 35–40 minutes Total: 50–55 minutes

1. Heat oven to 350°F. Grease two 9¼×5¼×2½-inch loaf pans.

2. In a large bowl, combine flour, oats, brown sugar, cinnamon, and salt; mix well.

3. In a medium bowl, combine milk, oil, and egg. Blend well.

4. Add milk mixture to dry ingredients. Stir just until dry ingredients are moistened.

5. Stir in carrot, zucchini, and walnuts until just blended.

6. Pour batter into loaf pan. Bake for 35 to 40 minutes or until golden brown and toothpick inserted in center comes out clean.

Cheesy Spoon Cornbread

1½ cups milk

½ cup cornmeal

1 TB. butter or margarine

¼ cup shredded cheddar cheese

½ tsp. baking powder

1 egg yolk, beaten

1 egg white, stiffly beaten

Makes about 2 cups
With its soufflé-like texture, carbohydrate-rich spoon bread is the perfect consistency for a young child.
Prep Time: 15 minutes Cook Time: 35–40 minutes Total: 50–55 minutes

1. Preheat oven to 375°F. Grease a 1-quart casserole dish.

2. In a medium saucepan, stir 1 cup milk into cornmeal.

3. Cook, stirring constantly, until mixture is very thick and pulls away from the sides of the pan. Remove pan from heat.

4. Stir in remaining milk, butter, cheese, and baking powder. In a medium bowl, mix 1 cup of this mixture into egg yolk. Return to pan. Gently fold in egg white.

5. Bake for 35 to 40 minutes or until a knife inserted in the center comes out clean.

Cinnamon French Toast

2 eggs

½ cup milk

½ tsp. vanilla extract

½ tsp. ground cinnamon

6 slices cinnamon bread

Makes 6 slices
A fun way of working in carbohydrates, fat, and protein.
Prep Time: 5 minutes   **Cook Time:** 10 minutes   **Total:** 15 minutes

1. In a medium bowl, whisk together eggs, milk, vanilla extract, and cinnamon.

2. Dip each piece of bread in egg mixture.

3. Cook until browned on both sides in a nonstick skillet or on a griddle.

Confetti Corn Cakes

1 tsp. canola oil

¼ cup red bell pepper, diced

¼ cup green bell pepper, diced

1 (8½-oz.) pkg. corn muffin mix

1 egg, slightly beaten

2 TB. melted butter or margarine

¾ cup milk

Makes about 10 pancakes
These make an attractive, high-carbohydrate snack or side dish.
Prep Time: 10 minutes   **Cook Time:** 10 minutes   **Total:** 20 minutes

1. In a medium skillet, heat oil over medium heat. Sauté peppers until tender, about 3 to 5 minutes.

2. Turn off heat, remove peppers from pan, and place in a medium mixing bowl along with corn muffin mix, egg, melted butter, and milk.

3. Blend ingredients until dry ingredients are just moist. Do not overmix.

4. Spray skillet with cooking spray. Heat.

5. Lightly coat a griddle or skillet with cooking spray and heat. Spoon out a scant ¼ cup of batter per pancake, spreading out in pan. When edges are firm, turn pancakes and cook 1 minute more.

Breads

Corny Corn Bread

1 cup milk

1 cup cottage cheese

2 eggs

½ cup packed shredded cheddar cheese (about 2 oz.)

1 cup cooked corn

2 (8½-oz.) pkg. corn muffin mix

Makes 18 pieces
Corn is a good source of lutein, a phytonutrient that helps eyesight.
Prep Time: 10 minutes **Cook Time:** 20 minutes **Total:** 30 minutes

1. Preheat oven to 400°F. Grease a 9×13-inch baking pan.

2. In a large bowl, combine milk, cottage cheese, and eggs.

3. Use an electric mixer to blend on medium speed for 1 to 2 minutes. Stir in cheese and corn, then stir in corn muffin mix until just blended. Do not over-mix.

4. Spoon batter into a prepared pan. Bake about 20 minutes, or until bread is light brown on top and tester inserted into center comes out clean.

Cottage Cheese Pancakes

1 cup cottage cheese

2 TB. milk

1 egg

1 cup pancake mix

Canola oil

Makes 12 (4-inch) pancakes
Cottage cheese sneaks protein and calcium into pancakes and other quick breads.
Prep Time: 5 minutes **Cook Time:** 15 minutes **Total:** 20 minutes

1. In a food processor or blender, combine cottage cheese and milk until smooth, about 2 minutes on high speed.

2. Transfer cottage cheese mixture to a bowl, and combine with egg, mixing well. Add pancake mix and blend with a wooden spoon, just to combine. Do not overmix.

3. Lightly coat a griddle or skillet with cooking spray and heat. Spoon out about 2 heaping tablespoons batter per pancake, spreading out in pan. When edges are firm, turn pancakes and cook 1 minute more.

Daddy's Delicious Crepes

4 eggs	2¼ cups milk
¼ tsp. salt	¼ cup melted butter
2 cups all-purpose flour	Butter or margarine for cooking

1. In a medium bowl, combine eggs and salt.

2. Take turns stirring in flour and milk, beating with whisk until smooth.

3. Add melted butter and whisk.

4. Heat a medium skillet on medium-high heat. Melt a dab of butter in the pan.

5. Pour in ¼ cup of crepe batter, swirling the pan around to coat the bottom evenly.

6. When the top of the crepe starts to look dry and the bottom is just beginning to brown (peek underneath to check), flip the crepe over with a spatula.

7. Cook 30 seconds more, then place on a plate. Cover and keep warm while you make the rest.

8. Fold crepes in quarters or rip into pieces for little ones.

Makes 10 to 12 crepes (using half the batter)

Elegant crepes, rich in protein and calcium, only *seem* hard to make.

Prep Time: 5 minutes
Cook Time: 20 minutes
Total: 25 minutes

Mother's Helper

Use half the batter now and freeze the rest (for up to 7 days).

Healthy Snack Chips

4 whole-wheat sandwich wraps or large whole-wheat pita bread	¼ cup canola or olive oil
	½ tsp. garlic or onion powder, if desired

1. Preheat oven to 425°F.

2. Lightly brush sandwich wraps with oil. Sprinkle with garlic or onion powder.

3. Cut each sandwich wrap with kitchen shears into 8 wedges.

4. Arrange in a single layer on an ungreased baking sheet. Bake for 8 minutes or until crisp and golden brown.

Makes 32 chips

Start kids with these high-fiber baked chips and they won't want the sodium-packed store-bought kind.

Prep Time: 5 minutes
Cook Time: 10 minutes
Total: 15 minutes

Herbed Buttermilk Biscuits

2 cups all-purpose flour

2 tsp. baking powder

1 tsp. dried dill weed

¾ tsp. caraway seeds

¼ tsp. salt

¼ tsp. baking soda

¼ cup margarine

1 cup buttermilk

Makes 14 biscuits
Offer these homemade biscuits instead of their higher-fat processed counterparts.
Prep Time: 10 minutes **Cook Time:** 15 minutes **Total:** 25 minutes

1. Preheat oven to 350°F.

2. In a medium bowl, stir together flour, baking powder, dill, caraway, and salt. Cut in the margarine until mixture resembles coarse meal.

3. Add buttermilk, stirring well to mix.

4. Turn dough out onto a well-floured surface and knead lightly 4 or 5 times.

5. Roll out dough to ¼-inch thickness and cut into 2½-inch rounds. Place biscuits on greased baking sheet. Bake for 10 to 12 minutes or until golden brown.

Laura's Oatmeal Walnut Waffles

1 cup milk

1 egg

¾ cup whole-wheat flour

3 TB. melted butter

1 tsp. baking powder

1 TB. brown sugar

1 cup old-fashioned rolled oats

½ cup finely chopped walnuts

Makes about 8 waffles
Nuts, oats, and whole-wheat flour provide fiber.
Prep Time: 10 minutes **Cook Time:** 20–30 minutes **Total:** 30–40 minutes

1. In a food processor or blender, place milk, egg, flour, butter, baking powder, and brown sugar. Process until blended.

2. Add oats and nuts and stir to blend.

3. Bake in preheated waffle iron.

Parmesan Snack Chips

4 whole-wheat sandwich wraps or large whole-wheat pita bread

¼ cup canola or olive oil

2 TB. grated Parmesan cheese

Makes 32 chips
Baked chips with fiber!
Prep Time: 5 minutes **Cook Time:** 10 minutes **Total:** 15 minutes

1. Preheat oven to 425°F.

2. Lightly brush sandwich wraps with oil. Sprinkle with cheese.

3. Cut each sandwich wrap with kitchen shears into 8 wedges.

4. Arrange in a single layer on ungreased baking sheet. Bake for 8 minutes or until crisp and golden brown.

Pumpkin Bread

3 cups all-purpose flour

1 cup whole-wheat flour

2 cups light brown sugar

2 tsp. baking soda

1 tsp. baking powder

2 tsp. ground cinnamon

1 tsp. ground nutmeg

1 cup canola oil

4 eggs

2 cups canned pumpkin

Makes 2 loaves
Loaded with vitamins and minerals, this bread is ideal for meals and snacks.
Prep Time: 10 minutes **Cook Time:** 50 minutes **Total:** 60 minutes

1. Preheat oven to 350°F. Grease two 9¼×5¼×2½-inch loaf pans.

2. In a large mixing bowl, combine flours, sugar, baking soda, baking powder, cinnamon, and nutmeg.

3. In a medium bowl, combine oil, eggs, and pumpkin. Mix well.

4. Add oil, eggs, and pumpkin to dry ingredients. Stir just until dry ingredients are moistened.

5. Divide batter evenly between the two loaf pans. Bake for 50 minutes or until a knife inserted near the middle comes out clean.

Breads

Pumpkin Pancakes

2½ cups plain yogurt plus ¼ cup sugar

1 TB. sugar

1 cup flour

2 tsp. baking soda

½ tsp. cinnamon

1 cup milk

2 TB. melted margarine or butter

1 egg

½ cup canned pumpkin

Makes about 12 pancakes
These pancakes pack the beta-carotene your child's body needs to produce vitamin A, along with calcium and protein.
Prep Time: 10 minutes **Cook Time:** 15 minutes **Total:** 25 minutes

1. In a small bowl, mix plain yogurt with ¼ cup sugar. Reserve.

2. Combine 1 TB. sugar, flour, baking soda, and cinnamon in a large mixing bowl.

3. In a medium bowl, combine milk, margarine, egg, pumpkin, and yogurt mixture.

4. Add wet ingredients to dry ingredients in larger bowl. Stir until just moist.

5. Lightly coat a griddle or skillet with cooking spray and heat. Using a ¼ cup measure, pour batter onto a hot griddle. Cook until bubbles begin to burst, then flip and cook until golden brown.

Whole-Grain French Toast Sticks

3 eggs

¾ cup milk

1 tsp. vanilla

1 tsp. ground cinnamon

4 slices whole-grain bread

2 TB. margarine

Makes 4 slices
Use eggs with added omega-3 fats for even more nutrition.
Prep Time: 5 minutes **Cook Time:** 10 minutes **Total:** 15 minutes

1. In a shallow bowl, mix eggs, milk, vanilla, and cinnamon. Beat well.

2. Soak each slice of bread in egg mixture.

3. Melt margarine in skillet.

4. Brown the soaked bread in skillet. Cut into strips.

5. Serve with applesauce for dipping.

Avocado Hummus Spread

1 avocado, sliced length-wise and pitted

1 cup white bean hummus (in Legume section)

1 TB. lemon juice

1. In a medium bowl, mash avocado. Add white bean hummus and lemon juice and mix well.

2. Use as a sandwich filling, dip, or cracker topping.

Makes about 2 cups
White beans are rich in folate and iron.
Prep Time: 10 minutes **Cook Time:** 0 **Total:** 10 minutes

Blue Cheese Dressing

½ cup blue cheese (made from pasteurized milk)

½ cup low-fat ricotta cheese

1–2 TB. milk (or more for thinner consistency)

1. Place blue cheese, ricotta cheese, and milk in a food processor or blender and blend until smooth.

2. Serve over salad greens or cooked, diced vegetables.

Makes 1 cup
Low-fat ricotta cheese cuts fat and adds calcium.
Prep Time: 5 minutes **Cook Time:** 0 **Total:** 5 minutes

Buttermilk Dressing

1 cup buttermilk

¼ cup mayonnaise

1 TB. Dijon mustard

2 tsp. dill

½ tsp. salt

1. In a small bowl, combine buttermilk, mayonnaise, mustard, dill, and salt.

2. Serve over cooked vegetables or tossed salad greens.

Makes 1¼ cups
This homemade dressing has far less sodium than store-bought versions of creamy dressings.
Prep Time: 5 minutes **Cook Time:** 0 **Total:** 5 minutes

Dips and Sauces

Herbed Yogurt Dip

8 oz. plain yogurt   Pinch salt

1 tsp. fresh chopped dill   Pinch onion powder

1 tsp. fresh basil

1. In a small bowl, combine yogurt, dill, basil, salt, and pepper.

2. Serve with cooked vegetables.

Makes 1 cup
A high-protein dip that also serves as a topping or add-in for mashed potatoes.
Prep Time: 5 minutes **Cook Time:** 0 **Total:** 5 minutes

Honey Orange Yogurt Dip

1 cup plain yogurt   1 TB. honey*

1 TB. orange juice

1. In a small bowl, mix orange juice and yogurt.

2. Serve with wedges of soft fruit, such as ripe bananas, peaches, melon, and plums, for dipping.

*Substitute sugar for honey in children under age 1.

Makes 1 cup
Kids will love to dip fruit into this calcium-packed dip.
Prep Time: 2 minutes **Cook Time:** 0 **Total:** 2 minutes

Laura's Easy Cheesy Sauce

2 TB. butter

2 TB. flour

1½ cups milk

1 cup shredded cheddar cheese

Pinch nutmeg

Salt and fresh ground black pepper to taste

Makes about 2½ cups
This sauce is brimming with calcium and vitamin D, and will help kids eat their greens.
Prep Time: 5 minutes   **Cook Time:** 5 minutes   **Total:** 10 minutes

1. In a medium saucepan, melt butter over medium heat.

2. Whisk in flour and cook until flour begins to turn golden.

3. Slowly whisk in milk. Continue to cook, whisking occasionally for 3 to 4 minutes until milk thickens.

4. Stir in cheese and cook until melted. Add nutmeg, salt, and pepper.

Nut Butter Dip

½ cup creamy peanut butter, almond butter, or soy nut butter

8 oz. vanilla or plain yogurt

Makes about 1½ cups
Use almond butter for even more calcium and vitamin E.
Prep Time: 5 minutes   **Cook Time:** 0   **Total:** 5 minutes

1. In a medium bowl, combine peanut butter and yogurt. Stir well.

2. Serve with sliced fresh fruit.

Dips and Sauces

Orange Ginger Dressing

½ **cup orange juice**

½ **cup canola oil**

½ **tsp. peeled and minced fresh ginger**

¼ **tsp. salt**

Makes 1 cup
Fresh ginger has a bit of a bite, so use less if desired in this phytonutrient-rich dressing.
Prep Time: 10 minutes **Cook Time:** 0 **Total:** 10 minutes

1. In medium bowl, mix orange juice, oil, ginger, and salt.
2. Serve over chopped salad greens or diced broccoli.

Raspberry Sauce

2 cups fresh or frozen raspberries, thawed

1 TB. sugar

2 tsp. cornstarch

2 TB. cold water

1 TB. orange juice

Makes about 2 cups
This simple sauce is filled with fiber and phytonutrients, protective plant compounds.
Prep Time: 0 **Cook Time:** 5 minutes **Total:** 5 minutes

1. In a small saucepan over low heat, cook raspberries and sugar for 2 to 3 minutes, stirring frequently.
2. In a small juice glass, mix cornstarch with water to dissolve.
3. Add cornstarch mixture to berries. Cook, stirring well, for 1 minute more.
4. Remove from heat and strain sauce through a fine sieve to remove seeds.
5. Cool. Serve over frozen yogurt or stir into plain yogurt.

Ricotta Cheese and Olive Spread

2 cups part-skim ricotta cheese   **¼ cup diced black olives**

½ tsp. dried parsley

1. In a small bowl, mix ricotta cheese, olives, and parsley.
2. Use as sandwich filling or as mix in or topping for baked white potatoes.

Makes 2 cups
Olives are a source of healthy fats for kids.
Prep Time: 5 minutes **Cook Time:** 0 **Total:** 5 minutes

Salsa and Cheese Dip

1 cup cottage cheese   **1 cup mild salsa**

1. In a small bowl, mix cottage cheese and salsa.
2. Serve with Healthy Snack Chips or use as a baked potato topping.

Makes 2 cups
A quick snack that provides protein and calcium.
Prep Time: 2 minutes **Cook Time:** 0 **Total:** 2 minutes

Dips and Sauces

Spinach Dip

1 (10-oz.) pkg. frozen,
chopped spinach, thawed
and drained well

1 cup cottage cheese

1 TB. dried parsley

⅓ cup mayonnaise

2 TB. lemon juice

Makes about 2 cups
Spinach and cottage cheese deliver calcium.
Prep Time: 10 minutes
Cook Time: 0
Total: 10 minutes

1. In a food processor, combine spinach, cottage cheese, parsley, mayonnaise, and lemon juice. Blend until smooth.

2. Serve with raw vegetables, toasted pita bread, or as a baked potato topper.

Very Cherry Sauce

2 cups pitted, fresh sweet
cherries, quartered

¼ cup orange juice

Makes about 2¼ cups
Cherries and orange juice supply a healthy dose of vitamin C.
Prep Time: 15 minutes
Cook Time: 0
Total: 8 hours (for marinating)

1. In a medium bowl, mix cherries and orange juice.

2. Marinate, covered overnight in the refrigerator.

3. Serve over plain yogurt, frozen yogurt, pancakes, waffles, or French toast.

Broccoli Carrot Frittata

1½ cups chopped broccoli
or 1 pkg. (10 oz.) frozen,
chopped broccoli, thawed
and drained

½ cup diced carrot (about
1 medium)

¼ cup water

8 eggs

¾ cup (3 oz.) shredded
cheddar cheese

½ cup milk

2 tsp. prepared mustard

Salt to taste

⅛ tsp. fresh ground black
pepper

Makes 6 small servings
This dish is nearly a meal in itself.
Prep Time: 10 minutes
Cook Time: 20 minutes
Total: 30 minutes

1. Coat a medium skillet with cooking spray.

2. Add broccoli, carrot, and water. Cover and cook over medium-high heat until carrot is crisp-tender, about 5 to 10 minutes.

3. Drain well. Return vegetables to pan. Set aside.

4. In a large bowl, beat together eggs, cheese, milk, mustard, salt, and black pepper until well blended. Pour over reserved vegetables.

5. Cover and cook over medium heat until eggs are almost set, about 15 minutes.

Cheesy Scrambled Eggs

2 eggs

2 TB. milk

Salt and fresh ground
black pepper, if desired

1 tsp. butter, margarine
or oil (or cooking spray)

¼ cup grated cheddar
cheese

Makes 2 eggs
Cheese adds B vitamins to this nutritious dish.
Prep Time: 1 minute
Cook Time: 5 minutes
Total: 6 minutes

1. In a small bowl, beat eggs, milk, salt, pepper, and cheese.

2. Heat butter in medium skillet over medium heat. Pour in egg mixture.

3. When mixture begins to set, gently draw an inverted pancake turner completely across bottom and sides of pan, to form large, soft curds.

4. Continue cooking until eggs are thickened and no visible liquid egg remains. Stir in cheese and serve.

Eggs

Egg Salad

4 large hard-boiled eggs, cooled and peeled

2 TB. mayonnaise

¼ cup plain yogurt

¼ cup relish

Makes about 2½ cups
Yogurt cuts the fat in this high-protein kid favorite.
Prep Time: 5 minutes **Cook Time:** 15 minutes **Total:** 20 minutes

1. In a medium bowl, mash eggs.
2. Add mayonnaise, yogurt, and relish. Mix well.

Fruited Omelet

2 eggs

2 TB. water

Pinch sugar

1 TB. butter or margarine

2 TB. plain yogurt

¼ cup sliced strawberries or ripe, peeled and finely chopped peaches

1 TB. confectioners' sugar, optional

Makes 1 medium omelet
Add whole-grain bread and milk and you've got a meal.
Prep Time: 5 minutes **Cook Time:** 5 minutes **Total:** 10 minutes

1. In a small bowl, beat together eggs, water, and sugar.
2. In a medium nonstick skillet, heat butter over medium-high heat.
3. Pour in egg mixture. Gently tilt pan and move uncooked portions toward the center to cook.
4. When eggs are set, remove from heat.
5. Spread omelet with yogurt and top with fruit. Fold in half and remove from pan. Top with confectioners' sugar.

Mediterranean Frittata

5 eggs

Salt and pepper to taste

1 tsp. dried basil

½ tsp. oregano

1 cup cottage cheese

5 TB. grated Parmesan cheese

2 TB. olive oil

1 medium tomato, seeded and chopped

1 medium zucchini, washed, halved lengthwise, and thinly sliced

Makes 8 small servings
Olive oil adds beneficial antioxidants.
Prep Time: 10 minutes Cook Time: 15 minutes Total: 25 minutes

1. In a medium bowl, beat eggs lightly with salt, pepper, basil, and oregano. Stir in cottage cheese, and half the Parmesan cheese.

2. In a medium nonstick skillet, lightly sauté tomatoes and zucchini in olive oil over medium heat until zucchini is lightly browned.

3. Pour eggs into skillet, and sprinkle with remaining Parmesan cheese.

4. Cook over medium-low heat until eggs are well set on bottom of pan, about 15 minutes. Cut into wedges and serve hot.

Mini Spinach Quiches

3 eggs

1 cup light cream

½ tsp. salt

1 (10-oz.) box frozen, chopped spinach, thawed and drained

2 cups Gruyère cheese, shredded

Makes 12 mini-quiche
Mini-quiche are just right for children with small appetites who need to pack in the calories.
Prep Time: 15 minutes Cook Time: 20 minutes Total: 35 minutes

1. Preheat oven to 400°F. Grease and flour 12 muffin-pan cups.

2. In a medium bowl, whisk eggs, cream, and salt.

3. Divide spinach evenly among muffin cups. Top with cheese, also divided evenly.

4. Top spinach and cheese with 3 to 4 tablespoons of egg/cream mixture. Bake for about 20 minutes.

5. With a sharp knife, remove quiche carefully from muffin pan and cool.

Eggs

Omelet

2 eggs

2 TB. water

⅛ tsp. salt (optional)

Dash fresh ground black pepper (optional)

1 tsp. butter, margarine, or oil (or cooking spray)

Makes 1 medium omelet
A quick dish that provides essential amino acids.
Prep Time: 5 minutes   **Cook Time:** 5 minutes   **Total:** 10 minutes

1. In a small bowl, beat together eggs, water, salt, and black pepper.

2. In a medium nonstick skillet, heat butter over medium-high heat.

3. Pour in egg mixture. Gently tilt pan and move uncooked portions toward the center to cook.

4. When the top has thickened and no visible liquid egg remains, fill, if desired. With a large pancake turner, fold omelet in half or roll.

Oven-Scrambled Eggs

6 eggs

6 TB. milk (any fat level)

½ tsp. salt (optional)

Fresh ground black pepper to taste (optional)

Makes 6 eggs
An easy way to serve up protein with an array of vitamins and minerals.
Prep Time: 5 minutes   **Cook Time:** 25 minutes   **Total:** 30 minutes

1. Preheat oven to 350°F. Grease a glass 13×9×2-inch baking pan

2. In a medium bowl, beat eggs, milk, salt, and pepper together.

3. Place eggs in oven. Cook for 7 minutes.

4. Open oven and remove baking dish. Using an inverted pancake turner, scrape pan to form large, soft curds.

5. Continue baking. Repeat mixing a few more times until eggs are thickened and no visible liquid egg remains, about 12 to 15 minutes.

Perfect Boiled Eggs

6 raw eggs

1. Put eggs in single layer in medium saucepan.

2. Add enough water to come at least one inch above them. Cover, and quickly bring to a boil, then turn off heat.

3. Remove pan from stove top and let eggs stand, covered, in the water for: 15 minutes for large eggs; 12 minutes for medium; 18 minutes for extra large.

4. Run cold water over eggs.

Makes 6 eggs
Use eggs enriched with DHA, a type of fat your little one needs for brain development and peak vision.
Prep Time: 0
Cook Time: 10–20 minutes
Total: 20 minutes

Scrambled Eggs

2 eggs

2 TB. milk (any fat level)

Salt and fresh ground black pepper, if desired

1 tsp. butter, margarine, or oil (or cooking spray)

Makes 2 eggs
Use olive oil instead of butter to cut back on saturated fat.
Prep Time: 1 minute
Cook Time: 5 minutes
Total: 6 minutes

1. In a small bowl, beat together eggs and milk.

2. In a medium nonstick skillet, heat butter over medium heat.

3. Pour in egg mixture. As mixture begins to set, gently draw an inverted pancake turner completely across bottom and sides of pan, forming large, soft curds.

4. Continue cooking until eggs are thickened and no visible liquid egg remains.

Eggs

Scrambled Egg and Salsa Sandwich

1 egg, scrambled

Mild salsa or ketchup

¼ cup grated cheddar cheese or other hard cheese

1 small whole-wheat pita pocket, cut in half

Makes 1 sandwich
This easy sandwich uses foods from four food groups.
Prep Time: 2 minutes **Cook Time:** 5 minutes **Total:** 7 minutes

1. Fill pita halves with egg, salsa, and cheese.

Turkey and Vegetable Strata

2 tsp. olive oil

1 cup chopped mushrooms

½ cup each: chopped green pepper, chopped red pepper

8 oz. 100 percent ground turkey breast

2 slices whole-grain bread, cut into 2-inch cubes

4 oz. shredded sharp cheddar cheese

6 eggs

2 cups milk

½ tsp. dried mustard

Makes 6 medium servings
Ground turkey keeps saturated fat levels on the low side.
Prep Time: 20 minutes **Cook Time:** 30–40 minutes **Total:** 50–60 minutes

1. Preheat oven to 350°F. Grease an 11×7-inch baking dish.

2. In a medium skillet, heat oil. Sauté mushrooms and pepper until tender. Remove from pan and place in a small bowl.

3. Crumble turkey into skillet and cook over medium heat until browned, stirring constantly.

4. Sprinkle bread cubes into prepared baking dish. Top with vegetable mixture, turkey, and cheese.

5. In a medium bowl, combine eggs, milk, and mustard and beat until well blended. Pour into baking dish over meat mixture.

6. Bake for 30 to 40 minutes or until eggs are set. Allow to cool for 5 to 10 minutes. Serve warm.

Laura's Salmon Burgers

2 cans salmon (6½ oz.
per can)

⅓ cup unseasoned bread
crumbs

1 egg

1 TB. finely chopped
shallots

1 TB. dried dill

Makes 4 burgers
Salmon harbors healthy omega-3 fats.
Prep Time: 5 minutes **Cook Time:** 10–15 minutes **Total:** 15–20 minutes

1. In a medium bowl, chop salmon with knife.
2. Add bread crumbs, egg, shallots, and dill. Combine with fork until blended well.
3. Heat oil in medium skillet over medium-high heat. Form salmon mixture into 4 equal-size patties.
4. Cook about 4 minutes each side.

Parmesan Fish

1 lb. firm white fish, such as
haddock or cod

2 TB. grated Parmesan cheese

2 TB. mayonnaise

1 cup chopped tomato

1 tsp. dried tarragon

Makes 1 pound
Choose a mild-tasting fish to tempt toddlers to eat this protein-rich dish.
Prep Time: 10 minutes **Cook Time:** 20 minutes **Total:** 30 minutes

1. Preheat oven to 350°F.
2. Coat a roasting pan with cooking spray. Place fish, skin side down, in pan.
3. In a small bowl, combine mayonnaise and cheese to make a paste. Spread mixture on fish.
4. Top with chopped tomato. Sprinkle tarragon on top of tomatoes.
5. Bake until fish is flaky, about 20 minutes or until lightly browned.

Tuna Pate

4 oz. cream cheese,
softened

1 TB. lemon juice

1 (7-oz.) can light tuna,
drained, flaked

1 TB. dried parsley

Makes about 2 cups
Use light cream cheese to decrease the fat.
Prep Time: 5 minutes **Cook Time:** 0 **Total:** 5 minutes

1. In a food processor or blender, blend cream cheese, lemon juice, and tuna.
2. Stir in parsley.
3. Use as a spread or sandwich filling.

Fruit

Apple Crisp

5 cups sliced apples (or pears or peaches)

2 TB. sugar

½ cup packed brown sugar

¼ cup rolled oats

¼ cup wheat germ

¼ tsp. ground cinnamon, nutmeg, or ginger

¼ cup butter or margarine

Makes about 6 cups
Wheat germ adds folic acid and other B vitamins.
Prep Time: 5–15 minutes
Cook Time: 30 minutes
Total: 35–45 minutes

1. Preheat oven to 375°F.

2. Place fruit in 13×9×2-inch glass baking dish. Toss with sugar (and flour if making blueberry crisp).

3. In a medium bowl, combine brown sugar, oats, wheat germ, and cinnamon. Cut in margarine until mixture resembles coarse crumbs.

4. Sprinkle sugar mixture over fruit fully.

5. Bake for 30 minutes or until fruit is tender. Cool to room temperature before serving.

TIP: Triple the topping recipe, but don't add butter. Store unused portion in airtight container until you're ready to make another fruit crisp. Add butter as needed.

Baked Apples

4 medium baking apples

½ cup raisins, chopped fine

2 TB. brown sugar

½ tsp. ground cinnamon

¼ cup 100 percent apple juice

Makes 4 apples
Raisins and apples provide fiber.
Prep Time: 10 minutes
Cook Time: 40–45 minutes
Total: 50–55 minutes

1. Preheat oven to 350°F.

2. Wash and core apples. Peel a strip from the top of each.

3. Place apples in a 2-quart casserole dish.

4. In a small bowl, combine raisins, brown sugar, and cinnamon. Spoon into the center of each apple, dividing mixture evenly.

5. Add juice to baking dish. Bake for 40 to 45 minutes.

6. Cool completely before serving.

Baked Pears

6 Bartlett pears, peeled, cut in quarters, and cored

¼ cup light brown sugar

¼ cup apple or pear juice

1 tsp. ground cinnamon

Makes 6 pears
Pears are filled with fiber.
Prep Time: 5 minutes Cook Time: 20–30 minutes Total: 25–35 minutes

1. Preheat oven to 400°F.

2. Place pears in 9×13×2-inch glass baking dish.

3. Mix brown sugar, juice, and cinnamon together in a small bowl. Spoon over pears and toss gently until coated.

4. Bake for 20 to 30 minutes or until tender. Spoon into individual dessert bowls.

Blueberry Cobbler

Filling:

4 cups fresh or frozen blueberries

1½ TB. cornstarch

¼ cup water

⅔ cup sugar

Topping:

1 cup all-purpose flour

¼ cup sugar

1 tsp. baking powder

½ tsp. ground cinnamon

3 TB. margarine

¼ cup milk

1 egg, beaten

Makes 6 medium servings
Blueberries are brimming with antioxidants.
Prep Time: 15 minutes Cook Time: 25 minutes Total: 40 minutes

1. Preheat oven to 400°F.

2. For filling, combine sugar, water, and cornstarch in a medium saucepan. Stir in blueberries. Cook until thickened, stirring constantly. Set aside.

3. In a medium bowl, combine flour, sugar, baking powder, and cinnamon to make topping.

4. Cut in margarine until the mixture resembles coarse crumbs.

5. In a small bowl, combine egg and milk. Add to flour mixture, stirring just to moisten.

6. Transfer filling to a 2-quart rectangular baking dish. Drop about 12 mounds or so atop filling.

7. Bake for 25 minutes or until a toothpick inserted into topping comes out clean.

Fruit

Cinnamon Applesauce

6 small apples   ¼ **tsp. ground cinnamon**

1 TB. sugar (optional)

1. Peel, core, and cut apples into small pieces.

2. Place apples in a microwave-safe glass dish with cinnamon and sugar.

3. Cook, uncovered, for 8 minutes, on high power. Stop to stir at 4 minutes.

4. Allow mixture to cool for 5 minutes, then place in a blender or food processor, and purée until smooth.

Makes about 1½ cups
Cinnamon brings out sweetness, so you need less sugar.
Prep Time: 10 minutes **Cook Time:** 10 minutes **Total:** 20 minutes

Grape and Cranberry Salsa

2 cups red seedless grapes, rinsed

Juice of 1 orange (about ⅓ **cup)**

1 (12-oz.) pkg. cranberries, fresh or frozen

½ **cup sugar**

1. Place grapes, cranberries, orange juice, and sugar in a heavy saucepan. Bring to boil over high heat.

2. Reduce heat to medium. Cook, stirring occasionally, for 10 minutes.

3. Let cool thoroughly. Store in refrigerator, covered tightly, for up to a week.

Makes 3 cups
Grapes are safe for young children when cooked, as in this vitamin C-rich side dish that's perfect with meat.
Prep Time: 5 minutes **Cook Time:** 15 minutes **Total:** 20 minutes

Peach Shortcake

1 (29-oz.) can yellow cling peaches in light syrup

¼ cup sugar

2 cups all-purpose flour

2 tsp. baking powder

½ cup margarine

1 beaten egg

⅔ cup milk

Makes 8 shortcakes
Canned peaches are just as nutritious as fresh.
Prep Time: 20 minutes **Cook Time:** 15 minutes **Total:** 35 minutes

1. Preheat oven to 425°F. Grease an 8×1½-inch round baking pan.

2. Cut peach halves into 1-inch slices. Reserve syrup.

3. In a medium bowl, stir together sugar, flour, and baking powder to make short-cake. Cut in margarine until mixture resembles coarse crumbs.

4. In a small bowl, combine egg and milk and add to dry ingredients. Stir until dry ingredients are just moistened.

5. Spread into prepared baking pan. Bake for 15 minutes, or until a toothpick inserted in the center comes out clean. Cool in pan on wire rack for 10 to 15 minutes.

6. Remove from pan. Cut into 8 equal pieces. To assemble each serving, split each piece into two layers. Spoon 4 to 5 peach pieces and 1 TB. syrup onto the bottom layer. Cover. Spoon 1 TB. of peach syrup on the top.

Roasted Peaches

4 ripe peaches (about 1 lb.)

2 tsp. lemon juice

Makes about 1 pound
Roasting brings out the natural sweetness of peaches, so you don't need to add sugar.
Prep Time: 5 minutes **Cook Time:** 20 minutes **Total:** 25 minutes

1. Preheat oven to 400°F.

2. Cut peaches in half and remove pits.

3. In a large bowl, toss peaches with lemon juice.

4. Arrange peaches, cut side up, in a small baking dish.

5. Roast for 20 minutes or until peaches are tender.

Fruit

Stewed Peaches

¼ cup sugar

¾ cup water

4 whole cloves

1½ lb. peaches, peeled and halved

Makes about 3 cups
Peaches provide potassium and are low in sodium. Peaches are also a good source of vitamin C and fiber.
Prep Time: 10 minutes
Cook Time: 10 minutes
Total: 20 minutes

1. In a medium saucepan over medium heat, combine sugar, water, and cloves. Bring to a boil.

2. Add peaches and return to boil. Reduce heat to low. Cover.

3. Simmer until tender, about 10 minutes or so.

Beef Barley Soup

1 TB. olive oil

1 medium onion, chopped

½ cup chopped carrot

½ cup chopped celery with leaves

3 lb. beef shank cross cuts, cut 1-inch thick

5 cups low-sodium beef broth or water

1 tsp. salt

Fresh ground black pepper to taste

⅓ cup medium pearl barley

Makes 6 servings
This dish combines meat, vegetables, and grain for a hearty meal.
Prep Time: 15 minutes
Cook Time: 70 minutes
Total: 85 minutes

1. Heat oil in a large saucepan over medium heat until hot.

2. Add onion, carrot, and celery. Cook and stir for 5 minutes or until tender.

3. Add beef, broth, salt, thyme, pepper, and bay leaf; bring to a boil. Reduce heat; cover tightly and simmer 1 hour.

4. Remove beef and cut meat from bones into 1-inch pieces.

5. Return boneless meat to the pan. Stir in barley.

6. Continue cooking for another hour or until beef and barley are tender.

Confetti Rice

2 cups water or low-sodium chicken or vegetable broth

1 cup rice

1 cup diced broccoli

¼ cup diced red bell pepper

¼ cup diced carrots

Makes 4½ cups
A colorful way for kids to get vegetables and grains.
Prep Time: 10 minutes
Cook Time: 20 minutes
Total: 30 minutes

1. In a medium saucepan over high heat, bring water or broth to a boil.

2. Add rice, broccoli, red bell pepper, and carrots. Cover and reduce heat to low.

3. Simmer for 20 minutes or until fluid is absorbed and rice is tender.

Crunchy Granola*

2 cups uncooked oatmeal

½ cup finely chopped wal-
nuts

½ cup wheat germ

¼ cup honey

¼ cup canola oil

½ cup finely chopped
raisins

½ cup finely chopped
dried apricots

Makes 4 cups
Store-bought granola can be high in fat and sugar; this fiber-packed version is neither.
Prep Time: 10 minutes **Cook Time:** 25 minutes **Total:** 35 minutes

1. Heat oven to 325°F. Grease a baking sheet.

2. In a medium bowl, mix oatmeal, walnuts, and wheat germ.

3. In a small bowl, combine honey and canola oil.

4. Add honey mixture to oatmeal mixture and mix well.

5. Spread on baking sheet. Bake for 15 minutes.

6. After 15 minutes, add raisins and apricots and toss well.

7. Return to oven and bake for 10 minutes longer.

*Contains honey. Do not serve to children under age 1.

Fruity Bulgur

2 tsp. canola or olive oil

1 cup chopped onions

1 cup bulgur

1½ cups low-sodium
chicken or vegetable
broth

¼ tsp. ground cinnamon

¼ cup chopped dried
apricots

⅓ cup chopped fresh
parsley

Makes about 3 cups
Bulgur can help your child meet his daily requirement for whole grains.
Prep Time: 10 minutes **Cook Time:** 20–25 minutes **Total:** 30–35 minutes

1. In a large saucepan, heat oil over medium heat. Sauté onions until soft, about 3 to 5 minutes.

2. Add bulgur to the saucepan and stir for 1 minute.

3. Add chicken broth and cinnamon and bring to a simmer.

4. Reduce heat to low. Cover pan and allow to cook until liquid has been absorbed, about 15 to 20 minutes.

5. Stir in dried apricots and parsley.

Oatmeal and Wheat Germ Cereal

1 TB. toasted wheat germ

2 TB. cup uncooked oat-meal

¼ cup diced banana or other soft fruit

¼ cup milk, or more as needed

Makes about 1 cup
A great way to work in whole grains, fruit, and milk—and no cooking involved!
Prep Time: 5 minutes **Cook Time:** 0 **Total:** 5 minutes

1. Place wheat germ, oatmeal, and banana in a cereal bowl.

2. Top with milk. Allow to sit for 1 minute or until cereal has absorbed some of the milk. Serve imme-diately.

Overnight Orange Tabbouleh Dinner Salad

¾ cup bulgur

1½ cups boiling water

2 oranges

1½ cups firm tofu, cubed

2 cups cucumber, peeled, chopped

1 TB. chopped fresh mint

1 TB. olive or canola oil

½ tsp. salt

Makes about 6 cups
Tofu is a cholesterol-free source of protein that takes on the flavors of any dish it's a part of.
Prep Time: 40 minutes **Cook Time:** 0 **Total:** 40 minutes (plus 4 hours to marinate)

1. In a medium bowl, combine bulgur and boiling water. Let stand 30 minutes. Drain excess liquid.

2. Meanwhile, grate 2 TB. orange peel. Peel oranges and section, saving juice. Cover oranges in their juice and refrigerate.

3. In a large bowl, stir together bulgur, orange peel, tofu, cucumber, mint, oil, and salt.

4. Cover and chill overnight or for at least 4 hours. Stir in reserved oranges and their juice and serve.

Grains

Quinoa Pilaf

2 tsp. canola or olive oil

1 cup chopped onions

½ cup carrots, finely diced

1 cup uncooked quinoa

2 cups low-sodium chicken broth or vegetable broth

⅓ cup chopped fresh parsley

Makes about 2½ cups
Add leftover shredded chicken or turkey to up the protein of this nutritious dish.
Prep Time: 10 minutes **Cook Time:** 25 minutes **Total:** 35 minutes

1. In a large saucepan, heat oil over medium heat. Sauté onions and carrots until soft, about 3 to 5 minutes.

2. Add quinoa to the saucepan and stir for 1 minute.

3. Add chicken broth and bring to a simmer.

4. Reduce heat to low. Cover pan and allow to cook until liquid has been absorbed, about 20 minutes.

5. Stir in parsley and serve.

Speedy Skillet Supper

2 cups cooked rice or other grain

2 cups diced cooked vegetables, such as carrots and broccoli

4 eggs, beaten, and seasoned with salt and pepper, if desired

1 cup shredded aged cheese, such as cheddar, Gouda, or Fontina

Makes 5 to 6 cups
This fast and easy dish provides carbohydrates, protein, fiber, and fat, along with an array of vitamins and minerals.
Prep Time: 5 minutes **Cook Time:** 10 minutes **Total:** 15 minutes

1. In a large nonstick skillet over medium heat, combine grain and vegetables. Toss well, and warm.

2. Pour on beaten eggs and scramble the entire mixture.

3. When eggs are cooked, top with cheese.

Spinach Rice

2 cups white rice, cooked

1 TB. olive oil

1 large onion, finely diced

1 red bell pepper, cored and finely diced

10 oz. mushrooms, sliced

1 (10-oz.) pkg. frozen, chopped spinach, thawed and squeezed dry

4 oz. feta cheese, crumbled

1 tsp. dried dill weed

Fresh ground black pepper to taste

1 egg, beaten

2 cups cottage cheese

3 TB. grated Parmesan cheese

Makes about 6 cups
One serving has nearly as much calcium as eight ounces of milk.
Prep Time: 30 minutes   **Cook Time:** 30 minutes   **Total:** 60 minutes

1. Preheat oven to 400°F.

2. Cook rice according to package directions. Let cool and set aside.

3. Spray a 4-quart baking dish with nonstick cooking spray.

4. In a large nonstick skillet over medium heat, heat oil. Add onion and red bell pepper. Sauté for about 5 minutes, then add mushrooms, cooking until tender.

5. In a large bowl, combine spinach, feta cheese, dill weed, black pepper, egg, and cottage cheese. Stir in cooked vegetable mixture and cooked rice.

6. Spoon the entire mixture into prepared baking dish. Smooth the top, and sprinkle with Parmesan cheese. Bake about 30 minutes, or until golden on top.

Legumes

Black Bean and Beef Burgers

1 slice firm bread, torn into small pieces

2 TB. tomato paste

2 TB. water

¾ lb. lean ground beef

⅔ cup canned black beans, drained, rinsed, and chopped well

2 TB. fresh parsley

1 tsp. dried thyme

½ tsp. salt, if desired

Makes 4 patties
Black beans cut fat and add fiber to burgers.
Prep Time: 10 minutes **Cook Time:** 10 minutes **Total:** 20 minutes

1. Preheat a gas grill or oven broiler.

2. In a medium bowl, mash bread, tomato paste, and water with a fork to make a paste.

3. Add beef, beans, parsley, thyme, and salt. Mix thoroughly.

4. Shape into 4 patties. Grill or broil until browned or cooked through, about 5 minutes on each side.

Easy Cheese-y Lentil Soup

¼ cup lentil soup

¼ cup cooked small macaroni, such as orzo

2 TB. grated cheddar cheese

Makes ½ cup
This high-potassium soup is the perfect consistency for babies and toddlers. Add macaroni to thicken for older children who feed themselves.
Prep Time: 2 minutes **Cook Time:** 3 minutes **Total:** 5 minutes

1. In a small saucepan, combine lentil soup and macaroni. Warm.

2. Transfer to a serving bowl. Stir in grated cheese.

Lentil Salad

1¼ cups dried lentils

¼ cup lemon juice

2 TB. olive oil

½ tsp. dried thyme

Fresh ground black pepper, if desired

2 cups cherry tomatoes, cut into quarters, or 2 cups chopped tomatoes

1 cup cucumber, peeled, diced, and finely chopped

4 oz. feta cheese

Makes about 6 cups
Lentils are low in sodium and high in potassium and they are easy for a youngster to eat.
Prep Time: 10 minutes **Cook Time:** 25 minutes **Total:** 35 minutes

1. In a large saucepan, place lentils and cover with water to 2 inches above lentils. Bring to a boil over medium high heat.

2. Cover pan, reduce heat, and simmer for 20 minutes, or until tender. When done, drain well and reserve.

3. Meanwhile, in a medium bowl, combine lemon juice, oil, thyme, and black pepper. Whisk until blended well.

4. Add tomatoes, cucumber, and cheese. Toss gently to mix well.

Pocket Bean Sandwich

¼ cup canned garbanzo or white beans, rinsed

1 small pita round, cut in half

2 TB. finely grated aged cheese, such as cheddar

Makes 1 sandwich
Any bean will do in this fiber-rich sandwich.
Prep Time: 5 minutes **Cook Time:** 0 **Total:** 5 minutes

1. In a small bowl, mash beans.

2. Fill each pita pocket half with mashed beans and cheese.

3. Microwave both halves for 20 seconds or until cheese has just melted. Let sit for 5 minutes to be sure sandwich is cool enough for child to eat.

Legumes

Pasta and White Bean Casserole

8 oz. small macaroni

¼ lb. lean ground beef

1 small onion, peeled and diced (about 1½ cups)

2 cups chopped fresh broccoli, or 1 (10-oz.) pkg. frozen broccoli, thawed, drained, and chopped

1 (16-oz.) can diced tomatoes, finely chopped (reserve liquid)

1½ cups low-sodium beef broth or water

1 (15½-oz.) can white beans, rinsed and drained

2 TB. plain bread crumbs

2 TB. grated Parmesan cheese

Makes about 8 cups
Use low-sodium canned diced tomatoes to reduce the sodium even further in this dish.
Prep Time: 15 minutes Cook Time: 20 minutes Total: 35 minutes

1. Prepare pasta according to package directions. Drain and reserve.

2. Preheat oven to 350°F.

3. Crumble beef into a large skillet and place over medium heat. Cook, stirring occasionally, until cooked through, about 4 minutes.

4. Add onion and broccoli to the skillet. Cook until vegetables are soft, about 5 minutes. Add tomatoes and bring to a boil, stirring occasionally. Boil 3 minutes.

5. Remove skillet from heat and add beef broth or water, beans, and salt and pepper to taste. Stir well.

6. In a large mixing bowl, combine broccoli and beef mixture with cooked pasta. Toss well. Transfer mixture to a 4-quart baking dish.

7. In a small bowl, mix bread crumbs and Parmesan cheese and sprinkle over casserole. Bake until heated through in the center, about 20 minutes.

White Bean Hummus

1 TB. canola or olive oil

1 (15-oz.) can white beans, drained and rinse

2 TB. lemon juice

½ tsp. salt

½ tsp. ground cumin

⅓ cup fresh parsley, minced

Makes about 2 cups
Beans are rich in fiber, free of cholesterol, and contain just a touch of fat.
Prep Time: 5 minutes Cook Time: 0 Total: 5 minutes

1. Place oil, beans, lemon juice, salt, and cumin in food processor and purée until smooth.

2. Transfer to a serving bowl and stir in parsley.

3. Serve as a vegetable dip, or spread on crackers or bread.

Rice 'N' Beans

2 cups cooked beans

2 cups cooked rice

1½ cups fresh tomato, diced

Salt and fresh ground black pepper to taste

Makes about 6 cups
The tomatoes in this dish boost the body's absorption of iron in the rice and beans.
Prep Time: 10 minutes **Cook Time:** 5 minutes **Total:** 15 minutes

1. In a large skillet, combine beans and rice. Mix gently.

2. Add tomatoes, salt, and black pepper.

3. Cover and heat for about 5 minutes.

Smashed Baked Beans on Toast

¼ cup canned or home-made baked beans

1 slice whole-grain toast

Makes 1 piece
Baked beans are full of fiber.
Prep Time: 5 minutes **Cook Time:** 0 **Total:** 5 minutes

1. With a fork, mash beans into a paste.

2. Spread on toast and serve.

Tofu Veggie Stir-Fry

1 lb. firm tofu, cut in ¾-inch cubes

1 cup reduced-sodium soy sauce

1 TB. canola oil

1 red bell pepper, cut in ¼-inch pieces

1 green bell pepper, cut in ¼-inch pieces

2 cups chunky pineapple, cut in ¼-inch pieces

1 TB. rice wine vinegar

2 TB. chopped cilantro

Makes 6 servings
Red bell pepper is a good source of vitamin C.
Prep Time: 20 minutes **Cook Time:** 20 minutes **Total:** 40 minutes

1. In a medium bowl, gently toss tofu cubes in ¼ cup soy sauce.

2. In a medium skillet, heat canola oil over medium-high heat, brown tofu. Remove from pan and set aside.

3. Add red and green bell peppers to pan and sauté for 5 minutes, stirring. Add pineapple and sauté another 2 minutes.

4. Reduce heat to medium low. Add remaining soy sauce, rice wine vinegar, and cilantro, combining well.

5. Gently stir in tofu and heat. Serve over cooked brown or white rice.

Meat

Beef Stew

2 TB. olive oil

1 lb. lean beef stew meat, cut into 1-inch chunks

½ cup all-purpose flour

¾ cup onion, chopped

9 cups low-sodium beef broth

1 tsp. dried basil leaves

⅛ tsp. ground black pepper

1½ cups sliced carrots

1½ cups sliced celery

1 (14.5-oz.) can stewed tomatoes

1½ cups orzo or elbow macaroni

Makes 8 to 10 medium portions
Beef is loaded with iron and zinc that little ones need to maximize body and brain development.
Prep Time: 15 minutes **Cook Time:** 30 minutes **Total:** 45 minutes

1. In a large saucepan, heat oil.

2. Coat beef with flour and add to pan. Add onion. Cook until beef is browned.

3. Add broth, basil, and black pepper to pan. Bring to a boil.

4. Reduce heat; simmer, covered, until meat is tender, about 1½ hours.

5. Add carrots, celery, and tomatoes. Cook 15 minutes longer.

6. Stir in pasta. Cook until pasta is tender, 10 to 15 minutes, stirring occasionally.

Classic Meatloaf

¾ lb. lean ground beef

¾ lb. ground pork

4 oz. canned tomato sauce

1 cup bread crumbs

1 egg

1 small onion, finely chopped

2 tsp. Worcestershire sauce

1 tsp. dried thyme leaves, crushed

½ tsp. salt

Makes 1 loaf
Just like Mom made, only leaner.
Prep Time: 10 minutes **Cook Time:** 60 minutes **Total:** 70 minutes

1. Preheat oven to 350°F.

2. In a large bowl, combine meat, tomato sauce, bread crumbs, egg, onion, Worcestershire sauce, thyme, and salt, mixing thoroughly.

3. Shape beef mixture into an 8×4-inch loaf on rack in broiler pan.

4. Bake for 1 hour or until internal temperature reaches 160°F.

5. When done, allow to stand 10 minutes before slicing.

Marinated Pork Tenderloin

1 cup frozen apple-juice concentrate, thawed

2 TB. Dijon mustard

½ cup olive oil

1 TB. dried rosemary

4 cloves garlic, peeled and minced

Fresh ground black pepper

2 lb. pork tenderloin

Makes 2 pounds
Apple juice concentrate adds flavor and cuts fat as a substitute for oil.
Prep Time: 5 minutes **Cook Time:** 30 minutes **Total:** 1 hour (due to marinating)

1. In a medium bowl, combine juice, mustard, oil, rosemary, garlic, and black pepper. Whisk, mixing thoroughly.

2. Place meat in a shallow glass dish. Pour marinade over pork, turning to coat. Cover. Place in refrigerator and allow to marinate for at least 30 minutes.

3. Preheat a gas grill or oven broiler. Grill or broil meat until done, about 15 minutes. (Use a meat thermometer to be sure meat is done.)

4. Transfer cooked meat to a cutting board and allow to rest for five minutes before slicing.

Hearty Meatloaf

1½ lb. lean ground beef

¾ cup quick or old-fashioned oats, uncooked

¾ cup onion, finely chopped

½ cup chili sauce

1 egg

2 cloves garlic, minced

1 tsp. dried thyme

1 tsp. fresh ground black pepper

½ tsp. salt

Makes 1 loaf
Oats improve the fiber profile and keep the meatloaf moist.
Prep Time: 10 minutes **Cook Time:** 55 minutes **Total:** 65 minutes

1. Heat oven to 350°F. In a large mixing bowl, combine beef, oats, onion, chili sauce, egg, garlic, thyme, black pepper, and salt, mixing thoroughly. Shape into an 8×4-inch loaf on rack in broiler pan.

2. Bake meatloaf for 50 to 55 minutes or until internal temperature reaches 160°F.

3. When done, let stand for 10 minutes before cutting.

Meat

Muffin Tin Meatballs

1 lb. ground beef

¼ cup cornflake cereal, crushed

1 tsp. salt

⅛ tsp. ground black pepper

1 egg

¼ cup ketchup

3 TB. brown sugar

Makes 6 meatballs
Cornflakes cut the fat by standing in for some of the beef.
Prep Time: 15 minutes   **Cook Time:** 30 minutes   **Total:** 45 minutes

1. Preheat oven to 375°F. In a large bowl, combine beef, cornflakes, salt, pepper, and egg. Mix well.

2. In a small bowl, stir together ketchup and brown sugar. Spoon 2 TB. of the ketchup mixture into the beef and mix well.

3. Spray muffin tin with vegetable cooking spray. Form 6 meatballs and place in muffin tin. Coat the top of each meatball with the remaining ketchup mixture.

4. Bake for 30 minutes.

Orange Marmalade Pork Chops

4 boneless pork loin chops, about ¾-inch thick (about 1 lb.)

2 tsp. canola or olive oil

½ tsp. salt

2 TB. cider vinegar

¼ cup orange marmalade

Makes 4 chops
A low-fat, fast, and tasty way to serve protein, B vitamins, and minerals to kids.
Prep Time: 5 minutes   **Cook Time:** 15 minutes   **Total:** 20 minutes

1. Heat a heavy skillet over medium-high heat.

2. Brush chops with vegetable oil; sprinkle salt on both sides.

2. Brown on each side for 5 to 7 minutes or until cooked. Remove chops from pan and keep warm.

3. Slowly add vinegar to skillet, scraping up any brown bits. Stir in marmalade.

4. Return chops to skillet; turning to coat. Serve.

Turkey Sloppy Joes

1 lb. ground 100 percent turkey breast

½ cup onion, chopped

1 (8-oz.) can diced tomatoes, not drained

2 TB. quick-cooking rolled oats

1 tsp. Worcestershire sauce

Makes 1 pound
This mildly seasoned favorite is lower in saturated fat and cholesterol than the beef version.
Prep Time: 10 minutes **Cook Time:** 15 minutes **Total:** 25 minutes

1. In a large skillet, cook turkey and onion until meat is brown.

2. Stir in tomatoes, oats, and Worcestershire sauce.

3. Bring to a boil, then reduce heat.

4. Simmer for 5 to 10 minutes or until mixture reaches desired consistency.

5. Serve to young children with the bun on the side.

Pasta

Chicken, Ziti, and Broccoli

8 oz. ziti, uncooked

1 TB. olive oil

3 cloves garlic, peeled and minced

8 oz. boneless, skinless chicken breast, cut into 1-inch pieces

½ cup low-sodium chicken broth

2 cups fresh or frozen, chopped broccoli florets, cooked

Makes about 6 cups
Pasta is fortified with several nutrients, including the iron and folic acid your child needs for healthy red blood cells.
Prep Time: 15 minutes Cook Time: 15 minutes Total: 30 minutes

1. Cook ziti according to package directions.

2. Meanwhile, heat oil in skillet over medium heat. Add garlic and cook for 1 minute, stirring constantly. Add chicken; toss until brown for 1 to 2 minutes.

3. Add chicken broth to pan and continue to cook for about 5 minutes or until chicken is done.

4. Drain cooked ziti well. Add to skillet along with broccoli and toss well.

Pasta Salad

1 cup orzo or elbow macaroni

2 TB. olive oil

3 TB. lemon juice

¼ tsp. fresh ground black pepper, if desired

1 tsp. dried dill

1 sweet green bell pepper, chopped into ¼-inch pieces

2 large tomatoes, chopped

4 oz. feta cheese, crumbled

1½ cups cottage cheese

Makes about 6 cups
Use low-fat cottage cheese to reduce some of the fat.
Prep Time: 25 minutes Cook Time: 0 Total: 25 minutes

1. Cook macaroni according to package directions.

2. When done, transfer to a colander and rinse with cold water. Drain thoroughly and pour into a large mixing bowl.

3. Add olive oil, lemon juice, black pepper, and dill. Toss.

4. Add pepper, tomatoes, feta cheese, and cottage cheese. Toss again.

Tuna Pasta Pomodoro

8 oz. uncooked pasta

1 batch Laura's Fresh Tomato Sauce (see Chapter 16)

2 (6.5-oz.) cans chunk light tuna, drained and flaked

Makes 4 cups
Pasta is a source of the B vitamin folic acid.
Prep Time: 10 minutes **Cook Time:** 15 minutes **Total:** 25 minutes

1. Cook pasta according to directions.

2. In a medium skillet, warm tomato sauce and tuna, stirring to break up tuna and mix well.

3. Drain hot, cooked pasta well. Add to skillet and toss.

Cheesy Lasagna

8 oz. 100 percent ground turkey breast

1½ cups plus ½ cup spaghetti sauce

2 medium eggs

1½ cups cottage cheese

1 tsp. dried basil

1 tsp. dried oregano

1 TB. dried parsley

6 oz. oven-ready lasagna noodles (9 pieces total)

8 oz. part-skim mozzarella cheese, grated

¼ cup Parmesan cheese, grated

Makes 6 medium servings
The ground turkey and part-skim mozzarella drive down the fat and cholesterol in this delicious entrée.
Prep Time: 20 minutes **Cook Time:** 25–30 minutes **Total:** 45–50 minutes

1. Preheat oven to 350°F.

2. In a medium skillet, brown turkey, breaking into crumbles. Drain fat from meat, and season with salt and pepper to taste.

3. In a medium bowl, mix together turkey and 1½ cups spaghetti sauce.

4. In a separate medium bowl, beat eggs; add cottage cheese, basil, oregano, and parsley.

5. To assemble, spread a small amount of sauce on bottom of an 11×7×2-inch baking dish. Layer 3 sheets of oven-ready noodles crosswise over sauce. On top of noodles, layer ½ cup cottage cheese-egg mixture, then ½ mozzarella cheese, then ½ of the meat-sauce mixture. For the next layer, place another 3 noodles crosswise in pan; repeat the steps in order with remaining ingredients. Top final layer of noodles with remaining ½ cup spaghetti sauce, spreading evenly across top.

6. Sprinkle entire top with Parmesan cheese. Cover with aluminum foil.

7. Bake for 25 to 30 minutes, or until bubbly. Let stand 10 minutes before serving.

Pasta

Macaroni and Cheese

8 oz. elbow macaroni, uncooked

2 cups sharp cheddar cheese, shredded

1 TB. dried parsley, plus pinch for garnish

½ tsp. freshly ground black pepper

2 cups cottage cheese

½ cup milk

¼ cup seasoned bread crumbs

¼ cup shredded Parmesan cheese

Makes 6 medium servings
Low-fat cottage cheese increases the protein, but not the saturated fat, in this kid-favorite food.
Prep Time: 15 minutes **Cook Time:** 30 minutes **Total:** 45 minutes

1. Preheat oven to 350°F. Spray a 2-quart baking dish with nonstick cooking spray, and set aside.

2. Cook macaroni according to package directions until tender but firm. Drain, then rinse with cool water. Set aside.

3. In a large bowl, combine macaroni, cheese, parsley, and black pepper.

4. In a food processor, blend cottage cheese and milk until smooth.

5. Pour over macaroni mixture and mix thoroughly. Pour entire mixture into baking dish.

6. In a small bowl, combine bread crumbs and Parmesan cheese. Sprinkle over the top of the macaroni mixture, along with pinch of dried parsley.

7. Bake for about 30 minutes, or until hot in the center. Allow to cool before serving.

Peanut Butter Noodles

12 oz. spaghetti or linguine

½ cup creamy peanut butter or soy nut butter

¾ cup boiling water

¼ cup soy sauce

3 TB. rice wine vinegar

½ tsp. sugar

1 cup cucumber, peeled and finely diced

Makes about 6 cups
The sauce provides the B vitamin folate. If you want, consider adding chopped scallions.
Prep Time: 5 minutes **Cook Time:** 15 minutes **Total:** 20 minutes

1. Cook spaghetti according to package directions.

2. Meanwhile, combine remaining peanut butter and water in a medium mixing bowl until smooth.

3. Stir in soy sauce, rice wine vinegar, and sugar. Mix well.

4. Drain spaghetti well. Place in a large bowl with cucumber and toss with peanut sauce mixture.

Stuffed Shells with Spinach

10 jumbo pasta shells

1 cup ricotta cheese

1 TB. fresh parsley, chopped

2 egg whites, beaten

1 cup frozen, chopped spinach, thawed and drained well

¾ cup marinara sauce

¼ cup mozzarella cheese

Cooking spray

Makes 10 shells
Eggs whites reduce the cholesterol.
Prep Time: 15 minutes **Cook Time:** 45 minutes **Total:** 60 minutes

1. Cook pasta shells according to package directions. Drain and separate.

2. Preheat oven to 350°F.

3. Spray bottom of a 13×9×2-inch baking dish with cooking spray.

4. In a medium bowl, combine ricotta cheese and parsley. Add egg whites and spinach and combine well.

5. Spread half of the marinara sauce in the baking dish. Fill pasta shells with ricotta cheese mixture and place in baking dish.

6. Pour remaining sauce over prepared shells and top with mozzarella cheese.

7. Cover dish with aluminum foil and bake for 45 minutes. Let stand 10 minutes before serving.

Pasta

Baked Ziti

8 oz. ziti, uncooked

½ lb. extra lean ground beef

2 medium onions, chopped

3 cups spaghetti sauce

2 cups ricotta cheese

2 TB. grated Parmesan cheese

1 egg, lightly beaten

1 tsp. dried parsley

½ tsp. garlic powder

Serves 6
Use ground turkey breast and low-fat ricotta cheese to reduce the calories, fat, and cholesterol in this family favorite.
Prep Time: 20 minutes **Cook Time:** 30 minutes **Total:** 50 minutes

1. Preheat oven to 350°F. Spray a 2-quart or 2-liter baking dish with nonstick cooking spray.

2. Cook ziti according to package directions. Drain, and rinse with cool water. Set aside.

3. In a large skillet, crumble beef. Add onions. Sauté until meat is cooked. Add spaghetti sauce.

4. In a large bowl, combine ricotta, Parmesan cheese, egg, parsley, and garlic powder. Mix thoroughly. Add cooked ziti and mix well.

5. Spread about ⅓ of the meat mixture in the bottom of prepared baking dish. Spoon ziti and cheese mixture into the pan.

6. Pour the remaining spaghetti sauce mixture into the pan. Cover with aluminum foil and bake for about 30 minutes.

Basic Pizza Dough

1½ cups all-purpose flour

½ cup whole-wheat flour

1 tsp. salt

½ tsp. sugar

1 pkg. active dry yeast

¾ cup water

2 tsp. canola or olive oil

Makes 1 pound dough, enough for two 12-inch pizzas
This dough has more fiber and other nutrients than store-bought versions.
Prep Time: 20 minutes **Cook Time:** 0 minutes **Total:** 20 minutes

1. In a food processor, combine flours, salt, sugar, and yeast.

2. In a small saucepan, combine water and oil; heat until very warm (between 120°F and 130°F).

3. With the food processor on, gradually add the warm water/oil mixture to flour mixture. Blend until the dough forms a ball, then process 1 minute more.

4. Transfer the dough to a floured surface and cover with plastic wrap. Allow to rest for 10 to 15 minutes before rolling. (You might also make the dough one day ahead and refrigerate. Bring to room temperature before using.)

Basic Pizza

1 lb. pizza dough

1 cup tomato sauce

½ cup grated Parmesan cheese

16 oz. grated mozzarella cheese (or cheddar, Fontina, or Gouda cheese)

Makes two 12-inch pizzas
Kids gravitate toward pizza, which actually contains foods from three food groups.
Prep Time: 10 minutes **Cook Time:** 25 minutes **Total:** 35 minutes

1. Heat oven to 400°F. Grease two 12-inch pizza pans.

2. Divide dough in half. Punch down each half to get rid of air bubbles.

3. Press dough into each pan, forming a ½-inch rim.

4. Bake crusts for 5 minutes or until golden brown.

5. Remove crusts from oven and top with sauce and cheese.

6. Return pans to oven and cook for additional 15 to 20 minutes.

Pizza

Chicken and Spinach Pizza

1 lb. pizza dough

2 cups cooked chicken, shredded

1 (10-oz.) pkg. frozen spinach, thawed and well drained

16 oz. grated mozzarella cheese (or cheddar, Fontina, or Gouda cheese)

½ cup grated Parmesan cheese

Makes two 12-inch pizzas
This alternative pizza packs flavor, along with fiber and protein.
Prep Time: 15 minutes **Cook Time:** 30 minutes **Total:** 45 minutes

1. Heat oven to 400°F. Grease two 12-inch pizza pans.

2. Divide dough in half. Punch down each half to get rid of air bubbles.

3. Press dough into each pan, forming a ½-inch rim.

4. Bake crusts for 5 minutes or until golden brown.

5. Remove crusts from oven and top with chicken, spinach, and cheeses, in that order.

6. Return pans to oven and cook for additional 15 to 20 minutes.

English Muffin Pizzas

1 whole-wheat English muffin, sliced

¼ cup marinara sauce

¼ cup grated cheese, such as mozzarella, cheddar, or Gouda

Makes 2 pizza halves
Whole-grain English muffins are usually enriched with vitamins and minerals.
Prep Time: 5 minutes **Cook Time:** 5 minutes **Total:** 10 minutes

1. Preheat oven broiler or toaster oven.

2. Top each half with equal amounts sauce and cheese.

3. Broil for 5 minutes or until cheese melts. Cool before serving to your child.

Pita Pizzas

1 small whole-wheat pita round, sliced around edges

¼ cup marinara sauce

¼ cup grated cheese, such as mozzarella, cheddar, or Gouda

Makes 2 pita pizzas
Add some cooked vegetables for even more fiber.
Prep Time: 5 minutes **Cook Time:** 5 minutes **Total:** 10 minutes

1. Preheat oven broiler or toaster oven.

2. Top each half with equal amounts sauce and cheese.

3. Broil for 5 minutes or until cheese melts. Cool well before serving to your child.

Tortilla Pizzas

4 (6-inch) flour tortillas

¼ cup mild salsa

1 cup shredded Monterey Jack or cheddar cheese

Makes 4 pizzas
Salsa is packed with lycopene, a beneficial plant compound.
Prep Time: 10 minutes **Cook Time:** 10 minutes **Total:** 20 minutes

1. Preheat oven to 350°F. Place tortillas on baking sheet.

2. Bake until crisp, about 5 minutes. Remove from oven, but leave tortillas on baking sheet.

3. Spread each tortilla with an equal amount of salsa and cover with an equal amount of cheese.

4. Bake until cheese melts, about 5 minutes.

Pizza

Vegetable Calzone

2 TB. olive oil, divided

16 oz. refrigerated or homemade pizza dough

½ cup grated cheddar cheese

2 cups cooked broccoli, chopped into ½-inch pieces

½ cup carrot, finely grated 1 cup ricotta cheese

Makes 1 turnover
This giant turnover is brimming with calcium from the cheeses and broccoli.
Prep Time: 10 minutes Cook Time: 30 minutes Total: 40 minutes

1. Preheat oven to 375°F. Grease baking sheet with 1 TB. oil.

2. On a floured surface, roll out pizza dough into a 24×12-inch oval.

3. Sprinkle cheddar cheese lengthwise on half of pizza dough to within a half inch of the edge.

4. Place broccoli over cheese. Sprinkle carrots over broccoli.

5. Spoon ricotta cheese on top of vegetables in dollops. Spread.

6. Fold dough in half over filling. Seal edge by pressing with tines of fork.

7. Transfer to baking sheets. Brush outside of calzone with remaining olive oil.

8. Bake for 25 to 30 minutes or until light golden brown. Allow to sit for 5 minutes before cutting.

Apple Chicken

1 lb. boneless, skinless chicken breast halves

½ tsp. ground cinnamon

½ tsp. salt

¼ cup all-purpose flour

¼ cup canola oil

½ cup apple juice

1 TB. cornstarch

½ cup apricot preserves

Makes 1 pound
Apple juice adds nutrition and makes the chicken moist.
Prep Time: 15 minutes Cook Time: 30 minutes Total: 45 minutes

1. Sprinkle chicken with cinnamon and salt. Coat with flour, one piece at a time.

2. In a large skillet, heat canola oil over medium heat. Add chicken and cook, turning frequently, for about 20 minutes or until light brown.

3. Transfer chicken to serving platter and keep warm.

4. Add apple juice to the skillet. Slowly whisk in cornstarch, mixing well. Stir in apricot preserves. Simmer until thickened, about 3 minutes.

5. To serve, pour sauce over chicken.

Chicken Roll-Ups

4 pieces boneless, skinless chicken breasts (about 1 lb.)

4 (1-oz.) slices Swiss cheese

2 cups baby spinach leaves, chopped

Makes 1 pound
Spinach and cheese add calcium to this dish.
Prep Time: 15 minutes Cook Time: 30–35 minutes Total: 45–60 minutes

1. Preheat oven to 350°F.

2. Place chicken breasts between two large pieces of plastic wrap.

3. Using a meat tenderizer, pound the chicken until it becomes uniformly thin (don't overdo it).

4. Arrange cheese then spinach on each piece of chicken. Roll up and secure with toothpicks.

5. Arrange in small baking dish and bake for 30 to 35 minutes.

Crunchy Chicken Nuggets

1 TB. canola or olive oil

½ cup all-purpose flour

¼ cup grated Parmesan cheese

1 cup cornflakes, crushed

¾ cup fat-free buttermilk

1 lb. boneless, skinless chicken breast, cut into small chunks or strips

Makes eight 2-ounce servings
Cornflakes add crunch and carbohydrates.
Prep Time: 15 minutes **Cook Time:** 10–15 minutes **Total:** 25–30 minutes

1. Preheat oven to 400°F. Grease baking sheet with oil.

2. Rinse chicken and pat dry with paper towels.

3. Measure flour and Parmesan cheese into a reseal-able 1-gallon plastic bag. Do the same for the crushed cornflakes in a separate 1-gallon plastic bag.

4. Pour buttermilk into a shallow bowl.

5. Add chicken pieces one at a time to the flour bag and shake until coated.

6. Dip each piece of chicken into buttermilk, covering thoroughly, and letting extra buttermilk drain off.

7. Place each piece of chicken chunk one at a time into the cornflake bag and shake to cover.

8. Place coated chicken pieces on a baking sheet. Cook for 5 minutes. Flip and cook for another 5 minutes, or until done.

Crunchy Turkey Cutlets

1 cup toasted wheat germ

¾ tsp. salt (optional)

2 eggs

4 skinless, boneless turkey cutlets or turkey breasts (about 1 lb.)

Cooking spray

Makes about four 4-ounce servings
Use eggs enriched with DHA to increase the amount of the important fat in your child's diet.
Prep Time: 15 minutes **Cook Time:** 20 minutes **Total:** 35 minutes

1. Preheat oven to 400°F. Spray baking sheet with cooking spray.

2. In a shallow dish, combine wheat germ and salt.

3. In another shallow dish, beat eggs until frothy.

4. Dip each piece of turkey into egg and then into wheat germ mixture. Dip and coat chicken again, coating thoroughly.

5. Arrange on a baking sheet. Lightly spray tops of turkey with cooking spray.

6. Bake about 20 minutes or until chicken is done.

Easy Almond Chicken

2 TB. olive oil

⅔ cup slivered almonds

1¼ cups onions, sliced

1 lb. boneless, skinless chicken breasts

1 (14.5-oz.) can low-sodium chicken broth

1½ tsp. ground cinnamon

½ cup dried apricots, diced

Makes 16 ounces
Apricots, packed with potassium, go well with chicken and work fruit into this entrée.
Prep Time: 10 minutes **Cook Time:** 20 minutes **Total:** 30 minutes

1. In a large nonstick skillet, heat oil over medium heat.

2. Add almonds, tossing to cook for about 3 to 5 minutes or until lightly browned.

3. Remove almonds from the pan with slotted spoon. Reserve.

4. Add onions to the skillet and cook over medium heat for 2 minutes.

5. Add chicken. Cook for 5 minutes, turning chicken once.

6. Add broth, cinnamon, and apricots. Cover and reduce heat to medium. Cook 5 minutes.

7. Remove cover, and simmer for 5 minutes or until fluid is reduced slightly. Serve over cooked couscous or rice.

Poultry

Honey* Dijon Chicken

1 lb. boneless, skinless chicken breasts or thighs

¼ cup Dijon mustard

¼ cup honey

2 tsp. canola oil

Makes 1 pound
Honey contains small amounts of vitamins and minerals.
Prep Time: 5 minutes   **Cook Time:** 35 minutes   **Total:** 40 minutes

1. Preheat oven to 350°F.
2. In a medium skillet, sear both sides of each piece of chicken.
3. Arrange chicken in baking dish lined with foil.
4. Bake chicken, covered with foil, for about 30 minutes.
5. Meanwhile, in a small bowl, mix mustard, honey, and canola oil.
6. Serve mustard and honey mixture over cooked chicken.

*Do not serve to children under the age of 1.

Lemon Caper Chicken

1 cup all-purpose flour

3 cloves garlic, peeled and minced

Juice of 2 lemons (about ⅓ cup)

¾ cup low-sodium chicken broth

3 TB. capers (optional)

Fresh ground black pepper to taste

Makes 1 pound
If you want, omit the garlic from this flavorful low-fat dish.
Prep Time: 5 minutes   **Cook Time:** 20 minutes   **Total:** 25 minutes

1. Coat each chicken breast in flour. Reserve.
2. Over medium heat, heat oil in a large skillet. Add garlic and cook for about 1 minute, stirring constantly.
3. Add chicken to the pan, browning on each side for about 2 to 3 minutes.
4. Add lemon juice, chicken broth, capers, and black pepper to the skillet.
5. Cover and cook for 10 minutes more, or until done. Serve with rice.

Roasted Rosemary Chicken

2 tsp. salt

4 cloves garlic, peeled and minced

2 TB. chopped rosemary

1 tsp. freshly ground black pepper

1 whole broiler-fryer chicken

2 TB. olive oil

Makes 1 chicken
Using a roasting rack allows chicken fat to drop off the meat, lowering its fat content.
Prep Time: 10 minutes **Cook Time:** About 2 hours, depending on chicken size **Total:** 2½ hours

1. Preheat oven to 400°F.

2. In a small bowl, mix salt, garlic, rosemary, and ground black pepper.

3. Place mixture in cavity of chicken.

4. Place chicken on a rack in roasting pan and roast for about 1 hour 45 minutes or until done.

Teriyaki Turkey Tenderloin

¼ cup low-sodium soy sauce

3 TB. dark brown sugar

1 tsp. ground ginger

½ tsp. garlic powder

1 lb. turkey tenderloin

Makes 1 pound
Turkey is low in total and saturated fat.
Prep Time: 10 minutes **Cook Time:** 30 minutes **Total:** 40 minutes

1. In a medium bowl, combine soy sauce, brown sugar, ginger, and garlic powder.

2. Add turkey to a bowl and marinate for 1 hour, covered, in the refrigerator.

3. Preheat oven to 350°F.

4. Transfer turkey to shallow baking dish.

5. Bake, uncovered, for 30 minutes or until turkey is done.

Turkey Loaf

2 lb. 100 percent ground turkey breast

1 (10-oz.) pkg. chopped spinach, thawed and well drained

8 oz. mozzarella cheese

½ cup whole-wheat bread crumbs

1 egg

¼ cup Italian salad dressing

Makes 2 loaves
Be sure to buy 100 percent ground turkey meat to insure the least total and saturated fat.
Prep Time: 20 minutes **Cook Time:** 50 minutes **Total:** 70 minutes

1. Preheat oven to 350°F.

2. In a medium bowl, combine turkey, spinach, cheese, bread crumbs, egg, and salad dressing. Mix well.

3. Shape into 2 equal size loaves on rack in broiler pan.

4. Bake meatloaf 40 to 50 minutes to medium doneness.

5. When done, let stand for 10 minutes before cutting.

Turkey in a Pouch

½ cup carrots, diced

½ lb. turkey tenderloin

½ cup onions, diced

2 slices sweet red pepper

½ tsp. dried rosemary, crushed

½ tsp. salt

Fresh ground black pepper to taste

Makes 8 ounces
Turkey is a lean source of protein.
Prep Time: 15 minutes **Cook Time:** 20–25 minutes **Total:** 35–40 minutes

1. Lay carrots on a 12×16-inch foil rectangle. Top with turkey. Arrange onions and pepper slices over tenderloin. Sprinkle with rosemary, salt, and pepper.

2. Fold edges of foil up to form a bowl shape. Bring two opposite foil sides together above food; fold edges over and down to lock fold. Fold short ends up and over.

3. Place turkey foil bundle on a baking sheet.

4. Bake for 20 to 25 minutes or until turkey reaches 170°F.

Walnut Chicken

1 lb. boneless, skinless chicken breasts, cut into several pieces

1 cup all-purpose flour

1 cup buttermilk

1 cup walnuts, finely chopped

Makes 1 pound
Walnuts add crunch, vitamins, and minerals.
Prep Time: 10 minutes **Cook Time:** 30 minutes **Total:** 40 minutes

1. Preheat oven to 350°F.

2. Place flour on a plate; buttermilk in a shallow dish; and walnuts on a separate plate.

3. Dip each piece of chicken in flour first, then buttermilk, then nuts.

4. Place in baking dish and bake until done, about 30 minutes.

Yogurt Baked Chicken

2 cups plain yogurt

½ tsp. dried basil

½ tsp. dried parsley

1 lb. boneless, skinless chicken thighs

2 cups cornflakes, crushed

Makes 1 pound
Dark chicken meat has slightly more flavor, fat, and iron than light meat.
Prep Time: 15 minutes **Cook Time:** 30 minutes **Total:** 45 minutes

1. Preheat oven to 350°F.

2. In a shallow bowl, mix yogurt with basil and parsley.

3. Coat each piece of chicken with yogurt. With fork, scrape excess yogurt from chicken, then coat with cornflakes.

4. Place coated chicken breasts in baking dish. Bake for about 30 minutes or until chicken is brown.

Sandwiches

Almond Butter and Apple Sandwich

2 slices whole-grain bread

2 TB. almond butter

½ apple, peeled and shredded or diced fine

Makes 1 sandwich
Apples add fiber to this wholesome sandwich.
Prep Time: 5 minutes Cook Time: 0 Total: 5 minutes

1. Spread almond butter on one piece of bread.
2. Top with apple and other slice of bread.

 Mother's Helper

Look for almond butter in the peanut butter section of your supermarket.

Cheese and Pear Quesadilla

2 (8-inch) flour tortillas

½ cup shredded Monterey Jack cheese

½ large ripe Bartlett pear, peeled and thinly sliced

Makes one 8-inch quesadilla
Pears provide vitamin C.
Prep Time: 5 minutes Cook Time: 5 minutes Total: 10 minutes

1. Sprinkle cheese on top of one of the tortillas.
2. Place pear slices on top of cheese.
3. Top with the other tortilla.
4. In a medium skillet, melt margarine over medium-high heat. Cook quesadilla, gently pressing down with spatula for 3 to 5 minutes or until golden brown.
5. Remove from pan and let sit for 5 minutes. Cut quesadilla into 8 wedges.

Chicken and Cheese Quesadilla

2 oz. chicken, cooked, shredded

¼ cup shredded cheddar cheese

2 (8-inch) flour tortillas

2 tsp. margarine

Makes one 8-inch quesadilla
A high-protein finger food that's great for meals or snacks.
Prep Time: 5 minutes **Cook Time:** 5 minutes **Total:** 10 minutes

1. Spread chicken on top of one of the tortillas.

2. Sprinkle cheese on top of chicken.

3. Top with the other tortilla.

4. In a medium skillet, melt margarine over medium-high heat. Cook quesadilla, gently pressing down with spatula for 3 to 5 minutes or until golden brown.

5. Remove from pan and let sit for 5 minutes. Cut quesadilla into 8 wedges.

Mini Guacamole Sandwich

2 slices cocktail or snack bread

2 TB. prepared guacamole

Makes 1 sandwich
Avocados are a good source of fiber.
Prep Time: 1 minute **Cook Time:** 0 **Total:** 1 minute

1. Spread guacamole on 1 slice cocktail bread.

2. Top with second slice and serve.

Open-Faced Pineapple Ricotta Sandwich

1 slice whole-grain bread

¼ cup ricotta cheese

¼ cup crushed pineapple, drained

Makes 1 sandwich
Creamy ricotta cheese contains calcium.
Prep Time: 2 minutes **Cook Time:** 3 minutes **Total:** 5 minutes

1. Toast bread.

2. Meanwhile, in a small bowl, mix ricotta cheese and pineapple.

3. Spread on toast and serve.

Sandwiches

Pinwheel Sandwiches

1 slice whole-grain bread **Sandwich filling**

1. Cut the crust from bread.
2. Using a rolling pin, gently flatten bread with fingers and palm of hand.
3. Spread with egg salad, tuna salad, or peanut butter.
4. Roll up and slice into 4 pieces.

Makes 4 pinwheels
Little mitts can handle this fun shape, so they may be more likely to eat this protein-filled sandwich.
Prep Time: 5 minutes **Cook Time:** 0
Total: 5 minutes

Peanut Butter Pancake Sandwich

2 small frozen pancakes or 2 small homemade pancakes

2 TB. peanut butter

½ apple, peeled, cored, and finely diced or shredded

1. Heat frozen pancake, if necessary, to thaw.
2. Spread one pancake with peanut butter and top with apple. Form into sandwich.

Makes 1 sandwich
Peanut butter packs beneficial phytonutrients.
Prep Time: 5 minutes **Cook Time:** 0
Total: 5 minutes

Peanut Butter and Banana Sandwich

2 slices whole-grain bread

2 TB. peanut butter

½ banana, peeled and cut lengthwise

1. Spread peanut butter on one piece of bread.
2. Top with banana and other slice of bread.

Makes 1 sandwich
Bananas are high in vitamin B6.
Prep Time: 5 minutes **Cook Time:** 0
Total: 5 minutes

Asparagus Strata

8 slices whole-grain bread, toasted

¼ lb. asparagus spears, cooked until crisp-tender

½ cup shredded reduced-fat cheddar cheese

2 TB. grated Parmesan cheese

2 cups milk

4 eggs

1 tsp. dried oregano

Makes 9 servings
Asparagus is rich in folate, a B vitamin.
Prep Time: 15 minutes **Cook Time:** 45 minutes **Total:** 90 minutes (due to refrigerator time)

1. Preheat oven to 350°F. Spray a 9-inch square baking dish with nonstick cooking spray.

2. Arrange 4 of the bread slices in the dish in a single layer. Scatter the asparagus over the bread.

3. Sprinkle the cheddar and Parmesan cheeses over the asparagus and top with remaining bread slices.

4. In a large bowl combine milk, eggs, and oregano.

5. Pour the egg mixture over the bread, cover, and refrigerate to allow the bread to absorb the egg mixture for 30 minutes.

6. Uncover the strata, and bake for 45 minutes or until the top is golden brown and the tip of a knife inserted into the center comes out clean.

Baked Acorn Squash

1 acorn squash

2 tsp. butter or margarine

4 tsp. brown sugar

Pinch cinnamon

Makes 1 squash
Acorn squash is naturally low in sodium and rich in potassium.
Prep Time: 10 minutes **Cook Time:** 30–40 minutes **Total:** 40–50 minutes

1. Heat oven to 400°F.

2. Cut squash lengthwise and scoop out seeds.

3. Place squash in a medium baking dish or pan.

4. In each squash cavity, place equal amounts of butter, brown sugar, and cinnamon.

5. Bake for 30 to 40 minutes or until squash is tender.

Vegetables

Baked Orange Sweet Potato

1 medium sweet potato, scrubbed well

2 TB. orange juice

Pinch cinnamon

Makes 1 potato
Sweet potatoes are a good source of vitamin B6. No butter or margarine is needed for this tasty fat-free side dish.
Prep Time: 5 minutes **Cook Time:** 45 minutes **Total:** 50 minutes

1. Preheat oven to 400°F.

2. Place sweet potato on the middle rack and bake for 45 minutes or until tender.

3. Remove from oven and slit lengthwise to cool. Scoop out inside of potato into a small bowl and mix with orange juice and cinnamon.

Baked Potatoes

4 medium Yukon Gold potatoes

Makes 4 potatoes
Potatoes in their natural state are very low in sodium.
Prep Time: 5 minutes **Cook Time:** 40 minutes **Total:** 45 minutes

1. Preheat oven to 400°F.

2. Wash potatoes thoroughly.

3. Spread in a single layer on a baking sheet.

4. Bake for 40 minutes or until tender.

5. Serve with sour cream or Herbed Yogurt Dip.

Cheese-y Potato Wedges

4 medium potatoes

1 TB. olive oil

2 TB. grated Parmesan cheese

¼ tsp. fresh ground black pepper

Makes 24 wedges
Much lower in fat than French fries.
Prep Time: 10 minutes **Cook Time:** 30 minutes **Total:** 40 minutes

1. Preheat oven to 400°F. Coat a baking sheet with cooking spray.

2. Wash potatoes well. Cut each potato into 6 wedges.

3. In a large bowl, place olive oil, Parmesan cheese, and black pepper. Mix well.

4. Add potatoes and coat well.

5. Arrange wedges on a baking sheet. Bake for 30 minutes or until potatoes are tender.

Cream of Broccoli Soup

6 cups broccoli flowerets or 2 (10-oz.) pkg. frozen broccoli

1 cup low-sodium chicken broth

2 TB. margarine

2 TB. all-purpose flour

½ tsp. dried thyme

½ tsp. salt

2 cups milk

Makes 8 cups
Broccoli is a surprising source of beta-carotene and vitamin C.
Prep Time: 10 minutes Cook Time: 10 minutes Total: 20 minutes

1. Cook broccoli until crisp-tender.

2. In a blender or food processor, combine broccoli and chicken broth. Cover and blend until smooth, about a minute or so.

3. Melt margarine in a medium saucepan. Stir in flour, thyme, and salt.

4. Add milk and stir. Cook and stir until slightly thickened and bubbly.

5. Cook 1 minute more and stir in broccoli mixture. Cook until heated through, stirring constantly.

Creamed Spinach

1 tsp. olive oil

1 large sweet onion, sliced

1 (10-oz.) box frozen spinach, defrosted and well-drained

¼ tsp. ground nutmeg

1 cup low-sodium chicken broth

3 TB. cream cheese

2 TB. lemon juice

1 tsp. salt

½ tsp. fresh ground black pepper

Makes 2 cups
A little added fat goes a long way to getting children to eat their spinach.
Prep Time: 5 minutes Cook Time: 5 minutes Total: 10 minutes

1. In a medium skillet, heat oil over medium-high heat. Add onions and sauté until translucent, about 2 minutes.

2. Add spinach and nutmeg. Cook for 1 minute.

3. Add chicken broth and bring to simmer for 1 minute.

4. Pour entire mixture into a blender or food processor. Add cream cheese, lemon juice, salt, and pepper.

5. Pulse until creamy. Serve warm.

Creamy Tomato Basil Soup

2 TB. olive oil

1 medium onion, chopped

2 cloves garlic, crushed

1 (16-oz.) can chopped tomatoes, drained

1 TB. chopped fresh basil or 1 tsp. dried basil

1⅔ cups milk

Salt and fresh ground black pepper to taste

Makes 4 cups
Tomatoes pack lycopene that helps prevent cell damage.
Prep Time: 15 minutes Cook Time: 15 minutes Total: 30 minutes

1. In a medium saucepan, heat oil. Add onion, sautéeing until tender. Add garlic and cook about 1 minute longer.

2. Add tomatoes and stir. Simmer, uncovered, over medium heat for about 10 minutes. Remove from heat.

3. Spoon half the soup mixture into a blender or food processor and purée until smooth. Return puréed mixture to saucepan.

4. Add basil and milk. Heat until hot, but not boiling. Serve lukewarm.

Easy Eggplant Parmesan

1 medium eggplant (about 1 lb.)

1 egg, beaten

¼ cup all-purpose flour

¼ cup grated Parmesan cheese

1 cup shredded mozzarella cheese

1 cup spaghetti sauce (or Laura's Fresh Tomato Sauce in Chapter 16)

Makes 4 servings
Baking the eggplant instead of frying reduces fat content.
Prep Time: 15 minute Cook Time: 25 minutes Total: 40 minutes

1. Preheat oven to 400°F. Grease a baking sheet.

2. Peel eggplant and cut crosswise into ½-inch slices.

3. Dip eggplant into egg, then into flour, turning to coat.

4. Place slices on baking sheet and bake for 12 to 15 minutes or until soft but not mushy.

5. Assemble by placing eggplant slices in a 12×7½×2-inch baking dish. Sprinkle with cheese. Top with sauce.

6. Return to oven and bake for 10 minutes or until hot.

Green Beans with Almonds

1 (9-oz.) pkg. frozen cut green beans

1 TB. butter

3 TB. slivered almonds, chopped well

1 tsp. lemon juice

Makes 1½ cups
Children love the mild taste of low-sodium green beans.
Prep Time: 5 minutes **Cook Time:** 10 minutes **Total:** 15 minutes

1. Prepare green beans according to package directions.

2. Meanwhile, in a medium saucepan over medium heat, melt butter. Add almonds and cook for 1 to 2 minutes.

3. Remove from heat and add lemon juice. Stir.

4. Add cooked beans to saucepan and stir well to coat.

Glazed Carrots

¼ lb. medium carrots, peeled and diced

1 TB. margarine or butter

1 TB. brown sugar

Pinch salt

Makes about 2 cups
Carrots contain beta-carotene.
Prep Time: 10 minutes **Cook Time:** 5 minutes **Total:** 15 minutes

1. Steam or microwave carrots until tender, but not mushy.

2. In a medium saucepan, combine margarine, brown sugar, and salt over medium heat until combined. Add carrots and toss.

3. Cook for 2 minutes longer.

Guacamole

2 TB. yogurt

2 ripe avocados, pitted and mashed

2 TB. mild salsa

1 tsp. lemon juice

Salt and pepper to taste

Makes about 2½ cups
Creamy avocados are loaded with potassium and kids love their mild taste.
Prep Time: 10 minutes Cook Time: 0 Total: 10 minutes

1. In a medium bowl, mix yogurt, avocado, salsa, and lemon juice. Season with salt and pepper, if desired.

2. Keep refrigerated until ready to use.

High-Calcium Mashed Potatoes

1 lb. potatoes (about 3 medium), diced

2 TB. sour cream

¼ cup evaporated milk

Salt and fresh ground pepper to taste

Makes about 4 cups
Evaporated milk has twice the calcium of regular; sour cream adds calcium, too.
Prep Time: 10 minutes Cook Time: 15–20 minutes Total: 25–30 minutes

1. Wash, peel, and dice potatoes.

2. In a medium saucepan, cook covered potatoes for about 15 to 20 minutes or until tender.

3. Drain well and return to pan.

4. Add sour cream, evaporated milk, salt, and pepper to pan. Beat with an electric mixer on low speed until light and fluffy.

Mock Mashed Potatoes

½ head chopped cauliflower (about 2 cups)

1 TB. butter or margarine

¼ cup grated Parmesan cheese

½ cup milk

¼ cup chopped fresh parsley

Makes about 2½ cups
Cauliflower contains powerful phytonutrients that fight disease.
Prep Time: 10 minutes Cook Time: 10 minutes Total: 20 minutes

1. Steam cauliflower until very tender.

2. Place cooked cauliflower, butter, Parmesan cheese, and milk in a food processor. Pulse until mixture reaches desired consistency.

3. Transfer to a serving bowl. Stir in parsley.

Roasted Maple Pumpkin

1 small pumpkin (about 2½ lb.)

2 TB. maple syrup

1 TB. butter or margarine

Makes 8 wedges
Pumpkins, rich in beta-carotene, are for more than carving.
Prep Time: 10 minutes **Cook Time:** 40 minutes **Total:** 50 minutes

1. Preheat oven to 400°F. Coat medium glass baking dish with cooking spray.

2. Cut pumpkin in half vertically. Discard seeds and membranes and cut into 8 wedges.

3. Place wedges in a baking dish. Drizzle maple syrup and butter over wedges.

4. Bake for 20 minutes. Turn wedges and bake for 20 more.

Potato Zucchini Pancakes

2 medium potatoes, peeled and rinsed

1 medium zucchini, peeled and rinsed

1 small onion, peeled

1 egg

¼ cup grated cheddar cheese

⅓ cup all-purpose flour

1 tsp. salt

½ cup canola oil, divided

Makes 8 pancakes
Canola oil is a source of healthy fat.
Prep Time: 20 minutes **Cook Time:** 20 minutes **Total:** 40 minutes

1. In a large bowl, combine grated potatoes, zucchini, and onion.

2. Place mixture in a colander. Place 2 paper towels over mixture and press down to drain as much moisture as possible.

3. Return vegetable mixture to a large bowl. Add egg, cheese, flour, and salt. Mix well.

4. In a medium skillet over medium heat, heat half the canola oil.

5. Using a ¼-cup measure, drop mixture into 4 mounds at a time. Using a spatula, flatten mounds to make 4-inch pancakes.

6. Cook for 5 minutes on each side.

7. Remove from pan and drain on a plate or baking sheet lined with paper towels. Repeat to make the other 4 pancakes.

Roasted Cream of Butternut Squash Soup

2 medium butternut squash

6 TB. butter, margarine, or cooking oil

2 small onions, chopped

1 tsp. ground ginger

½ cup low-sodium chicken broth

3 cups milk

Makes 6 cups
Kids won't have a clue this soup contains vegetables that are good for them.
Prep Time: 10 minutes
Cook Time: 60 minutes
Total: 70 minutes

1. Preheat oven to 400°F.

2. Cut squash lengthwise and scoop out seeds. Spray a baking sheet with vegetable cooking spray, and place squash on it, cut side down.

3. Roast until soft (about 45 minutes).

4. Meanwhile, melt margarine over medium heat in a medium saucepan. Add onions and cook until clear; add ginger and chicken broth.

5. When squash is done and cool enough to handle, scoop squash from skin and add to saucepan. Stir thoroughly.

6. Transfer saucepan mixture to a blender or food processor and purée.

7. Return to saucepan and add milk. Warm gently. Serve immediately.

Sautéed Spinach and Golden Raisins

10 oz. fresh spinach

1 TB. olive oil

2 TB. golden raisins, chopped well

2 cloves garlic, peeled and minced (optional)

½ tsp. salt

Makes about 2 cups
Filled with fiber and flavor.
Prep Time: 10 minutes
Cook Time: 5 minutes
Total: 15 minutes

1. Remove tough stems from spinach and wash and drain well.

2. In a large skillet, heat olive oil over medium-high heat.

3. Add raisins and garlic and sauté for about 30 seconds, being careful not to burn garlic.

4. Add spinach and cook until wilted, about 3 minutes. Stir in salt.

Scalloped Potatoes

½ cup onion, chopped

2 TB. margarine

½ tsp. salt

Fresh ground black pepper to taste

2 TB. flour

1½ cups milk

3 medium potatoes, peeled and thinly sliced

Makes 6 cups
Potatoes provide vitamins C and B6, and potassium.
Prep Time: 15 minutes Cook Time: 35 minutes Total: 50 minutes

1. Preheat oven to 350°F. Grease a 1-quart casserole dish.

2. In a medium saucepan, sauté onion in margarine until translucent. Stir in salt and fresh ground black pepper.

3. Add flour and milk. Cook until thick and bubbly, stirring constantly. Remove from heat.

4. Put half the sliced potatoes in the prepared casserole dish, and cover with half the sauce. Repeat.

5. Cover with aluminum foil and bake for 35 minutes. Remove foil and bake 30 minutes more. Let stand for 10 minutes before serving.

Sweet Potatoes 'N' Apples

2 TB. butter or margarine

1 large apple, peeled, cored, and sliced

4 cups cooked and cooled, peeled sweet potatoes, sliced (about 2 lb.)

¼ cup apple juice

2 TB. brown sugar

⅛ tsp. ground cinnamon

Makes about 5 cups
Apples and apple juice add vitamin C to this delicious dish.
Prep Time: 15 minutes Cook Time: 10 minutes Total: 25 minutes

1. In a large saucepan, melt butter and sauté apples until very tender.

2. Add sweet potato to the pan and mash until smooth. Stir in apple juice, brown sugar, and cinnamon.

Sweet Potato Oven Fries

1½ lb. scrubbed sweet potatoes

1 TB. olive oil

1 tsp. salt

Makes about 1½ pounds
Far lower in fat and sugar than the candied version.
Prep Time: 10 minutes
Cook Time: 30 to 35 minutes
Total: 40 to 45 minutes

1. Heat oven to 400°F. Coat a baking sheet with cooking spray.

2. Cut each potato lengthwise into 8 wedges.

3. In a large bowl, combine oil and salt. Add sweet potatoes and toss to coat.

4. Arrange sweet potatoes on a prepared baking sheet and roast for 20 minutes. Open oven, and toss with spatula.

5. Bake another 10 to 15 minutes or until golden brown.

Spaghetti Squash and Diced Tomatoes

1 medium spaghetti squash

1 (14½-oz.) can seasoned diced tomatoes

Salt and fresh ground pepper, if desired

Makes 4 to 6 cups
A colorful way to serve up vegetables, and a good source of fluid.
Prep Time: 5 minutes
Cook Time: 50 minutes
Total: 55 minutes

1. Heat oven to 400°F.

2. Slice squash lengthwise. Spray a baking sheet with vegetable cooking spray and place squash on it, cut side down.

3. Roast until soft, about 40 minutes. When done remove from oven and flip over so cut side is up. Allow to cool for 5 minutes.

4. Place diced tomatoes in medium skillet and warm.

5. With a fork, remove squash from skin, discarding seeds. Squash will be string-like. Transfer to a skillet.

6. Toss squash with diced tomatoes. Season as desired. Chop spaghetti squash before serving to little ones.

Winter Squash Casserole

3 eggs

⅓ cup firmly packed
brown sugar

¼ tsp. ground cinnamon

¼ tsp. ground nutmeg

¼ tsp. ground ginger

½ tsp. salt, optional

1 (10-oz.) pkg. frozen
winter squash, thawed

1 (16-oz.) can solid
packed pumpkin

Makes 6 servings
Winter squash is a good source of fiber.
Prep Time: 10 minutes **Cook Time:** 35 minutes **Total:** 45 minutes

1. Preheat oven to 350°F. Grease a round 2-quart baking dish.

2. In a large bowl, beat together eggs, sugar, cinnamon, nutmeg, ginger, and salt (if desired), until blended.

3. Stir in squash and pumpkin.

4. Pour into a baking dish.

5. Bake for 30 to 35 minutes.

Sweet Endings and Snacks

Apple Tapioca Pudding

¼ cup sugar

3 TB. tapioca

2 cups apple juice

1 cup apple, peeled, cored, and finely diced

Makes 4 cups
A high-energy snack.
Prep Time: 10 minutes
Cook Time: 5 minutes
Total: 15 minutes

1. In a medium saucepan, mix sugar, tapioca, and apple juice. Let stand for 5 minutes.

2. Over medium heat, cook mixture, stirring constantly, until it comes to a full boil. Remove from heat.

3. Stir in apple. Cool for 20 minutes.

Baked Custard

4 eggs

½ cup sugar

1½ tsp. pure vanilla extract (or almond extract)

3 cups milk, heated until very hot, but not boiling

Ground cinnamon or nutmeg, if desired

Makes 6 servings
A sweet way to work protein into your child's diet.
Prep Time: 10 minutes
Cook Time: 25–30 minutes
Total: 35–40 minutes

1. Preheat oven to 350°F.

2. In a medium bowl, beat together eggs, sugar, vanilla, and salt until well blended. Stir in milk.

3. Place 6 lightly greased 6-ounce custard cups or 1 lightly greased 1½-quart casserole in a large baking pan.

4. Pour egg mixture into cups or a casserole dish. Sprinkle with ground nutmeg or cinnamon.

5. Place pan on rack in oven. Pour very hot water into pan to within ½ inch of top of cups or 1 inch of top of casserole.

6. Bake custard until knife inserted near center comes out clean, about 25 to 30 minutes for cups or about 35 to 40 minutes for casserole.

7. Promptly remove custard cups or casserole dish from hot water and transfer to wire rack. Allow to cool 10 minutes.

Cheese Tarts

1 cup cottage cheese

½ cup sour cream

¼ cup sugar

1 tsp. vanilla extract

¼ tsp. ground cinnamon

24 mini-muffin sized phyllo-dough shells

Makes 24 tarts
Bite-size treats that supply calcium.
Prep Time: 10 minutes Cook Time: 0 Total: 10 minutes

1. In a blender or food processor, blend cottage cheese until smooth.

2. Add sour cream, sugar, vanilla, and cinnamon, and blend until just mixed. Transfer to a medium mixing bowl.

3. Spoon about a tablespoon of filling into each phyllo-dough shell.

Chocolate Dipped Strawberries

4 oz. semisweet chocolate

1 pint strawberries

Makes 1 pint
A vitamin C and fiber-rich alternative to candy.
Prep Time: 10 minutes Cook Time: 5 minutes Total: 15 minutes

1. Rinse strawberries well, but do not remove steps. Blot dry with a paper towel. Reserve.

2. Melt chocolate in the top pan of a double boiler, stirring constantly.

3. When chocolate has melted, remove top portion of the double boiler.

4. Holding one strawberry at a time, dip into chocolate, coating completely except for stem area.

Chocolate Tapioca Pudding

½ cup sugar

3 TB. quick-cooking tapioca

3 cups milk

1 egg, beaten well

3 oz. semisweet baking chocolate

1 tsp. vanilla

Makes 3 cups
Protein-packed and chocolate, too!
Prep Time: 10 minutes **Cook Time:** 5 minutes **Total:** 15 minutes

1. In a medium saucepan, mix sugar, tapioca, milk, egg, and chocolate. Let stand 5 minutes.

2. Cook mixture over medium-high heat, stirring constantly, until mixture comes to a boil.

3. Remove from heat. Stir in vanilla. Cool 20 minutes in the refrigerator.

Cinnamon Toast

1 slice whole-grain bread

1 tsp. sugar

½ tsp. ground cinnamon

1 tsp. butter or margarine

Makes 1 slice
A sweet treat with fiber.
Prep Time: 1 minute **Cook Time:** 2 minutes **Total:** 3 minutes

1. Toast bread.

2. Meanwhile, in a small bowl, mix sugar and cinnamon.

3. Spread butter on bread and top with cinnamon/sugar mixture.

Cottage Cheese and Raisin Toast

1 slice whole-grain bread   **1 tsp. chopped raisins**

¼ cup cottage cheese

1. Toast bread.
2. In a small bowl, combine cottage cheese and raisins. Mix well.
3. Spread cottage cheese mixture on toast.

Makes 1 slice
Raisins are a choking hazard whole, so chop this carbohydrate-rich fruit well.
Prep Time: 1 minute   **Cook Time:** 1 minute   **Total:** 2 minutes

Creme Puffs

½ cup butter or margarine   **1 cup all-purpose flour**

1 cup water   **4 eggs**

¼ tsp. salt

1. Preheat oven to 375°F. Grease 2 baking sheets.
2. In a medium saucepan over medium heat, bring butter, water, and salt to a boil. Remove from heat.
3. Add flour to a pan. Stir vigorously until mixture forms a ball that pulls away from the side of the pan.
4. Add eggs to the pan, one at a time. Beat well after each egg, until smooth.
5. Drop batter onto baking sheets in 12 large mounds, about 3 inches apart.
6. Bake 50 minutes. Remove from the oven and transfer to wire rack to cool.
7. Eat as is, or slice top off of each and fill.

Makes 12
Don't reserve these protein-packed puffs for dessert. Kids can eat them plain, or with their favorite sandwich filling.
Prep Time: 0   **Cook Time:** 60 minutes (10 minutes in saucepan; 50 minutes in oven)   **Total:** 60 minutes

Fruity Brown Rice Pudding

Cooking spray

½ cup cooked brown rice

½ cup mixed diced golden raisins and dried cranberries

2 eggs

3 TB. brown sugar

1 tsp. vanilla extract

1 cup 1 percent low-fat milk

Makes 6 servings
This high-fiber dessert is a great way to use up leftover brown rice.
Prep Time: 10 minutes **Cook Time:** 35–45 minutes **Total:** 45–55 minutes

1. Preheat oven to 350°F.

2. Spray 4 (6-oz.) custard cups with cooking spray. Place custard cups in a large baking pan, leaving about an inch between cups.

3. Place 2 TB. of the rice and 2 TB. of the fruit into each cup.

4. In a medium bowl, beat together eggs, sugar, and vanilla. Blend well.

5. Stir in milk. Pour over rice and fruit in cups.

6. Pour very hot water into a baking pan to within a half inch of top of custard cups.

7. Bake about 35 to 45 minutes, or until a knife inserted near the center comes out clean.

8. When done, remove custard cups immediately from the roasting pan. Cool on a wire rack for 5 to 10 minutes.

Fruit Slurry

3 cups frozen fruit (such as strawberries, blueberries, raspberries, or melon)

1 tsp. vanilla extract

1 cup plain yogurt

2 TB. sugar

Makes 4 cups
Use any berry to include beneficial phytonutrients.
Prep Time: 10 minutes **Cook Time:** 0 **Total:** 10 minutes

1. Blend frozen fruit, vanilla extract, yogurt, and sugar in a food processor or blender until smooth.

2. Serve immediately.

Graham Cracker Sandwich Treats

1 ripe medium banana

⅓ cup peanut butter, almond butter, or soy nut butter

10 whole-wheat graham cracker squares

Makes 5 sandwiches
These treats are rich in healthy fats, vitamins, and minerals.
Prep Time: 10 minutes **Cook Time:** 0 **Total:** 2 hours (due to freezing time)

1. In a small bowl, mash banana and peanut butter.

2. Place a heaping tablespoon of the mixture on a graham cracker square. Cover with another square to make a sandwich.

3. Wrap each sandwich in plastic wrap and freeze for two hours.

Laura's Sweet Potato Custard

4 medium sweet potatoes, cooked

2 TB. melted butter or margarine

4 large eggs

1½ cups milk

3 TB. light brown sugar

½ tsp. salt, if desired

Pinch nutmeg

Makes 8 servings
A delicious way to have vegetables for dessert.
Prep Time: 10 minutes **Cook Time:** 60 minutes **Total:** 70 minutes

1. Preheat oven to 325°F. Place rack in center of oven.

2. Scoop sweet potatoes out of their skins and place in a medium mixing bowl.

3. Add melted butter, then add eggs one at a time, beating with an electric mixer after each addition.

4. Add milk, brown sugar, and nutmeg and beat until smooth.

5. Pour mixture into 8-inch square glass baking dish. Place baking dish in roasting pan. Fill with water to halfway up sides of baking dish. Place roasting pan with baking dish in oven. Bake until custard is set, about one hour.

Melon Slush

1 cantaloupe   ½ cup sugar

1 honeydew melon   3 TB. lemon juice

Makes 5 cups
The melons offer potassium and vitamin C as well as carbohydrates.
Prep Time: 10 minutes **Cook Time:** 0 **Total:** 3 hours (for freezing)

1. Wash outside of cantaloupe and honeydew melon with mild soap and dry.

2. Cut melons in half and remove seeds. Cut into thick chunks. Discard rind.

3. In a food processor, blend sugar and lemon juice. Gradually add melon chunks and process until smooth.

4. Pour mixture into a large shallow baking dish. Freeze for 2 hours.

5. Remove pan from freezer and place in a mixing bowl. Beat, on high speed, until fluffy. Return to the shallow baking dish and freeze until firm, about an hour.

No-Cook Orange Nut Butter Balls

½ cup peanut butter, almond butter, or soy nut butter

½ cup honey*

¼ cup orange juice concentrate

1½ cups nonfat dry milk

2 cups oatmeal, uncooked

Makes about 24 small balls
Make these with almond butter to get more vitamin E.
Prep Time: 20 minutes **Cook Time:** 0 **Total:** 20 minutes

1. In a large bowl, combine peanut butter, honey, orange juice, milk, and oatmeal thoroughly.

2. Shape into small balls.

*Do not serve to children under age 1.

Orange Blueberry Slush

4 cups fresh or thawed frozen blueberries

1 (6-oz.) can frozen orange juice concentrate

Makes 3 cups
A fun way to get vitamin C and fiber.
Prep Time: 5 minutes **Cook Time:** 0 **Total:** 2–4 hours (due to freezing time)

1. In a food processor or blender, combine blueberries and orange juice concentrate and blend until mixture is liquid.

2. Pour into an 11×17-inch baking pan. Cover and freeze for about 2 hours or until firm.

3. Using a heavy spoon, break mixture into pieces. Place pieces in a food processor or blender and blend until smooth but not completely melted.

4. Spoon into a 9×5-inch loaf pan. Cover with plastic wrap and freeze until firm, then serve.

Peach Berry Yogurt Tarts

1½ cups peach yogurt

1½ cups ricotta cheese

6 prepared graham cracker tart shells

¼ cup diced strawberries

Makes 6 tarts
A calcium-packed sweet treat little ones will love.
Prep Time: 10 minutes **Cook Time:** 0 **Total:** 10 minutes

1. In a medium bowl, mix yogurt and ricotta cheese with a whisk until creamy.

2. Spoon ⅙ mixture into each tart shell and top with strawberries.

Pineapple Cottage Cheese

¼ cup cottage cheese

¼ cup crushed pineapple

Makes ½ cup
Pineapple is rich in vitamin C, and is naturally sweet.
Prep Time: 2 minutes **Cook Time:** 0 **Total:** 2 minutes

1. In a small bowl, combine cottage cheese and pineapple.

Pineapple Raspberry Yogurt Parfait

1 (20-oz.) can crushed pineapple in its juice (drain and reserve juice to drink)

8 oz. plain or vanilla yogurt

1½ cups fresh or thawed frozen raspberries

½ cup whole-grain flake cereal

Makes 4 parfaits
Whole-grain cereal adds fiber, vitamins, and minerals.
Prep Time: 10 minutes Cook Time: 0 Total: 10 minutes

1. In a small bowl, combine pineapple with half the yogurt.

2. In small dessert bowls or juice glasses, layer yogurt mixture with berries and granola. Repeat.

Raisin Bread Pudding

2 cups milk

1 cup sugar

2 eggs

1 tsp. ground nutmeg

1 tsp. pure vanilla extract

8 slices raisin bread, cut into 1-inch cubes

Makes 8 medium servings
Sweet, but high in calcium and protein, too.
Prep Time: 10 minutes Cook Time: 40–45 minutes Total: 50–55 minutes

1. Preheat oven to 350°F. Spray a 2-quart baking dish with cooking spray.

2. In a large bowl, combine milk, sugar, eggs, nutmeg, and vanilla. Blend until smooth.

3. Fold in bread cubes.

4. Pour into prepared dish. Bake for 40 to 45 minutes, or until knife inserted in middle comes out clean. Remove from oven and allow to cool on a wire rack before serving.

Pineapple Orange Freeze

4 oz. calcium-added orange juice

2 TB. pineapple chunks, drained

2 TB. vanilla frozen yogurt

Makes about ¾ cup
Fortified orange juice supplies as much calcium as milk.
Prep Time: 5 minutes **Cook Time:** 0 **Total:** 5 minutes

1. Combine orange juice, pineapple, and yogurt in a blender or food processor.
2. Whip on high speed for 2 to 3 minutes, or until frothy. Serve immediately.

Yogurt Cereal Treat

½ cup plain yogurt

½ cup applesauce or puréed baby fruit

Pinch cinnamon

2 TB. toasted wheat germ

Makes about 1 cup
Any fortified cereal will work to add vitamins and minerals to this dish that's perfect for babies and toddlers.
Prep Time: 5 minutes **Cook Time:** 0 **Total:** 5 minutes

1. In a serving bowl, combine yogurt, applesauce, cinnamon, and wheat germ.
2. Allow to sit for a few minutes to soften up the cereal.

Glossary

allergens   Proteins found in foods not broken down during cooking or digestion that trigger the body's immune response.

amino   Refers to compounds containing nitrogen, including the amino acids in protein. Nitrogen is necessary for building body proteins. The protein in food provides nitrogen; carbohydrates and fats don't contain any.

anaphylaxis   The most dangerous and life-threatening result of a food allergy, it causes blood vessels to widen so much that blood pressure falls precariously low. It can result in a dangerously abnormal heartbeat that can be fatal if not treated promptly.

antibodies   Proteins produced by the immune system to defend the body against allergens.

atherosclerosis   A condition that chokes off blood supply by encouraging deposits of fatty substances, cholesterol, and other junk in arteries to the point of narrowing them significantly or completely blocking them.

electrolytes   Sodium, potassium, and chloride. These three minerals play an important role in regulating the body's fluid balance, muscle contraction, and the transmission of nerve impulses.

endocrine disrupters   Compounds that mimic or block the body's natural hormones. Endocrine disrupters have been implicated in birth defects, developmental and growth problems, low sperm counts in men and early puberty in girls, and an increased risk for certain hormone-dependent cancers.

enriched   Grains that contain the nutrients lost during the refining process.

extrusion reflex A baby's instinctive way of rejecting something that could choke her. In younger infants, it's an automatic response to anything other than liquid in their mouth.

fat-soluble Capable of dissolving in fat.

food neophobia The fear (phobia) of unfamiliar, or new (neo) foods.

fortified Grains that supply nutrients not originally present in the grain, such as iron and the B vitamin folic acid.

glucose The basic single sugar unit that circulates in the blood and provides fuel for cells. With the exception of corn syrup, food does not supply glucose.

gluten The protein portion of some grains, including wheat, barley, oats, and rye, that can sometimes trigger an allergic reaction in susceptible babies. Gluten intolerance can show up at any age, but may first appear during infancy.

hydrogenation The process of forcing hydrogen atoms into vegetable oils to transform unsaturated fats into trans fatty acids. Hydrogenation creates tastier, firmer fats with a longer shelf life that are ideal for processed foods.

irradiation Using ionizing radiation to rid foods of bacteria and parasites. Irradiation does not change the nutritional content of foods, nor does it make food radioactive.

metabolism Refers to all the body functions that together provide energy, build tissue, and regulate bodily processes.

methemoglobinemia Causes a defect in the iron attached to hemoglobin, the part of the red blood cell that carries oxygen to cells. Symptoms include lack of energy, shortness of breath, and a bluish tinge to the skin, and are considered a medical emergency.

myelin The sheath surrounding nerve cells that serves to protect them while preventing "short circuits" in communication.

pasteurization The process of heating juice and other liquids, including milk, to a high heat to kill bacteria that can make you sick.

water-soluble Capable of dissolving in water.

In a Pinch: Recipe Substitutions

You're missing a critical ingredient and your child is clamoring for a meal. No problem. Improvise with these hassle-free stand-ins.

This Is Equal To ...	This
1 tsp. double-acting baking powder	¼ tsp. baking soda + ½ tsp. cream of tartar OR ¼ tsp. baking soda + ½ cup buttermilk
1 cup all-purpose flour	¾ cup whole wheat flour
1 cup packed brown sugar	1 cup white sugar OR 1 cup white sugar + 1½ TB. molasses
2 cups tomato sauce	¾ cup tomato paste + 1 cup water
¼ cup dry bread crumbs	¼ cup crushed cornflakes OR ¼ cup other flake cereal

continued

This Is Equal To ...	This
1 oz. unsweetened chocolate	3 TB. unsweetened cocoa powder + 1 TB. shortening or canola oil
1 TB. cornstarch	2 TB. all-purpose flour
½ cup maple syrup	½ cup honey
1 cup butter	1 cup margarine
1 cup buttermilk	1 cup plain yogurt
1 cup whole milk	½ cup evaporated milk + ½ cup water
1 TB. fresh herbs	1 tsp. dried herbs
Chicken	Turkey

C

Vitamins and Minerals in the Foods Your Child Eats

No one nutrient is more worthy than any other, but there are some that stand out when it comes to your child's health. In Chapter 11, you read about vitamins and minerals considered central to a developing child's well-being. This section goes a step further with detailed lists of foods rich in calcium, iron, magnesium, zinc, potassium, and vitamins A, B6, B12, folate (a B vitamin), C, E, and K.

Use these tables as a resource to learn about what vitamins and minerals are in the food your child eats. Wondering whether bananas have more potassium than orange juice? Maybe you'd like to know if plain milk supplies more calcium than chocolate? You'll find the answers here.

Each table is made up of foods in descending order of their nutrient content. That means you can get a sense for how many nutrients one food has relative to another. Don't worry about how many micrograms of vitamin B12 your one-year-old needs every day, or whether your two-year-old is getting the exact amount of zinc she requires. When you feed your child a balanced diet as described in this book, she'll most likely meet her nutrient needs over the course of a few days.

The information provided in this section is from the United States Department of Agriculture (USDA). The facts listed here are just a smattering of what the USDA has to offer consumers and health professionals. For more information about foods and the nutrients they provide, visit www.nal.usda.gov/fnic/foodcomp/search.

Calcium

Food	Amount	Calcium (Milligrams)
Whole Grain Total cereal	¾ cup	1104
Cheese, ricotta, whole milk	1 cup	509
Yogurt, plain, low-fat	1 cup	415
Yogurt, fruit, low-fat	1 cup	345
Milk, fat-free	1 cup	306
Potatoes, au gratin	1 cup	292
Spinach, frozen, cooked	1 cup	291
Milk, chocolate, low-fat	1 cup	288
Milk, whole	1 cup	276
Yogurt, plain, whole milk	1 cup	275
Collards, cooked	1 cup	266
Cheese, Swiss	1 oz.	224
Black-eyed peas, cooked	1 cup	211
Cheese, mozzarella, part-skim, low moisture	1 oz.	207
Cheese, cheddar	1 oz.	204
Basic 4 cereal	1 cup	196
Beans, white, canned	1 cup	191
Waffles, from recipe	1	191
Soybeans, cooked	1 cup	175
Molasses, blackstrap	1 TB.	172
Tofu, firm, prepared with calcium sulfate and magnesium chloride	¼ block	163
Cheese, American	1 oz.	162
Cheese, cottage, 2% milk fat	1 cup	156

Iron

Food	Amount	Iron (Milligrams)
Whole Grain Total cereal	¾ cup	22
Frosted Mini Wheats cereal	1 cup	15
Clams, raw*	3 oz.	12
Cheerios	1 cup	10
Cream of Wheat, cooked	1 cup	10
Soybeans, cooked	1 cup	9
Wheat Chex cereal	1 cup	9
Kix cereal	1⅓ cup	8
Rice, enriched, cooked	1 cup	8
Beans, white, canned	1 cup	8
Oats, instant	1 packet	8
Lentils, cooked	1 cup	7
Spinach, cooked	1 cup	6
Textured Vegetable Protein ("Burger" crumbles)	1 cup	6
Beans, kidney, cooked	1 cup	5
Cap'n Crunch cereal	¾ cup	5
Barley, raw	1 cup	5
Beans, garbanzo, cooked	1 cup	5
Apple Cinnamon Cheerios	¾ cup	5
Beef, cooked	3 oz.	3
Ground beef, cooked	3 oz.	2
Turkey, roasted	¾ cup	2
Lamb, cooked	3 oz.	2
Chicken, light meat, cooked	3 oz.	1

Thoroughly cook raw animal foods.

Magnesium

Food	Amount	Magnesium (Milligrams)
Bulgur, dry	1 cup	230
Oat bran, raw	1 cup	221
Spinach, cooked	1 cup	156
Soybeans, cooked	1 cup	148
Beans, white, canned	1 cup	134
Artichokes, cooked	1 cup	101
Black-eyed peas, cooked	1 cup	91
Halibut, cooked	3 oz.	91
Oat bran muffin	1	89
Beans, baked, canned	1 cup	86
Rice, brown, long-grain, cooked	1 cup	84
Almonds	1 oz.	78
Cashews	1 oz.	77
Couscous, dry	1 cup	76
Orange juice	6 oz.	72
Lentils, cooked	1 cup	71
Milk, canned, evaporated, nonfat	1 cup	69
Plantain, raw	1 medium	66
Pollock, cooked	3 oz.	62
Rice, white, dry	1 cup	57
Potato, baked, flesh and skin	1 medium	57
Pumpkin, canned	1 cup	56

Zinc

Food	Amount	Zinc (Milligrams)
Oysters, cooked	3 oz.	76
Whole Grain Total cereal	¾ cup	17
Product 19 cereal	1 cup	15
Beef, cooked	3 oz.	9

Food	Amount	Zinc (Milligrams)
Frosted Wheaties cereal	¾ cup	8
Crab, cooked	3 oz.	6
Ground beef, cooked	3 oz.	5
Lamb, cooked	3 oz.	5
Cheerios	1 cup	5
Pork, cooked	3 oz.	4
Turkey, dark meat, cooked	3 oz.	4
Chili with meat	1 cup	4
Beans, white, canned	1 cup	3
Beans, garbanzo, canned	1 cup	3
Wheat Chex cereal	1 cup	2
Lobster, cooked	3 oz.	2
Beans, baked, canned	½ cup	2
Yogurt, plain, fat-free	1 cup	2
Turkey, light and dark meat, cooked	3 oz.	2
Turkey, light meat, cooked	3 oz.	2
Wheat germ	2 TB.	2
Rice, white, cooked	½ cup	1

Potassium

Food	Amount	Potassium (Milligrams)
Beans, white, canned	1 cup	1189
Winter squash	1 cup	896
Plantain	1 medium	893
Spinach	1 cup	839
Papaya	1 medium	781
Beans, baked, canned	1 cup	746
Lentils, cooked	1 cup	731
Prune juice	1 cup	707
Sweet potato, baked in skin	1 medium	694

Potassium   (continued)

Food	Amount	Potassium (Milligrams)
Black-eyed peas, cooked	1 cup	690
Potato, baked in skin	1 medium	610
Yogurt, fat-free	1 cup	579
Tomatoes, stewed	1 cup	528
Beets, cooked	1 cup	519
Molasses, blackstrap	1 TB.	498
Orange juice	1 cup	496
Halibut, cooked	3 oz.	490
Beans, garbanzo, canned	1 cup	477
Marinara sauce	½ cup	470
Vegetable juice	1 cup	467
Broccoli, cooked	1 cup	457
Yogurt, fruit, low-fat	1 cup	443
Cantaloupe	1 cup	431
Banana	1 medium	422
Honeydew melon	1 cup	388
Raisins	¼ cup	250

Vitamin A

Food	Amount	Vitamin A (Micrograms)
Carrot juice, canned	1 cup	2256
Pumpkin, canned	1 cup	1906
Sweet potato, cooked, baked in skin	1 medium	1403
Carrots, cooked	1 cup	1341
Kale, cooked	1 cup	955
Spinach, cooked	1 cup	943
Pumpkin pie, prepared from recipe	1 piece	660
Carrots, raw	½ cup	331

Food	Amount	Vitamin A (Micrograms)
Cream of Wheat, cooked	1 packet	376
Oatmeal, instant	1 packet	320
Milk, canned, evaporated, nonfat	1 cup	302
Butternut squash, cooked	½ cup	200
Mixed vegetables, cooked	½ cup	200
Cabbage, cooked	½ cup	180
Cheese, ricotta, whole milk	½ cup	150
Milk, low-fat	1 cup	141
Cantaloupe	½ cup	140
Ice cream, soft-serve French vanilla	½ cup	140
Milk, 2% reduced fat	1 cup	134
Peas, cooked	½ cup	130
Margarine	1 TB.	117
Egg, whole	1 large	90
Mandarin oranges	½ cup	53
Broccoli, cooked	½ cup	50

Vitamin B6

Food	Amount	Vitamin B6 (Milligrams)
Whole Grain Total cereal	¾ cup	2.8
Product 19 cereal	1 cup	2.0
Beans, garbanzo, canned	1 cup	1.1
Frosted Wheaties cereal	¾ cup	1
Cheerios	1 cup	.7
Potato, baked, flesh and skin	1 medium	.6
Cap'n Crunch cereal	¾ cup	.6
Cream of Wheat, cooked	1 packet	.6
Beef, top sirloin, cooked	3 oz.	.5
Plantain	1 medium	.5

Vitamin B6   (continued)

Food	Amount	Vitamin B6 (Milligrams)
Chicken, breast meat, cooked	½ breast	.5
Carrot juice, canned	1 cup	.5
Turkey, light meat, cooked	3 oz.	.5
Pork loin, cooked	3 oz.	.4
Sweet potato, baked in skin, cooked	1 medium	.4
Cod, cooked	3 oz.	.4
Bananas	½ cup	.3
Potatoes, mashed	½ cup	.3
Lentils, cooked	1 cup	.3
Halibut, cooked	3 oz.	.3
Sweet potato, canned	½ cup	.2
Broccoli, cooked	½ cup	.1

Vitamin B12

Food	Amount	Vitamin B12 (Micrograms)
Clams, raw*	3 oz.	42
Whole Grain Total cereal	¾ cup	6
Crab, blue, cooked	3 oz.	6
Product 19 cereal	1 cup	6
Salmon, cooked	3 oz.	5
Textured Vegetable Protein ("Burger" crumbles)	1 cup	4
Trout, rainbow, cooked	3 oz.	4
Pollock, cooked	3 oz.	4
Tuna, light, canned in water	3 oz.	3
Ground beef, cooked	3 oz.	2
Flounder and sole, cooked	3 oz.	2
Frosted Mini Wheats cereal	1 cup	2
Beef, cooked	3 oz.	2

Food	Amount	Vitamin B12 (Micrograms)
Cottage cheese, 2% milk fat	1 cup	2
Yogurt, plain, fat-free	1 cup	1
Milk, fat-free	1 cup	1
Turkey, light and dark meat	3 oz.	1
Scallops, cooked	6 large	1
Haddock, cooked	3 oz.	1
Milk, 2% reduced fat	1 cup	1
Cheese, Swiss	1 oz.	1
Wheat Chex cereal	1 cup	1

Thoroughly cook raw animal foods.

Folate

Food	Amount	Folate (Micrograms)
Whole Grain Total cereal	¾ cup	807
Cap'n Crunch cereal	¾ cup	711
Frosted Wheaties cereal	¾ cup	676
Product 19 cereal	1 cup	676
Wheat Chex cereal	1 cup	404
Lentils, cooked	1 cup	358
Black-eyed peas, cooked	1 cup	358
Cheerios	1 cup	336
Beans, garbanzo, cooked	1 cup	282
Spinach, cooked	1 cup	263
Beans, black, cooked	1 cup	256
Beans, kidney, cooked	1 cup	230
Rice, white, enriched, cooked	1 cup	195
Cream of Wheat, cooked	1 cup	177
Frosted Mini Wheats cereal	1 cup	176
Spaghetti, enriched, cooked	1 cup	172
Beans, white, canned	1 cup	170

Folate *(continued)*

Food	Amount	Folate (Micrograms)
Broccoli, cooked	1 cup	168
Noodles, egg, enriched, cooked	1 cup	166
Orange juice	1 cup	110
Strawberries	½ cup	20

Vitamin C

Food	Amount	Vitamin C (Milligrams)
Peppers, sweet, red, raw	1 cup	283
Peaches, frozen, sliced, sweetened	1 cup	235
Papayas, raw	1 medium	188
Apricot nectar, canned with ascorbic acid	1 cup	137
Orange juice	1 cup	124
Peppers, sweet, green, raw	1 cup	120
Strawberries	1 cup	106
Broccoli, cooked	1 cup	101
Brussels sprouts, cooked	1 cup	97
Orange slices	1 cup	96
Grapefruit juice	1 cup	94
Cranberry juice cocktail, bottled	1 cup	90
Papaya	1 cup	87
Broccoli, cooked	1 cup	74
Kiwi fruit	1 medium	71
Orange	1 medium	70
Sweet potato, canned	1 cup	67
Whole Grain Total cereal	¾ cup	60
Cantaloupe	1 cup	59
Tomato juice	1 cup	45

Food	Amount	Vitamin C (Milligrams)
Raspberries	1 cup	32
Tomato	1 medium	32

Vitamin E (Alpha-Tocopherol)

Food	Amount	Vitamin E (Milligrams)
Product 19 cereal	1 cup	14
Whole Grain Total cereal	¾ cup	14
Almond butter	2 TB.	8
Almonds	1 oz.	7
Sunflower oil	1 TB.	6
Safflower oil	1 TB.	5
Special K cereal	1 cup	5
Soy beverage	1 cup	3
Carrot juice, canned	1 cup	3
Marinara sauce	½ cup	3
Pumpkin, canned	1 cup	3
Peanut butter	2 TB.	3
Avocado	¼ whole	2
Spinach, cooked	½ cup	2
Canola oil	1 TB.	2
Papaya	1 medium	2
Peanut oil	1 TB.	2
Corn oil	1 TB.	2
Olive oil	1 TB.	2
Raisin Nut Bran cereal	1 cup	2
Peanuts	1 oz.	2
Wheat germ	2 TB.	2
Sweet potato, canned	½ cup	1
Broccoli, cooked	½ cup	1
Asparagus, cooked	½ cup	1

Vitamin E (Alpha-Tocopherol) *(continued)*

Food	Amount	Vitamin E (Milligrams)
Tomatoes, stewed	½ cup	1
Carrots, cooked	½ cup	1
Blackberries	½ cup	1

Vitamin K

Food	Amount	Vitamin K (Micrograms)
Kale, cooked	1 cup	1146
Spinach, cooked	1 cup	889
Turnip greens, cooked	1 cup	851
Brussels sprouts, cooked	1 cup	229
Broccoli, cooked	1 cup	220
Spinach, raw	1 cup	145
Broccoli, raw	1 cup	89
Cabbage, cooked, drained	1 cup	73
Black-eyed peas, cooked	1 cup	63
Coleslaw	¾ cup	56
Carrot juice, canned	1 cup	37
Soybeans, cooked	1 cup	33
Kiwi fruit	1 medium	31
Asparagus, cooked	4 spears	30
Lettuce, cos or romaine	½ cup	29
Artichokes, cooked	1 cup	25
Peas	½ cup	18
Canola oil	1 TB.	17
Prunes	¼ cup	16
Blackberries	½ cup	14
Blueberries	½ cup	14
Grapes	½ cup	12
Cauliflower, cooked	½ cup	11
Carrots, cooked	½ cup	11

Charting Your Child's Growth

Growth indicates health, so it's natural for parents to be curious about whether their child is growing properly. This appendix provides growth charts devised by the Centers for Disease Control and Prevention—the same tools pediatricians use to track growth in children beginning at birth.

There are 16 charts in this section, 8 for each gender in 2 age categories:

0–36 months
Length for age
Weight for age
Head circumference for age
Weight for length

2–20 years
Stature (height) for age
Weight for age
Body Mass Index for age
Weight for stature (height)

Growth charts relate your child's growth to the average values for a particular age group. The curved lines on the charts represent percentiles. A percentile is based on a scale of 100 children. For example, if your child is in the fiftieth percentile for weight, half the children his age weigh more and half weigh less. Children tend to grow along their own percentile curve; however, sudden and major deviations in growth may be of concern to your pediatrician. Plot the growth by locating values that pertain to your child on the bottom of each chart and along the sides. Mark the point on the chart where the two intersect.

When your child reaches the age of two, you can plot his Body Mass Index (BMI) on a growth chart in relationship to his age. BMI is an indicator of body fat. BMI-for-age charts help identify children at risk for becoming overweight or who are overweight. A child with a BMI-for-age measuring above the eighty-fifth percentile is considered at risk for becoming overweight; a child with a BMI-for-age above the ninety-fifth percentile is overweight.

Here's how to calculate your child's BMI:

1. Weigh your child naked.
2. Confirm his height in inches.
3. Multiply his weight in pounds by 704.
4. Divide the result in #3 by his height in inches.
5. Divide the result in #4 by his height in inches again. That's his BMI.

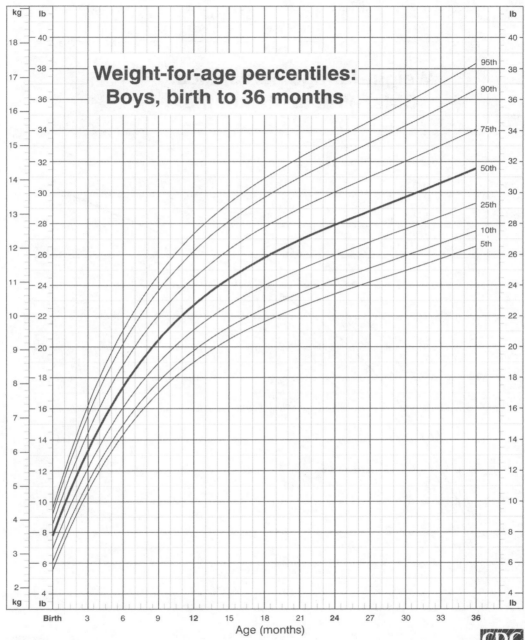

Weight-for-age percentiles:
Boys, birth to 36 months

Age (months)

Published May 30, 2000.
SOURCE: Developed by the National Center for Health Statistics in collaboration with
the National Center for Chronic Disease Prevention and Health Promotion (2000).

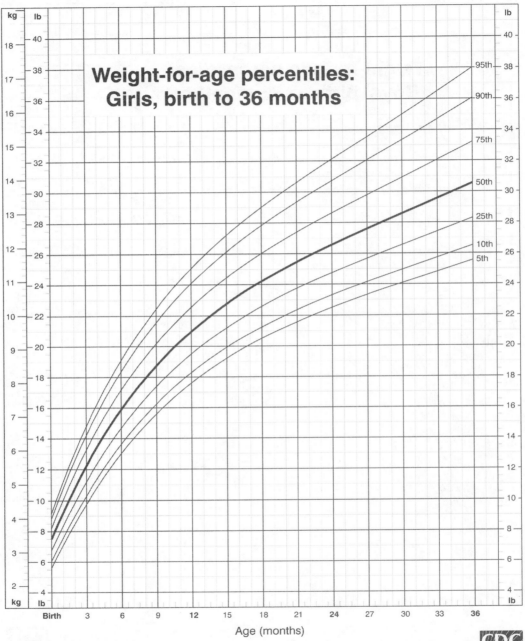

Weight-for-age percentiles: Girls, birth to 36 months

Published May 30, 2000.
SOURCE: Developed by the National Center for Health Statistics in collaboration with
the National Center for Chronic Disease Prevention and Health Promotion (2000).

SAFER · HEALTHIER · PEOPLE™

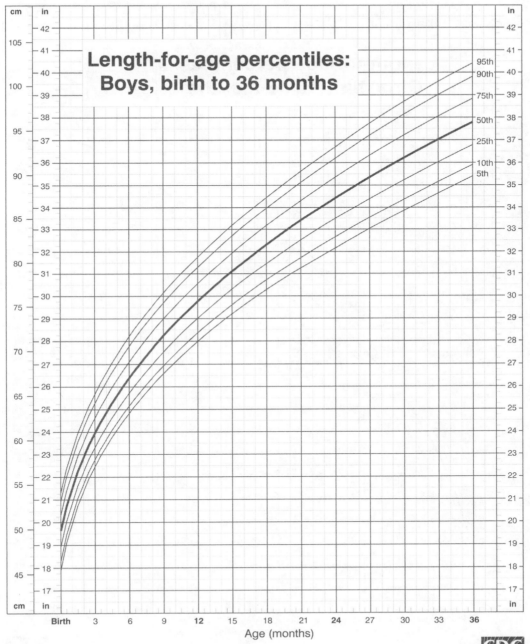

Length-for-age percentiles: Boys, birth to 36 months

Published May 30, 2000.
SOURCE: Developed by the National Center for Health Statistics in collaboration with
the National Center for Chronic Disease Prevention and Health Promotion (2000).

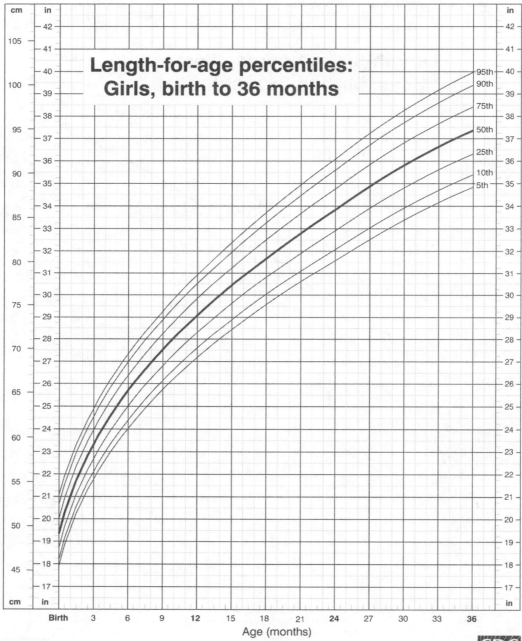

Length-for-age percentiles:
Girls, birth to 36 months

Published May 30, 2000.
SOURCE: Developed by the National Center for Health Statistics in collaboration with
the National Center for Chronic Disease Prevention and Health Promotion (2000).

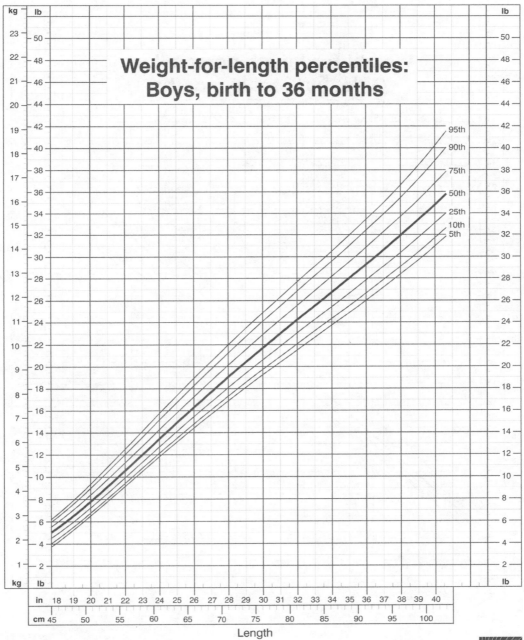

Weight-for-length percentiles: Boys, birth to 36 months

Published May 30, 2000 (modified 6/8/00).
SOURCE: Developed by the National Center for Health Statistics in collaboration with
the National Center for Chronic Disease Prevention and Health Promotion (2000).

CDC
SAFER · HEALTHIER · PEOPLE™

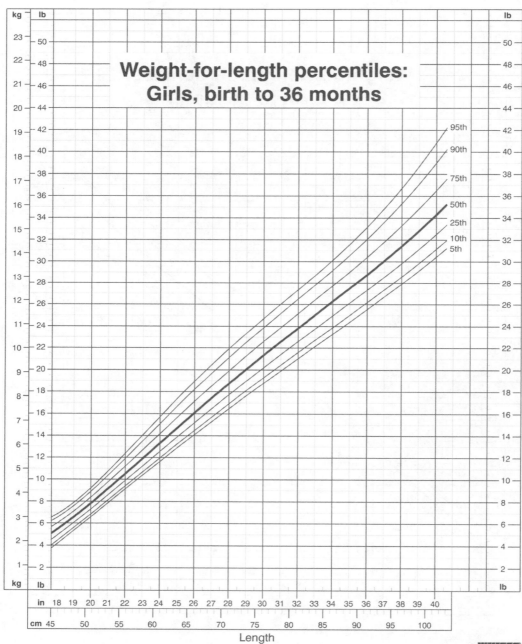

Weight-for-length percentiles: Girls, birth to 36 months

Published May 30, 2000 (modified 6/8/00).
SOURCE: Developed by the National Center for Health Statistics in collaboration with
the National Center for Chronic Disease Prevention and Health Promotion (2000).

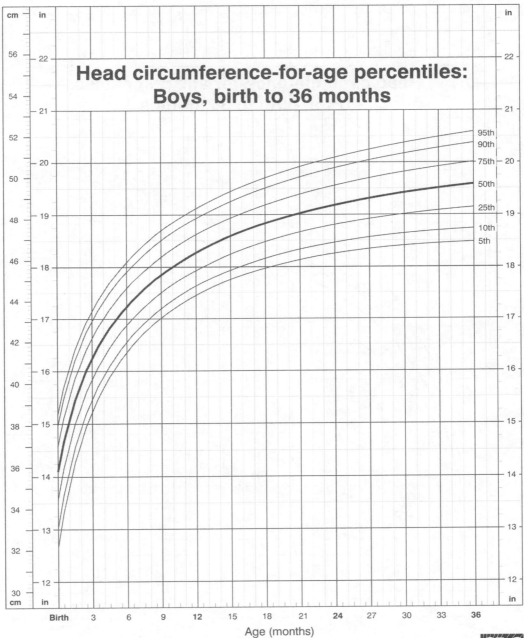

Head circumference-for-age percentiles: Boys, birth to 36 months

Age (months)

Published May 30, 2000.
SOURCE: Developed by the National Center for Health Statistics in collaboration with
the National Center for Chronic Disease Prevention and Health Promotion (2000).

SAFER · HEALTHIER · PEOPLE™ ʿS

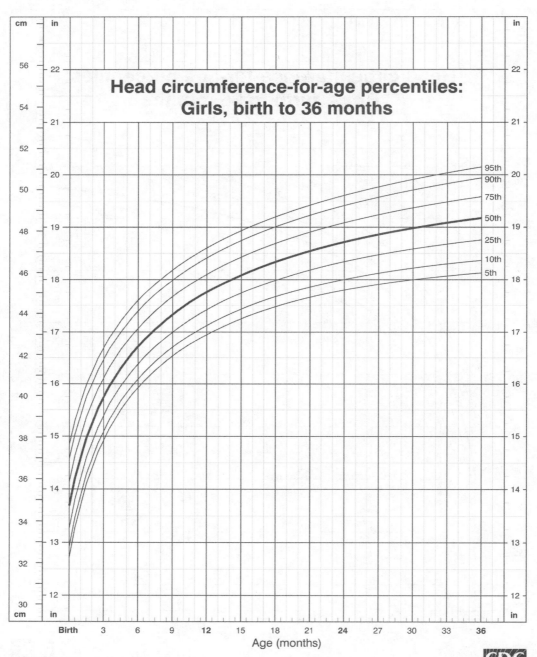

Head circumference-for-age percentiles: Girls, birth to 36 months

Published May 30, 2000.
SOURCE: Developed by the National Center for Health Statistics in collaboration with
the National Center for Chronic Disease Prevention and Health Promotion (2000).

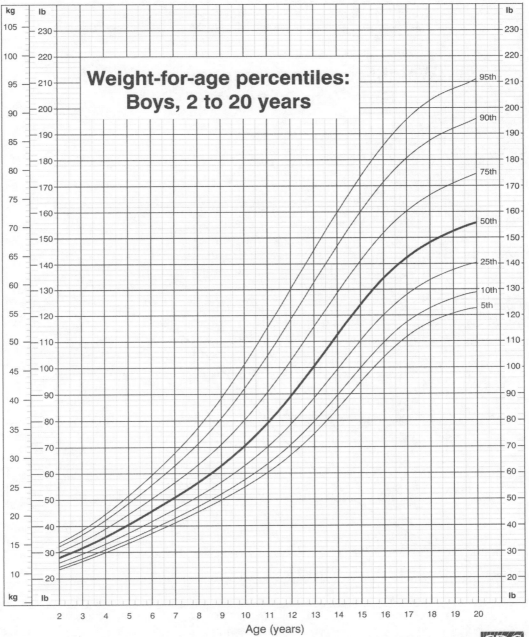

Weight-for-age percentiles: Boys, 2 to 20 years

Published May 30, 2000.
SOURCE: Developed by the National Center for Health Statistics in collaboration with
the National Center for Chronic Disease Prevention and Health Promotion (2000).

SAFER · HEALTHIER · PEOPLE™

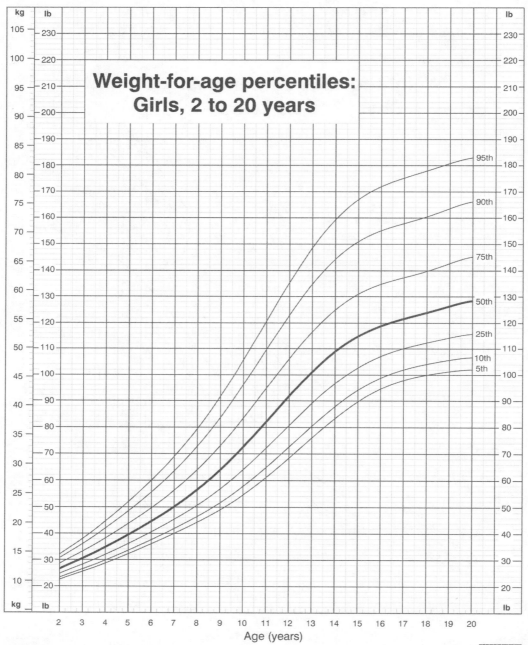

Weight-for-age percentiles:
Girls, 2 to 20 years

Published May 30, 2000.
SOURCE: Developed by the National Center for Health Statistics in collaboration with
the National Center for Chronic Disease Prevention and Health Promotion (2000).

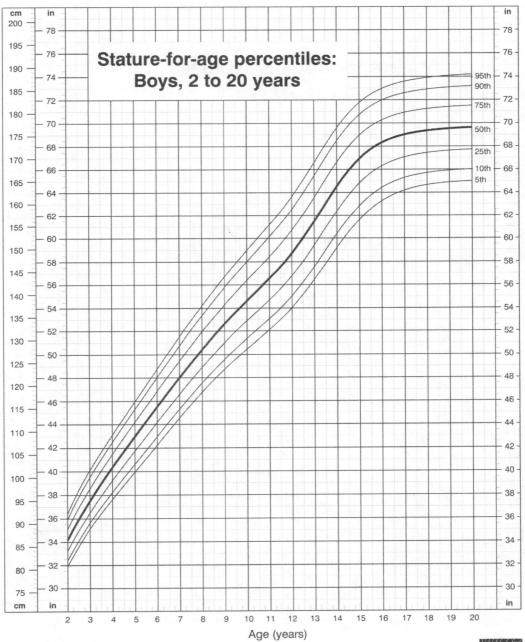

Stature-for-age percentiles:
Boys, 2 to 20 years

Age (years)

Published May 30, 2000.
SOURCE: Developed by the National Center for Health Statistics in collaboration with
the National Center for Chronic Disease Prevention and Health Promotion (2000).

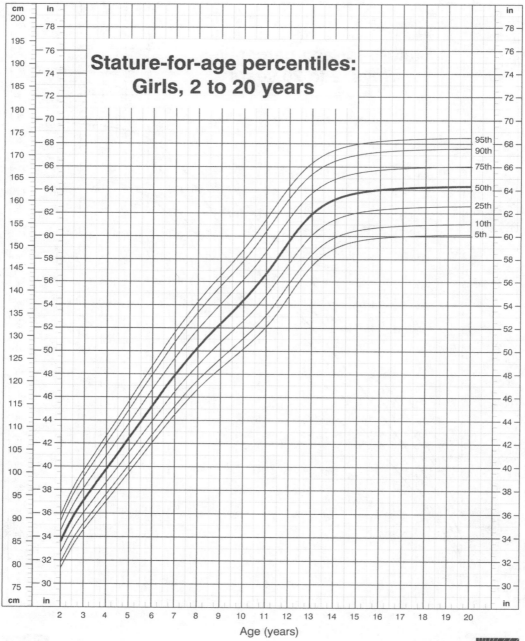

Stature-for-age percentiles:
Girls, 2 to 20 years

Age (years)

Published May 30, 2000.
SOURCE: Developed by the National Center for Health Statistics in collaboration with
the National Center for Chronic Disease Prevention and Health Promotion (2000).

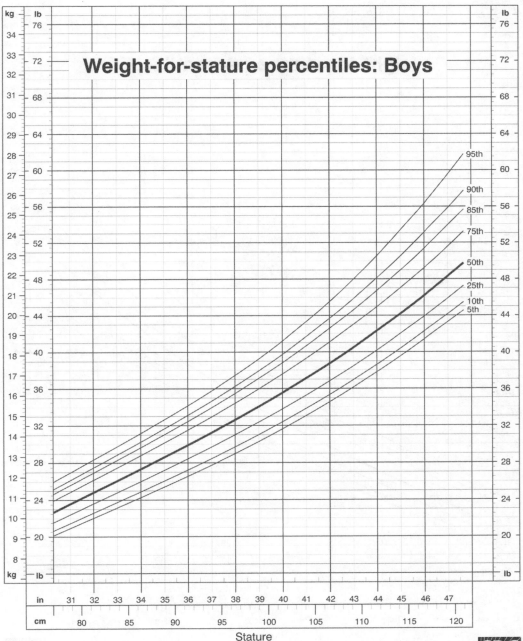

Weight-for-stature percentiles: Boys

Published May 30, 2000 (modified 11/21/00).
SOURCE: Developed by the National Center for Health Statistics in collaboration with
the National Center for Chronic Disease Prevention and Health Promotion (2000).

SAFER·HEALTHIER·PEOPLE™

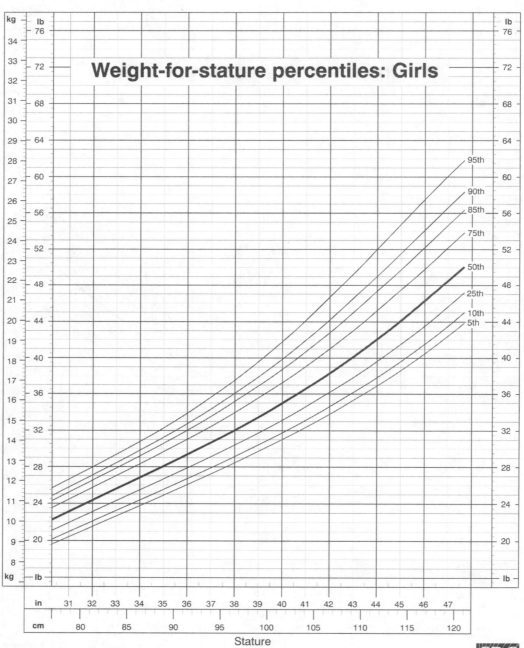

Weight-for-stature percentiles: Girls

Published May 30, 2000 (modified 11/21/00).
SOURCE: Developed by the National Center for Health Statistics in collaboration with
the National Center for Chronic Disease Prevention and Health Promotion (2000).

SAFER·HEALTHIER·PEOPLE™

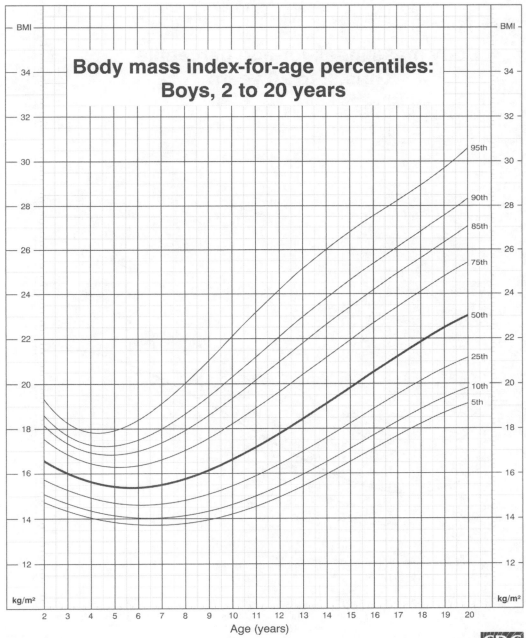

Body mass index-for-age percentiles: Boys, 2 to 20 years

Published May 30, 2000.
SOURCE: Developed by the National Center for Health Statistics in collaboration with
the National Center for Chronic Disease Prevention and Health Promotion (2000).

SAFER · HEALTHIER · PEOPLE™

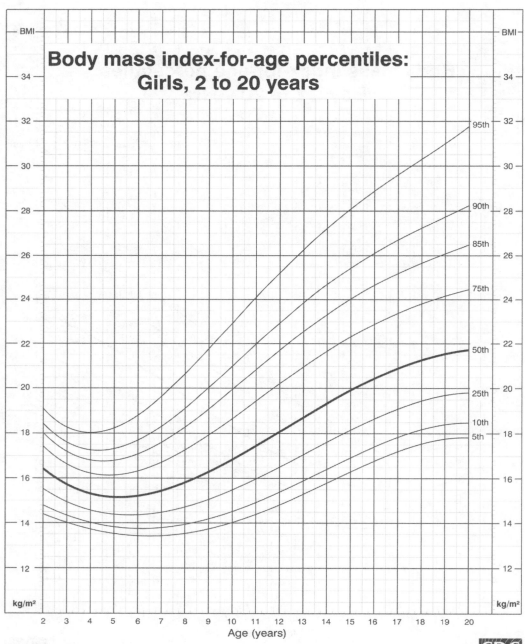

Body mass index-for-age percentiles:
Girls, 2 to 20 years

Published May 30, 2000.
SOURCE: Developed by the National Center for Health Statistics in collaboration with
the National Center for Chronic Disease Prevention and Health Promotion (2000).

SAFER·HEALTHIER·PEOPLE™

Appendix E

Resources

American Academy of Allergy, Asthma & Immunology
www.acaai.org

American Academy of Family Physicians
www.aafp.org

American Academy of Pediatric Dentistry
www.aapd.org

American Academy of Pediatrics
www.aap.org

American Dental Association
www.ada.org
312-440-2500

American Dietetic Association
www.eatright.org
1-800-877-1600

Attention Deficit Disorder Association
www.add.org
484-945-2101

Centers for Disease Control and Prevention
www.cdc.gov
1-800-232-4674

Children's Health Environmental Coalition
www.checnet.org
323-938-9918

Dietary Guidelines for Americans 2005
www.healthierus.gov

Environmental Protection Agency
www.epa.gov

Environmental Working Group
www.ewg.org

Food Allergy and Anaphylaxis Network
www.foodallergy.org
1-800-929-4040

Food Safety and Inspection Service
202-720-7943
www.fsis.usda.gov

International Food Information Council
202-296-6540
www.ificinfo.org

Keep Kids Healthy
www.keepkidshealthy.com

Kids Health
www.kidshealth.org

National Center for Education in Maternal and Child Health
www.ncemch.org

National Institute of Child Health and Human Development (NICHD)
Clearinghouse
www.nichd.nih.gov

Nutrition Explorations
www.nutritionexplorations.com

Organic Consumers Association
www.organicconsumers.org

Organic Trade Association
www.ota.com

Produce for Better Health Foundation
www.5ADay.gov

United States Department of Agriculture
www.usda.gov

United States Department of Health and Human Services
www.hhs.gov

United States Food and Drug Administration/Center for Food Safety and Applied Nutrition
www.cfsan.fda.gov

United States Maternal and Child Health Bureau
www.mchb.hrsa.gov/default.htm

Vegetarian Resource Group
www.vrg.org

Weight Control Information Network
www.niddk.nih.gov/health/nutrit/win.htm

Index

G

S